WALKING IN CROATIA

About the Author

Rudolf Abraham (www.rudolfabraham.co.uk) is an award-winning writer and photographer whose love of travel and remote places has taken him from the Balkans to eastern Turkey, Central Asia and Patagonia. He first visited Croatia in 1998, lived in Zagreb from 1999–2001 and continues to make several trips a year to his favourite country in Europe.

Other Cicerone guides by the author
The Mountains of Montenegro
Torres del Paine: A Trekker's Guide (2010)

WALKING IN CROATIA

by
Rudolf Abraham

2 POLICE SQUARE, MILNTHORPE, CUMBRIA LA7 7PY
www.cicerone.co.uk

Text, maps and photographs © Rudolf Abraham 2010

Second edition 2010
ISBN-13: 978 1 85284 614 5

First edition 2004
ISBN-13: 978 1 85284 406 6

Printed by KHL Printing, Singapore
A catalogue record for this book is available from the British Library.
Author photo by Ivana Jović Abraham. All other photographs by Rudolf Abraham.

Acknowledgements

A number of people gave their time, advice and encouragement during the preparation of the first edition of this guide. In particular I would like to thank my mother and father, obitelj Jović, Liz Barrett, Aaron Taylor and Sarah Cohen, and Ante Vukušić and family. For the second edition I would like to thank the Croatian National Tourist Board, who made arrangements for revisiting a number of national parks in June 2009. Finally, for her advice, and company on a number of these routes, and for her help with the language section I must thank my wife Ivana – with whom I first discovered Velebit, and to whom this book is dedicated.

Advice to Readers

Readers are advised that, while every effort is made by our authors to ensure the accuracy of guidebooks as they go to print, changes can occur during the lifetime of an edition. Please check Updates on this book's page on the Cicerone website (www.cicerone.co.uk) before planning your trip. We would also advise that you check information about such things as transport, accommodation and shops locally. Even rights of way can be altered over time. We are always grateful for information about any discrepancies between a guidebook and the facts on the ground, sent by email to info@cicerone.co.uk or by post to Cicerone, 2 Police Square, Milnthorpe LA7 7PY, United Kingdom.

Front cover: Sveti Nikola, Hvar (Walk 21)

CONTENTS

Main Velebit ridge above Paklenica (Walk 12, Stage 3)

Warning

Mountain walking can be a dangerous activity carrying a risk of personal injury or death. It should be undertaken only by those with a full understanding of the risks and with the training and experience to evaluate them. While every care and effort has been taken in the preparation of this guide, the user should be aware that conditions can be highly variable and can change quickly, materially affecting the seriousness of a mountain walk. Therefore, except for any liability which cannot be excluded by law, neither Cicerone nor the author accept liability for damage of any nature (including damage to property, personal injury or death) arising directly or indirectly from the information in this book. Information regarding emergency services in Croatia may be found in 'What to do in an Emergency' on page 61. In addition, walkers in Croatia should be aware of the landmine risk in some areas (see 'Landmines' on page 63).

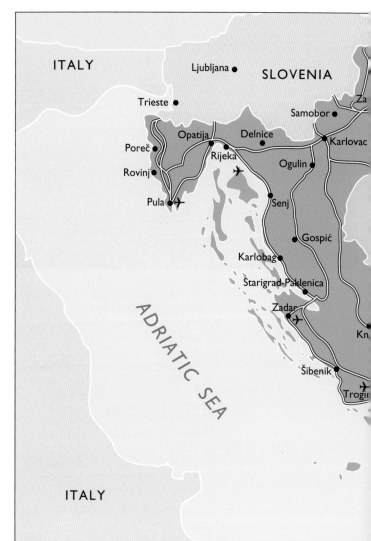

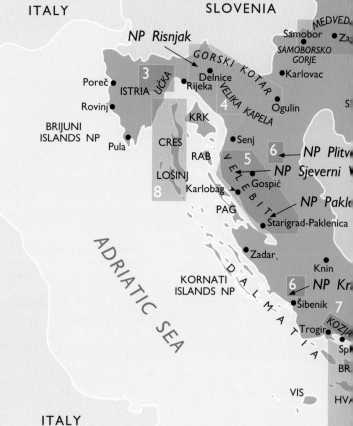

AUSTRIA

ITALY

SLOVENIA

MEDVED

NP Risnjak

Samobor • Zag

SAMOBORSKO GORJE

GORSKI KOTAR

Poreč •

3

UČKA

Delnice •

• Karlovac

ISTRIA

Rijeka

VELIKA KAPELA

Rovinj •

4

• Ogulin

S

BRIJUNI ISLANDS NP

KRK

Pula •

• Senj

6 ← *NP Plitv*

CRES

5

NP Sjeverni V

RAB

VELEBIT

Karlobag

• Gospić

LOŠINJ

8

PAG

NP Pakle

• Starigrad-Paklenica

ADRIATIC SEA

DALMATIA

• Zadar

• Knin

KORNATI ISLANDS NP

6 ← *NP Kr*

• Šibenik

7

KOZJA

Trogir •

Sp

BR

VIS

HV

ITALY

8

HUNGARY

ždⁿ

ovar

roatia

SLAVONIA
PAPUK

ko polje

Slavonski Brod

ra

BOSNIA-HERCEGOVINA

Osijek ●

Vukovar ●

NP Kopački rit

2

Ilok ●

SERBIA

Location of the Walks

Part 1: Walks around Zagreb
Part 2: Walks in Slavonia
Part 3: Walks in Istria
Part 4: Gorski kotar
Part 5: Velebit
Part 6: Plitvička jezera and Krka
Part 7: Mosor, Kozjak and Biokovo
Part 8: The Islands

NP = NATIONAL PARK

ŠOKOVO

tarska

PELJEŠAC

LA

↑ MLJET

NP Mljet

Dubrovnik ●

MONTENEGRO

KOSOVO

Map Key

- - - - - - - - - - route

.... other paths

~~~~~~ road (sealed roads and forest tracks)

▲ peak (with altitude in metres)

⌒ cave or sinkhole

· spring or water source

╫╫╫●╫╫╫ railway line/station

♠ mountain hut or shelter

⌐ ruin, castle or other monument

☦ church or chapel

■ other building

	1600m
	1500m
	1400m
	1300m
	1200m
	1100m
	1000m
	800m
	600m
	400m
	200m
	sea level

Rossijevo sklonište below Pasarićev kuk, Northern Velebit (Walk 11, Stage 2)

PREFACE TO THE SECOND EDITION

When I wrote the first edition of this guide, in 2003, Croatia was already beginning to see a steady rise in overseas visitors. Since then, numbers have skyrocketed, there has been a huge surge in property buying, and a plethora of guidebooks have appeared. If you're looking for quiet, undiscovered coastline, then, alas, you've arrived rather too late. (Although this coastline does remain one of the most beautiful and unspoilt on the Mediterranean, and is still less busy than most others).

Nevertheless – and quite incomprehensibly to this writer – the mountainous areas, including Velebit and Gorski kotar, which offer some of the finest scenery and without any doubt the best hiking in Croatia, still see remarkably few visitors. Although I have added some new routes and areas to this edition, it is these wild, remote and as yet relatively little known mountain ranges which remain the core subject of this guide.

Rudolf Abraham
March 2010

St Mark's church, Korčula, with the Pelješac peninsula and Sveti Ilija in the background (Walks 18 and 19)

Winter on Risnjak, Gorski kotar (Walk 8)

INTRODUCTION

My love affair with Croatia began more than a dozen years ago, with my first visit to a snow-bound Velebit in the middle of winter. Within a year I had moved to Zagreb where I lived and worked as an English teacher for two years, making frequent trips into the mountains and seeing in the new millennium in a bitterly cold tent, once again on Velebit. I have been returning to Croatia ever since.

Long popular as a summer destination with German and Italian visitors, but largely overlooked by the vast majority of western travellers since its independence from the Federal Republic of Yugoslavia, the past few years have seen the Croatian coast literally flooded with western, and in particular English and French, visitors. This

is not to say that the Croatian coastline is busier than any other attractive and sunny part of Europe during the summer months – indeed, it remains less crowded than most places, and much less spoilt. And while most visitors head straight for the coast – the lovely Dalmatian towns and villages and the glittering isles of the Croatian archipelago – the rest of the country remains largely untouched.

Visitors cannot fail to notice the rugged mountains, which rise up suddenly, often spectacularly, beyond the narrow ribbon of coastal cities and rocky beaches. It is these mountains – the limestone massifs of Velebit, Gorski kotar, Mosor and Biokovo, extending in furrowed ranges from Slovenia in the north to Montenegro in the south – which so dramatically divide the Adriatic from the continental interior, contributing as much to the particular character of the country as the more celebrated coastline. More significantly, from the point of view of this guide they provide a superb, and as yet remarkably unspoilt, arena for the mountain walker or alpinist.

Often only a few hours from the coast by way of steep and rocky trails, these mountains have much to commend them as a walking destination. Ranging from gently sloping, forested hills to rugged tops and limestone crags, they form a landscape of outstanding beauty; at their most spectacular they are a karst labyrinth of domed peaks and cavernous sinkholes, sun-bleached ridges and rocky dells. They are not a wilderness experience in the traditional sense (then again, little in Europe is). Trails are for the most part well established and clearly marked, mountain huts are plentiful and local walkers abound. But the scenery is as lovely as it is varied, the terrain rewarding, and the views often breathtaking. And despite their modest elevation – Velebit rises to less than 1800m – there is still plenty to be found that is challenging. Furthermore, in contrast to many of the mountain areas in neighbouring Slovenia, Velebit and Gorski kotar remain well within the capabilities of the moderately well-equipped walker during the winter months, despite heavy snowfall.

Finally, the very proximity of these areas to the coastal scenery and

islands, and to historic cities such as Dubrovnik, Split and Korčula, is a considerable attraction in itself. These cities boast some quite stunning Roman and medieval architecture – Dubrovnik often being touted, with considerable justification, as the best-preserved medieval city on the Mediterranean.

To complement these better-known features of the country, the walks in this guide provide a more intimate view of Croatia and its people, and a counterbalance to the bustle of its coastline during the summer months (after which the coast largely reverts to its sleepy Dalmatian self). While the walls of Dubrovnik throng with sightseers, and the rocky beaches steadily swell with the returning tide of western tourism, the walker will be able to sit comfortably on a high pass below Zavižan, perhaps with a fine selection of dried meats and cheeses and other local delicacies spread on a convenient rock, flask in hand, and survey the splendour of a dazzling sunset across the Croatian archipelago.

GEOGRAPHY AND GEOLOGY

Croatia, my Croatian friends told me long before I first visited their country, is like a bird in flight. Look at a map and you'll see this quite clearly: the great wings spread back across Slavonia, poised between beats; the head hanging low in Istria, and protruding out into the Adriatic; the body and tail stretching down through Lika and Dalmatia; the belly splintering into the myriad isles of the Croatian archipelago. It is an attractive image, and one which has stuck (certainly it is more poetic than the comparison between Croatia's rather peculiar shape and a boomerang).

From a walking or a mountaineering point of view, the most interesting areas are the successive ranges of mountains running parallel to the Adriatic coast – the belly and tail of the bird, to take the analogy further. Collectively known as the Dinaric Alps, and including the massifs of Gorski kotar, Velebit, Mosor and Biokovo, these rise steeply from the narrow band of settlements and cultivation along the coast, frequently to 1500m and in some cases to over 1700m, forming a formidable natural barrier between the rocky coastline and the continental interior.

The dominant characteristic of these mountains is their stunning karst formations. (The term 'karst' is actually derived from the limestone Kras region near Trieste, and was first coined in the 19th century following a study of the area.) These include saucer-shaped or cone-shaped dells and depressions (*dolina* and *uvala*), known locally as *vrtača*, or in the case of larger examples as *dabar* or *duliba*; bare tops and crags, known locally as either *stijene* or *kukovi*; rivers which disappear underground only to re-emerge as karst springs, either in the foothills of the mountains or as submarine springs, *vrulja*; and numerous caves and sinkholes, *špilja* and *jama* respectively, which in many cases reach astonishing depths (Lukina jama on Velebit is among the ten deepest sinkholes in the world). These features

Karst landscape on Northern Velebit, from Premužićeva staza (Walk 11)

are at their most impressive on Velebit and Biokovo.

Karst is formed by the destructive chemical effect of rainwater on limestone, and by the enlargement of surface drainage holes and of the various horizontal and vertical cracks and fissures in the rock as the water percolates downwards. As a consequence all rainwater rapidly disappears underground, and the landscape is characterised by a dearth of surface streams matched only by the abundance of sub-surface streams, caverns and sinkholes.

Although in many places now denuded and bare, and typified by poor vegetation, the Dinaric Alps were once heavily forested. Progressive deforestation (both by foreign powers and the local population) and overgrazing since well before the Middle Ages led to extensive soil erosion, exposing the underlying rock to chemical and mechanical weathering. The Republic of Venice, in particular, is frequently singled out for its role in the process, drawing much of the timber for its fleet from Dalmatian forests. Local restrictions on the sale of timber to foreign powers (in the case of the Republic of Dubrovnik, as early as the 13th century) failed to check the process, and archives from the town of Zadar, dating from 1803, state that the forests of the surrounding mountains were by then so devastated that not even a piece of firewood could be found.

The Croatian archipelago encompasses a quite mind-boggling number of islands of various shapes and sizes, ranging from the tiny Jabuka (meaning 'apple') to Marco Polo's Korčula. In total they number some 1185, bringing the actual length of the already very indented coastline to well over 5500km. Generally elongated, they follow the northwest–southeast orientation of the coastal ranges, and represent all that remains above sea level of a low, outlying range of hills once part of the Dinaric Alps. Beaches are typically rocky or of fine shingle, while Lopar has the distinction of being one of Croatia's few truly sandy beaches.

Slavonia, by contrast, is an extensive plain, and is extremely fertile. (It was the fertility of the land which, in the aftermath of the Second World War, encouraged many people from Dalmatia to move to Slavonia.) Its eastern border meets Serbia on the Danube, and its northern and southern borders are defined by the Drava and the Sava respectively. Low, wooded hills dot various areas such as that north of Poæega, while the landscape becomes progressively flatter towards the eastern border with the Danube and to the northeast, where it stretches off into the Hungarian plains.

Croatia's geographical position places it on the fringe of that rather ill-defined territory known in the West as the Balkans, though most Croatians prefer not to attach that label to their country – and may politely inform you

Zagreb's Gornji grad ('Upper Town') in winter

that the Balkans begin somewhere southeast of the River Sava.

CLIMATE

Croatia experiences two contrasting climatic types: continental inland and in the mountains, and Mediterranean along the coast and on the islands.

The Adriatic coast experiences hot, dry summers and relatively mild, but frequently rainy winters, being protected from the harsher inland climate by the mountain barrier of the coastal ranges. Forest fires pose a major threat both on the lower mountain slopes and on the islands – a fact confirmed by the great blackened tracts of land on Mosor and Hvar. Slavonia is somewhat more humid in the summer months, and considerably colder during the winter, with heavy

snowfalls. Zagreb generally lies under a few inches of snow over the winter months, but during the summer can become a stifling oven, leading most residents to escape to the coast.

Summers can be extremely hot on Mosor and Biokovo and water shortages can be something of a concern for the walker. The best times to visit are therefore spring and autumn. On Velebit daytime temperatures during the summer usually hover around 20–25°C; at night they can drop to almost freezing. On balance summer remains the most pleasant time to visit both Velebit and Gorski kotar, although southern Velebit tends to be rather hot. Nevertheless, the position of the Dinaric Alps so close to the coast ensures that they get considerable precipitation throughout the year

19

CROATIA CLIMATE DATA	Jan	Feb	Mar	Apr	May	Jun	Jul	Aug	Sept	Oct	Nov	Dec
ZAGREB												
Abs max temp (°C)	19.4	22.2	26	29.4	33.7	37.6	40.4	39.8	33.5	28.3	25.4	22.5
Abs min temp (°C)	-24.3	-27.3	-18.3	-4.4	-1.8	2.5	5.4	3.7	-0.6	-5.6	-13.5	-19.8
Mean average temp (°C)	-0.1	2	6.2	10.9	15.7	19.1	20.8	20	16	10.8	5.7	1.3
Total precipitation (mm)	47	40.6	52.2	63.1	76.4	96.7	81.6	89.3	85.9	74.2	81.8	64.2
Max snow cover (cm)	49	51	63	16	0	0	0	0	0	0	50	56
SPLIT												
Abs max temp (°C)	17.4	22.3	23.2	27.7	33.2	38.1	38.6	38.1	34.2	27.4	25.8	18.1
Abs min temp (°C)	-9	-8.1	-6.6	0.3	4.8	9.1	13	11.2	8.8	3.8	-4.5	-6.3
Mean average temp (°C)	7.9	8.2	10.6	14.1	19	23	25.8	25.5	21.4	17.1	12.4	9.2
Total precipitation (mm)	77.3	62.8	63.4	62.6	55.4	49.7	26.1	42.7	71	76.5	112.9	103.5
Max snow cover (cm)	21	6	7	0	0	0	0	0	0	0	0	14
ZAVIŽAN (N VELEBIT)												
Abs max temp (°C)	12.5	13.7	16.5	17.1	22.1	24.4	27.6	27.2	27.2	20.6	19.2	14.6
Abs min temp (°C)	-24.5	-28.6	-22.6	-14.5	-9.8	-3.1	0.2	-2	-3.8	-11.5	-16.8	-24.2
Mean average temp (°C)	-4	-4.2	-1.9	1.4	6.5	10.1	12.5	12.4	8.9	5.2	0.4	-2.7
Total precipitation (mm)	146.8	146.2	155.9	175.9	151.8	139.3	90.1	131.2	167.1	196.6	229.5	197.2
Max snow cover (cm)	240	287	320	298	272	106	3	5	22	87	142	212

Source: www.klima.hr

(although all water rapidly disappears underground), and heavy rain and storms can unleash themselves upon the unsuspecting walker at any time. The author has been lost in the clouds on Vaganski vrh in August and lashed by hailstorms on Rožanski kukovi in July.

The Dinaric Alps experience bitterly cold winters, when they are inundated with snow and frequently swept by blizzards. Gorski kotar and Velebit in particular receive abundant snowfall during the winter months, and become largely snowbound. They are, for all that, extremely beautiful at this time of year and remain far more accessible to the winter walker than the mountains in neighbouring Slovenia. Snow usually lies on Velebit for about 132 days per year, and winters with well over 2m of snow are not unheard of. While this snow generally provides an acceptable base for walking, it is not that unusual to disappear suddenly up to your waist in submerged juniper thicket. Microclimates also occur in the deep karst dells of the Dinaric Alps in the form of temperature inversions, which are reflected in local vegetation patterns.

A number of winds buffet Croatia from different directions – all of them bearing their own names, and all of them well known and discussed by locals. The most important of these from a mountaineering point of view is the *bura*. A cold northeasterly, the *bura* is the result of cold air accumulating behind Velebit in the Lika basin, where it is effectively trapped until it escapes through the cols and high passes of Velebit to descend in terrible gusts upon the Adriatic. These gusts frequently reach gale force, and the Venetian traveller Alberto Abbé Fortis, writing in the 18th century, even claimed that on occasions the *bura* would pick up young children and dash them against the walls of houses, and throw down horses loaded with salt. There is a saying in Croatia that the *bura* is born in Lika, lives on Velebit and dies on the sea; and a frequently heard observation in the villages beyond the Velebit Channel is *puše bura* ('the bura is blowing').

The *jugo*, as its name implies (*jug* meaning 'south'), is a moderate southerly which typically brings cloud and rain to the coastal mountains, and is traditionally associated with bad temper and ill health. (Under the Republic of Dubrovnik, crimes committed when the *jugo* was blowing generally earned a more lenient sentence for their perpetrator, following the belief that the wind had, at least partially, driven them to commit the crime or induced their fit of rage.) There is also the *maestral*, a brisk sea breeze which tends to blow from the morning to the early afternoon, and the *široko*, a warm, dry southeasterly from north Africa, roughly equivalent to the *sirocco* in other parts of the Mediterranean.

HISTORY

The earliest evidence of human habitation in Croatia dates back to the Palaeolithic era, most famously in the form of humanoid bones and stone tools unearthed in a cave at Krapina, not far from Zagreb, and dated to around 65,000BC. Evidence of the presence of Neolithic man is widespread, from the Starčevo culture (c6000–4500BC), which reached into eastern Slavonia at least as far as Vučedol (near Vukovar), to the Danilo culture (around 4500BC), which flourished around Šibenik, and notably on the island of Hvar. These early fishing and farming communities were characterised by the cultivation of cereals and the domestication of livestock, the development of 'tell' settlements and the introduction of copper working. Further traces of Neolithic man have been found at Smilčić (near Zadar), on a number of islands including Cres and Lošinj, and among the caves of Velebit. Finds from the later Vučedol culture, which flourished aound 2800–2500BC, include some remarkably beautiful pottery objects – the most famous of which figures on the reverse of the modern 20Kn note. Finds from the Bronze Age include axe-heads discovered in Slavonia and on Hvar, datable to around 2000BC. From the middle of the second millennium BC the Dalmatian coast was joined by sea routes to Italy and the Aegean, leading to an increase in trade and an expansion of external contacts; and with the beginning of the Iron Age we gradually enter the annals of recorded history.

The Illyrians

The precise origin of the Illyrians remains a matter of some conjecture, but from about 800BC they come to dominate the history of the eastern

Panorama of Southern Velebit and Paklenica, seen across the Velebit Channel from the village of Jovići (Walk 12)

Adriatic. An Indo-European people, the Illyrians were in effect composed of numerous tribes scattered throughout the region from the Veneto to Albania, some perhaps more deserving of the title 'Illyrian' than others. Among the most important of these tribes were the Liburni (famed pirates, also noted for the size and fertility of their flocks who originally controlled the coast from Istria to the River Krka); the Delmatae (inhabiting the coast and hinterland, including the Dinaric mountains, and noted for their near unassailable hill forts); and the Japodes (inhabiting the area behind the Liburni, north to the Sava and west to Velebit, whom Strabo describes as living on Mount Albion – perhaps Velebit). A number of them (Histri, Delmatae, Ardiaei) were to leave their names in the region (Istria, Dalmatia, Adriatic), and by the early 3rd century BC the Ardiaei had formed

a powerful kingdom in the south, centred around Scodra (Lake Shkodër in modern Albania).

At roughly the same time, or from the 6th century BC, Greek settlements and trading posts began to be established on the Adriatic coast and on the islands, notably at Korkyra meliana ('black Korčula'), Issa (Vis), Pharos (Hvar) and Tragurion (Trogir), which assured the spread of Greek culture on the islands and along the coast. The 4th century BC also saw the arrival of the Celts, who subjugated the Illyrians in Pannonia (an area roughly corresponding to modern Slavonia) and settled around the middle Danube and in the Sava and Drava valleys, bringing with them the fruits of the La Tène culture.

The Illyrian kingdom reached the height of its power during the 3rd century BC under King Agron and, following his death, Queen Teuta, with the

23

defeat of the Aetolian Greeks (in turn famed for their victory over the invading Gauls). Following this Teuta despatched enormous plundering expeditions against Epirus, and particularly the city of Phoenice, which was then emerging as a centre of commerce and trade with Rome. It was perhaps Illyrian interference with this trade, combined with the murder of a Roman envoy sent to complain against Illyrian piracy, which prompted the Romans to launch their attack on Illyria in 229BC, with 200 ships and a massive contingency of infantry and cavalry. Thereafter a Roman protectorate was established over the Greek coastal cities and islands.

The Roman period

The Romans conducted a succession of campaigns against the Illyrians, initially against Scodra in the south (where they defeated the Illyrian King Gentius in 168BC and made considerable gains in Macedonia), but subsequently against the Japodes, the Delmatae and the Pannonians (35–33BC). The Roman province of Illyricum was placed under senatorial control in 27BC, when it stretched from Istria in the north to the River Drin in the south, and east to the River Sava; it passed to imperial control with the full conquest of the Pannonian tribes during 13–11BC, which extended its territory to the Danube. Following the great Illyrian revolt of AD6–9, Pannonia became a separate province and Upper Illyria was renamed Dalmatia.

Establishing their capital at the old Illyrian stronghold of Salona (Solin, near Split), the Romans built

Roman arena at Pula

roads and cities and developed trade, exploiting the wealth of minerals and timber offered by the territory as well as the agriculturally rich farmland of Pannonia (though initially it remained largely devastated by years of war). Among the most important Roman settlements were Jadera (Zadar), Parentium (Poreč) and Polensium (Pula), while a defensive boundary (the Roman limes) was established across the interior. At the end of the 3rd century AD the Emperor Diocletian (whose palace still graces the city of Split) initiated a number of massive administrative reforms, with Dalmatia being split between the two dioceses of Pannonia and Moesia, and Pannonia itself being subdivided into a number of separate administrative units. Byzantine influence on the coast was to become increasingly prominent following the dedication of Constantinople in 330 as the new capital of the Roman, and later the Byzantine, empire.

Invasions

The fourth and fifth centuries were marked by a succession of Hunnish and Gothic invasions. The Visigoths swept into the region during the period 379–401, while in 450 the Huns appeared in northern Pannonia, followed by the Ostrogoths, who made considerable gains in Pannonia, Italy and Dalmatia, although Dalmatia was regained by Byzantium in 535.

The Slavs, originally from Ukraine and the steppes north of the Black Sea, began migrating into the valleys of the Danube and the Sava some time after AD500. They had settled in the Dinaric mountains by about 600, and reached the Adriatic some time early in the 7th century, settling at Zadar, Šibenik and Nin, among other places. In the second half of the 6th century the Avars, a nomadic people of Turkic and Mongol stock, swept south into the region. Launching a series of devastating raids, they sacked Salona in 612–615, and in 622–626 laid siege to Constantinople.

In the chaotic wake of the Slavic and Avar invasions, a people known as the 'White Croats' were invited by the Emperor Heraclius to move into the region and fight against the Avars in 626. A Slavic (or at least Slavicised) people, these White Croats were at that time living in an area north of the Carpathians. Moving southwest as requested, they successfully defeated the Avars, after which they settled in the region to which they would eventually give their name, Croatia. They were followed by the Serbs, who migrated from their home (known as 'White Serbia', also north of the Carpathians), and settled east of the Croats. Although the historical accuracy of this account has been questioned, the existence of a 'White Croatia' north of the Carpathians is confirmed by medieval Arab geographers, and by a 9th century history written by Orosius for King Alfred of England.

The arrival of Charlemagne at the close of the 8th century brought first Pannonian and then Dalmatian Croatia under Frankish sovereignty, with all of Dalmatia save some key cities and islands being formally ceded by Byzantium to the Franks in 812. These campaigns were followed by a gradual and more widespread conversion to Christianity. Prince Ljudevit from the Sava region staged a major but unsuccessful rebellion against the Franks in 819–822, possibly supported or encouraged by Byzantine diplomacy. Byzantium regained its control of Dalmatia in 868–878, when it became one of a number of Byzantine themes, with its capital at Zadar.

Croatia's golden age

The second half of the 9th century saw a gradual increase in power and autonomy, which would lead to Croatia's brief but much vaunted golden age. This was reflected in a move towards religious autonomy; the adoption of Glagolitic (the written form of Old Church Slavonic) instead of Latin by the local priests; and the appearance of local Croatian dukes in a position of rule. Višeslav was the first known Croatian duke, ruling from Nin in 800 but acknowledging Byzantine sovereignty, while Trpimir ruled from the stronghold of Klis around 852. In 888 Branimir pledged his loyalty to the Pope and assumed the title Duke of the Croats.

After successfully repelling the first of many Hungarian attacks, Tomislav became the first king of

Croatia in 925. However, power struggles within the ruling class followed Tomislav's death, and it was not until the reign of Petar Krešimir IV (1058–1074) that Dalmatia was regained from Byzantine control, and Dalmatian and Pannonian Croatia unified for the first time into a single state. Petar was succeeded by Zvonimir (1075–1089), who had the title king of Croatia and Dalmatia conferred upon him by Pope Gregory VII. However, the country once more fell into disunity after his death, which effectively marked the end of the Croatian royal house (known as the Trpimirović dynasty, after its founder Trpimir). Popular legend tells that Zvonimir was actually murdered by his own people, and that his dying curse upon them was that they should be forever ruled by foreign powers. Indeed, Croatia would see some 900 years of foreign rule before regaining its independence in the 1990s.

Hungarian and Austrian rule

In 1091 Hungary invaded northern Croatia under King Ladislav, with the support of Zvonimir's widow, finally defeating the last pretender to the throne, Petar Svačić, on Mount Gvozd (the modern Petrova gora). In 1102 a treaty was signed between the 12 Croat tribes and the Hungarian King Koloman, with the Hungarian Arpad dynasty inheriting the rights of the Croatian kings, and a Hungarian ban or governor being installed. The Dalmatian nobility accepted

Dubrovnik city walls, with patron saint Sveti Vlaho

Koloman's rule, but this was to be limited by Venice's increasing power in the Adriatic.

It was during this period that the city of Dubrovnik (or Ragusa) rose to prominence. Founded in the first half of the 7th century by refugees from Epidaurus (Cavtat), a city recently devastated by the Avars and the Slavs, Dubrovnik soon grew rich on maritime trade, and in the 12th century developed into an independent republic. In 1190 Dubrovnik signed treaties against external enemies, in particular Venice, as well as trading agreements with the pirates at Omiš. (Much later, the city would once again demonstrate its political acumen by signing a treaty with the Ottomans guaranteeing trading rights.) In the 14th century its territory stretched from the Kotor inlet in the south to the northern tip of the

Pelješac peninsula, and included the islands of Lastovo and Mljet.

In the 12th century Venice launched a series of attacks on the coastal cities of Dalmatia, as well as on a number of its islands. In 1202 the Venetian Doge Dandolo enlisted the support of the armies of the Fourth Crusade (which would go on to sack Constantinople two years later, with the wily old Doge playing a prominent role in the affair) to capture Zadar – following which an infuriated Pope excommunicated the entire expedition. In 1205 Dubrovnik also fell to Venice. The Mongol invasions of the 13th century saw their pursuit of King Bela of Hungary to the Adriatic coast, which they ravaged before being recalled to their homeland on the death of Genghis Khan. The power struggles which followed

27

the death of Bela in 1270 were used by Venice as an opportunity to take Šibenik and Trogir. Between 1342 and 1382 King Ludovik I of Hungary re-established control over Croatia, persuading Venice to relinquish its grip on Dalmatia; and in 1358 Dubrovnik was returned to Hungary, although it maintained its own government and from this date existed as an independent republic. The country slid into anarchy on Ludovik's death, with Tvrtko I of Bosnia emerging briefly as the most powerful figure in the region and carving out a small kingdom before his death in 1391. Following this, the Croatian nobility misguidedly turned to Ladislas of Naples, who was crowned king of Zadar in 1403. Ladislas soon sold Zadar to Venice for a miserable 100,000 ducats, and by 1420 Venice controlled the whole

of Dalmatia, a grip it would not relinquish until the arrival of Napoleon.

The overwhelming defeat of Serbian, Croatian and Bosnian forces by the Ottomans at the battle of Kosovo in 1389, together with the fall of Constantinople in 1453, saw the Balkan peninsula opened up to Turkish invasion. Bosnia was conquered in 1463 and Herzegovina in 1482, and thousands of refugees trekked north. In 1493 the Croatian nobility were decimated at the battle of Krbavsko polje in Lika, and city after city fell to the Ottoman advance. In 1526 the Hungarian forces under Ludovik II were defeated at the battle of Mohacs, and 1529 saw the Ottomans lay siege to Vienna. The Austrian Archduke Ferdinand was elected king of Croatia by its *sabor* (parliament) under the proviso that he would help defend

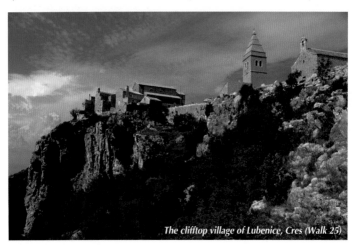

The clifftop village of Lubenice, Cres (Walk 25)

the country against the Ottomans; but by the end of the century only a small area around Zagreb, Karlovac and Varaždin remained under Austrian control. Austria established the Vojna Krajina (military frontier) across the war-ravaged and largely depopulated Croatian hinterland, and settled the area with large numbers of Vlachs (mountain inhabitants of both Orthodox and Catholic faiths), who were granted a degree of independence in return for their services as frontier soldiers. The Croatian parliament objected furiously to their settlement on Croatian soil and to their exemption from the system of feudal taxes imposed on the rest of the population by the Austrians. Yet the Vlachs were to remain in the Krajina for over 450 years, to be expelled only at the close of the appalling events of 1991–1995.

During the 16th century the Uskoks, fugitives from the Ottoman advance based in Senj, conducted their long reign of terror against the Turks, with refugees joining them as partisans. The rout of the Ottoman forces at the second siege of Vienna in 1683 marked a reversal of their fortunes in the Balkans, and in 1699 the Treaty of Sremski Karlovci saw all Turkish claims to Croatia and Hungary renounced. During the following century, a flood of Croatian and Serbian immigrants settled in Slavonia.

The arrival of Napoleon at the end of the 18th century brought new changes to the region, as well as renewed hopes of Croatian unity. However, although the Venetian republic disintegrated in 1797, with Dalmatia being transferred to Austria by the Treaty of Campo Formio that same year, the administrative division of Dalmatia and Slavonia was maintained, much to Croatian disgust. In 1805 Napoleon's victory over the Austrian forces at Austerlitz resulted in Dalmatia being ceded to France, and in the creation of the Illyrian Provinces. Dubrovnik was occupied by Napoleon's troops the following year, following which the Republic of Dubrovnik was dissolved and became part of the new Illyrian Provinces. Napoleon instigated a number of reforms in Dalmatia to counteract the years of neglect suffered by the region. These included a tree plantation programme, in an attempt to restore the denuded forests; the establishment of primary schools, high schools and the University of Zadar to combat illiteracy; the draining of the marshes to combat rampant malaria; the construction of new roads and hospitals; and the introduction of new crops. Yet these reforms remained largely unpopular, due in part to French opposition to the clergy, and to the fact that new taxes were introduced upon the locals in order to pay for the reforms.

In 1815 the Congress of Vienna returned Dalmatia to Austria, while placing the rest of Croatia under Austria's Hungarian province. This saw a restoration of power to the former Italian élite in Dalmatia, and

Tiled roofs and cloister of Franciscan monastery, Dubrovnik

the imposition of Hungarian language and culture upon Croatia as a whole. The reaction to all of this was the Illyrian Movement, which surfaced in the 1830s and marked the beginning of a national awakening, or national revival, in Croatia. Typically at this time upper-class Dalmatians spoke Italian, while German or Hungarian were spoken in northern Croatia. Perhaps not surprisingly then, the Illyrian Movement centred on a revival of the Croatian language.

In 1834 the first 'Illyrian' newspaper was published, written in the Zagreb dialect. Its appearance prompted the Croatian parliament to call for the teaching of Slavic language at schools, this being followed by calls for the unification of Dalmatia and Slavonia, and in 1837 'Illyrian' was voted the national language. In 1843 Vienna banned the use of the

word 'Illyrian' in Croatia: thereafter it was superseded by the term Croatian.

During the revolutions of 1848 Croatia agreed to intervene against a Hungarian revolutionary movement on the side of the Hapsburgs in return for greater autonomy for Croatia, and 40,000 troops were despatched under the command of ban Josip Jelačić. Born in 1801, this celebrated figure (whose equestrian statue stands in Zagreb's main square, the eponymous Trg bana Jelačić) was both a loyal officer in the Austrian army and a firm supporter of the Illyrian Movement, and was elected ban of Croatia in 1848. However, the battles were indecisive, and ultimately Jelačić was not the only component of the force which finally broke Hungarian resistance. Opposition to any form of revolutionary regime grew in Austria; the emperor revoked all revolutionary and constitutional changes, and the Croatian parliament was closed.

The creation of the Austro-Hungarian dual monarchy in 1867 placed Croatia and Slavonia within Hungarian administration, leaving Dalmatia under Austrian control, and the Croats found themselves with even less independence and self-government than under the Hapsburgs.

Against this background two schools of political thought developed within 19th-century Croatia, both directed towards the emancipation of the country from foreign rule. The old Illyrian Movement became the National Party, led by the charismatic Bishop Josip Juraj Strossmayer. Strossmayer, who also supported the cause of Serbian independence, believed (with considerable justification) that the differences between Croats and Serbs were being magnified by foreign manipulation, and that this could be combated only by south Slavic unity (Jugoslavenstvo), although he felt that this should be within the framework of the Austro-Hungarian Empire, rather than complete independence. The opposing movement was the Party of Rights, led by Ante Starčević. Militantly anti-Serbian, he promulgated the idea of an independent Croatia consisting of Slavonia, Dalmatia, the Krajina, Slovenia, Istria, part of Bosnia and Herzegovina.

During this period, the Orthodox church encouraged Serbs to form a national identity based upon their religion, which together with the attacks of Starčević led to a gradual polarisation of the two populations and an increasing sense of a separate, Orthodox identity within a largely Catholic Croatia. The Hungarians exploited the situation by supporting the Serbian cause, dividing the country still further. Organised resistance to Austro-Hungarian rule first erupted in Dalmatia, and in 1905 Croat representatives in Rijeka and Serbian representatives in Zadar joined forces to call for a unification of Dalmatia and Slavonia, with a guarantee of Serbian equality.

The Kingdom of Serbs, Croats and Slovenes

With the collapse of the Austro-Hungarian Empire at the end of the First World War in 1918, Croatia feared that it might be further dissected by foreign powers (certainly the Treaty of London, signed in 1915, seemed to suggest that an Allied victory would be followed by Croatia effectively being carved up between Italy and Serbia). Pula, Rijeka and Zadar were quickly gobbled up by Italy, and to prevent further territory being lost, a Croatian delegation, the Yuguslav Committee, persuaded the Serbian government to agree to the establishment of a parliamentary monarchy ruling over the two countries. On 1 December 1918 the first communal Yugoslav state, the Kingdom of Serbs, Croats and Slovenes, was founded. It was to last until 1941, although it was never recognised by the Treaty of Versailles.

However, problems with the new regime soon became apparent: currency reforms benefited Serbia at the expense of Croatia; a treaty with Italy gave Istria, Zadar and a number of islands to Italy; and a new constitution abolished the Croatian sabor and centralised power in Belgrade. Opposition was spearheaded by Stjepan Radić, the leader of the Croatian Peasant Party. However, in 1928 he was murdered in parliament: the constitution was suspended, and what amounted to a military dictatorship ensued under King Peter's successor, Alexander.

Almost immediately the Croatian Liberation Movement, better known as the Ustaša, was set up with the stated aim of establishing an independent Croatian state, by force if necessary, under Ante Pavelić, a Bosnian Croat. After making contact with anti-Serbian Macedonian revolutionaries in Sofia, he fled to Italy, where he established training camps under the auspices of Mussolini. Pavelić masterminded the assassination of Alexander on a state visit in Marseilles, following which he was imprisoned by Mussolini and the training camps closed. Alexander's successor, his cousin Prince Paul, attempted to advance the cause for Croatian autonomy, but progress was cut short by the events of the Second World War.

The Second World War

Germany invaded Yugoslavia on 6 April 1941, installing the Ustaša as rulers of the Nezavisna Država Hrvatska or NDH (Independent State of Croatia), headed by Pavelić, and ushering in what is arguably the darkest chapter of Croatian history. Between 1941 and 1945 a range of decrees issued by Pavelić were implemented against the 'enemies' of the regime: primarily Jews, Gypsies and Serbs. These took the form of horrific local pogroms, with almost 80 per cent of the Jewish population sent to extermination camps in Nazi Germany, and Serb extermination camps set up (most notoriously at Jasenovac, south of Zagreb) to carry out the unwritten Ustaša demand that one third of the Serbian population should be killed, one third expelled and one third converted to Catholicism. The estimated number of Serb deaths varies enormously, but is possibly about 80,000.

However, the Ustaša drew their support from only a minority of the population, centred around Lika and western Herzegovina, and owed their authority primarily to the support of Hitler and Mussolini. That their support would remain minimal in Dalmatia was guaranteed by an agreement to cede large chunks of the coast and islands to Italy. Armed Četnik resistance to the Ustaša began under General Dražo Mihailović, but soon degenerated into massacres of Croats in eastern Croatia and Bosnia. The National Liberation Partisans under Tito, with their notions of 'Brotherhood and Unity' and a unified Yugoslav state, attracted both Croats and Serbs appalled by the cycle of reciprocal massacres, as well as anti-Fascists in general. The initial Allied support for the Četniks was re-channelled to the Partisans, who by 1943 controlled much of Croatia.

The Federal Peoples' Republic of Yugoslavia

Following the end of the Second World War, the Federal Peoples' Republic of Yugoslavia was established on 29 November 1945, consisting of six republics and two autonomous provinces. Tito initiated a number of constitutional reforms and formally broke with Stalinism in 1948. But the channelling of money from the wealthier Croatia and Slovenia to Belgrade and to the less prosperous republics, combined with the suppression of organised religion (following the perception that it had played its part in polarising the population, leading to the bloody inter-ethnic fighting of the Second World War) and the over-representation of Serbs in government positions and the security forces, led to increasing dissatisfaction in Croatia, which culminated in the 'Croatian Spring' of 1971. Croatia's increasingly vocal criticism of Belgrade's policies and calls for greater autonomy and constitutional reform were swiftly answered with purges, jail sentences and repression. Following Tito's death in 1980, the Serb and Croat nationalist aspirations which he had largely driven underground in 1971 slowly rose to the surface.

Against a background of sweeping changes and the collapse of communism in eastern Europe and the former Soviet Union, and the repression of the Albanian minority in Kosovo

Church of St Euphemia, Rovinj, Istria

in 1989, free elections were held in April 1990, with Franjo Tuđman and the HDZ (Croatian Democratic Union) elected to power with 40 per cent of the vote. Mass dismissals of Serbs from the public service sector, combined with an unrelenting Serbian media campaign heralding the rebirth of the Ustaša, prompted Croatia's 600,000 strong Serb community in the Krajina and eastern Slavonia to demand autonomy, while Serb extremists within Croatia staged provocations intended to draw federal military intervention. In March 1991 a Serb unit took over the headquarters of Plitvička jezera National Park: the resultant fighting between them and the Croatian police claimed the first victims of the war in Croatia, from both sides.

Independence

In May 1991, following the deaths of 12 Croatian policemen in Borovo Selo, a village near Osijek, a referendum was held, with over 90 per cent voting in favour of Croatian independence. Independence was formally declared on 25 June 1991. In response, the Krajina Serbs held their own referendum and voted to remain part of Yugoslavia. JNA (Yugoslav People's Army) forces entered Slovenia, which had also declared its independence, but were comprehensively defeated in five days. In Croatia, the war was to take a very different course.

In June 1991 heavy fighting broke out in the Krajina and eastern Slavonia, after which the Serb-dominated JNA increasingly intervened on its own authority in support of Serbian

Premužićeva staza, Northern Velebit (Walk 11)

irregulars. European Community mediation persuaded Croatia to freeze its declaration of independence to prevent the country spiralling into further bloodshed, but in the three months following 25 June a quarter of Croatian territory fell to Serb militias and the JNA. In September, the Croatian government ordered the blockade of federal military installations within Croatia; in response the JNA blockaded the Adriatic and laid siege to the historic town of Vukovar on the Danube. The United Nations declared an arms embargo on all republics of the former Yugoslavia. In October the JNA and Montenegrin militia positioned themselves on the hills above Dubrovnik, beginning a siege which would last until June the following year and draw widespread international media attention. In November Vukovar finally fell, having been almost razed to the ground by relentless air and artillery bombardment, and many of the surviving inhabitants were massacred. To this day, though largely rebuilt, Vukovar remains a haunting reminder of the war of the 1990s. By December, thousands of people had died in the fighting in Croatia, and more than half a million fled their homes.

Early in 1992 United Nations negotiations under its envoy Cyrus Vance were followed by the deployment of a 12,000 member UN Protection Force (UNPROFOR). The ceasefire declared in January 1992 largely held, and was accompanied by the withdrawal of the JNA, although significantly it did not mark a return to pre-war borders or provide for their future settlement. Moreover, for the Krajina it only temporarily froze the existing situation, without offering a permanent solution. In January, the European Community caved in to pressure from Germany and recognised Croatian independence. A few months later, the storm which had been brewing over Bosnia finally broke, plunging the country into a war of almost unimaginable barbarity.

In January 1993 the Croatian army launched an offensive in the south Krajina, recapturing large tracts of territory. In May 1995 Croatian forces entered occupied western Slavonia, quickly regaining control of the area; the Krajina Serbs responded by shelling Zagreb. Some 15,000 Serbs fled Slavonia, despite assurances of their safety from the Croatian government. In August Croatia launched a massive military offensive on the Serb stronghold of Knin. The Serb army fled northward, together with over 100,000 civilians whose roots in the area stretched back some four and a half centuries. Attacks followed on the few who stayed. In December 1995 the Dayton Accord was signed in Paris, and Croatia's international borders were recognised.

The years following the war have seen a gradual trickle of refugees returning to Slavonia and a massive increase in tourism in Dalmatia – although the war in Kosovo in

1998 and the NATO bombing of Serbia in 1999 did little to encourage this. In recent years, tourism has skyrocketed, with some 9.4 million foreign visitors in 2008. Croatia was accepted into the Council of Europe in 1996, and in January 1998 Vukovar and its surroundings were finally reintegrated into Croatia. The Prevlaka peninsula (the southernmost tip of Croatia) was disputed by Croatia and Montenegro following the war, and a small UN mission (known as UNMOP) remained there to oversee the demilitarisation of the peninsula until 2002.

President Tuđman died at the end of 1999, following which the HDZ were ousted and the SDP (Social Democratic Party) voted into power, with Stipe Mesić assuming presidency and Ivica Račan being elected prime minister. The HDZ returned to power in 2003 with Ivo Sanader as prime minister; on his resignation in 2009, he was succeded by Jadranka Kosor, Croatia's first female prime minister. Croatia achieved candidate status in its bid for EU membership in 2004, and it looks scheduled to finally join in 2011 – though this is not entirely certain.

Today Croatia is a quiet place, where the level of political excitement does not rise much higher than a dispute over fishing rights with neighbouring Slovenia. The economy is improving, yet prices remain high for most locals, with a typical salary being only a quarter of its equivalent in the UK. This state of affairs was perhaps best illustrated by the comments of a German tourist interviewed on television about prices along the coast: 'I don't find it expensive – in fact, prices are the same as in Germany. But I have absolutely no idea how the local population can afford anything.'

ARCHITECTURE, ART AND CULTURE

Croatia boasts some stunning architectural treasures. The country's finest Roman architectural remains are to be found at Split and Pula: the magnificent complex of Diocletian's palace at the former, and the incredibly well-preserved amphitheatre at the latter. Other important Roman sites include Zadar and Salona (Solin, in Split), while numerous smaller finds are on display at the archaeological museum in Split. In Poreč, the Euphrasian Basilica (commissioned by Bishop Euphrasius in 535–550) contains some particularly beautiful Byzantine mosaics.

Croatia's coastal towns are a wonderfully seductive amalgamation of Romanesque, Renaissance, Venetian and Baroque architecture. Particularly attractive are Dubrovnik, Hvar, Korčula, Trogir and Zadar; the most impressive walled medieval towns are Dubrovnik and Korčula. Baroque architecture is perhaps at its richest in Varaždin and Osijek, while nobody can claim to have really seen Croatia without spending some time in its capital, Zagreb, the centre of which is a lovely assortment of Secessionist and neo-Baroque styles.

Sculpture of Vladimir Nazor, Zagreb

FESTIVALS IN CROATIA

The country's major festivals include: the Dubrovnik Summer Festival (July–August); the Alka, a form of jousting tournament held in Sinj (August); the Zagreb International Folk Festival (July); the Pula Film Festival (July); and the Rijeka Carnival (second largest in Europe) as well as the Samobor Carnival (both February); while Independence Day (25 June) will undoubtedly involve some form of local celebrations, wherever you are. Finally, those on Korčula should not miss the Moreška, an elaborate sword dance which is performed about twice a week during August.

Perhaps the most venerated of Croatian artists is the sculptor Ivan Meštrović (1883–1962), whose colossal Gregorius of Nin stands behind Diocletian's palace in Split. His former house and studio in Zagreb, the Meštrović Atelier, is one of the finest museums in Croatia. (For a note on Croatian literature see Appendix D.)

WILDLIFE AND PLANTS

Mammals

Croatia's mountains and forests play host to a wide range of mammals including three large carnivores, the brown bear, grey wolf and lynx.

The brown bear (*Ursus arctos*) inhabits the forests of Gorski kotar and highland Velebit, although your chances of seeing more than the odd track in the snow are slim indeed.

(After more than a decade of hiking in Croatia, I have yet to see anything more than just this in the wild.) Sadly, the brown bear is still hunted for sport in Croatia (and overseas visitors pay top dollar to slaughter them), and you will see hunting and baiting towers in some parts of Gorski kotar. Croatia's brown bear population is estimated at around 400. The grey wolf (*Canis lupus*) inhabits some of the remoter parts of the Dinaric Alps, its population currently lying somewhere around 200 – although again, sightings are extremely rare (I have yet to meet anyone who has ever seen one). Although the grey wolf is protected in Croatia, over half of recorded deaths are by illegal shooting. The Eurasian lynx (*Lynx lynx*) is present on Risnjak and Velebit but, again, sightings are rare.

Wild pigs (*Sus scrofa*) roam the forests of Slavonia, Gorski kotar and Velebit, as do somewhat less reclusive species such as red deer (*Cervus elaphus*) and roe deer (*Capreolus capreolus*). Mouflon, or wild mountain sheep (*Ovis aries musimon*), are particularly common on Biokovo. Other mammals include the wild cat (*Felix silvestris*), chamois (*Rupicapra rupicapra*), red squirrel (*Sciurus vulgaris*), pine marten (*Martes martes*) and common dormouse (*Glis glis*). Incidentally, Croatia's currency (the kuna) is named after the marten – *kuna* in Croatian – the pelts of which were used as a unit of trade and measure of currency in the Middle Ages, and are recorded in this context as early as 1018.

CONSERVATION INITIATIVES

The website of the **State Institute for Nature Protection** (www.dzzp.hr) has information on protected areas and species. The **LIFE 'Conservation and Management of Wolves in Croatia' Project** has several offices in Croatia (Bogovićeva 1a, 10000 Zagreb; tel: +385 (0)1 487 4744). See its website, www.life-vuk.hr for more information on wolves in Croatia. See the website of the **Large Carnivore Initiative for Europe** (www.lcie.org) for further details on the status of brown bear, grey wolf and lynx in Europe, along with links to project brochures.

Refugium Ursorum Kuterevo (Velebitsko utočište za mlade medvjede Kuterevo, www.kuterevo-medvjedi.hr, tel: +385 (0) 53 799 222) is a sanctuary for orphaned brown bear cubs, in the village of Kuterevo on northern Velebit.

Reptiles and Amphibians

The rocky limestone of Croatia's coastal ranges and islands provides an ideal habitat for snakes, and in the summer your chances of encountering one are fairly high. Two venomous species which you should be particularly alert for are the nose-horned viper (*Vipera ammodytes*), known

Dice snake (Natrix tessellata), Plitvička jezera national park (Walk 13)

locally as *poskok*, and the common viper or adder (*Vipera berus*), known locally as *šarka* or *šarulja*. The former grows up to 60cm in length, and sometimes to 95cm. It is either light grey or brownish copper, with a dark-black zigzag pattern along its back, and is recognisable by the soft horn at the end of its snout. The nose-horned viper is Europe's most venomous snake, and a bite from its 1cm fangs is something to be avoided. There is a well-preserved specimen at the hut PD Zavižan. Both *poskok* and *šarka* are to be found on rocky hill-sides, under low bushes and around dry-stone walls; the latter may also be found in forest clearings. The meadow viper (*Vipera ursini*) and its sub-species the karst adder (*Vipera ursine macrops*) are also venomous, although supposedly much more

Edible frog (Rana kl. esculenta), Lonjsko polje (Walk 5)

39

docile than either of the above species. In any case, walking boots and hiking poles will usually alert a snake to your approach and give it time to slither off, and snakes will usually only bite in self-defence.

Non-poisonous snakes include the leopard snake (*Elaphe situla*), the four-lined snake (*Elaphe quatuorlineata*), the black whip snake (*Coluber viridiflavus*), Dahl's whip snake (*Coluber gemonensis*) and the Montpellier snake (*Malpolon monpessulanus*).

A number of lizards are also common, including the sand lizard (*Lacerta agilis*), Dalmatian wall lizard (*Podarcis melisellensis*), Horvath's rock lizard (*Lacerta horvathi*), Mosor rock lizard (*Lacerta mosorensis*), green lizard (*Lacerta viridis*) and the slightly larger Balkan green lizard (*Lacerta trilineata*).

Amphibians include the fire salamander (*Salamandra salamandra*) and the less common alpine salamander (*Salamandra atra*), moor frog (*Rana arvalis*), marsh frog (*Rana ridibunda*), edible frog (*Rana kl. esculenta*) and Balkan stream frog (*Rana graeca*). Croatia also constitutes part of the extremely limited distribution of the olm (*Proteus anguinus*), a type of sightless salamander.

Birds

Of the various birds inhabiting Croatia, the largest is the griffon vulture (*Gyps fulvus*), which has a wingspan of some 2.5m. It once nested among the crags of Velika and Mala Paklenica, but the last surviving pair were poisoned a few years back, and the species now only survives in Croatia at the sanctuary in Beli on the

Grey heron (Ardea cinerea), Kopački rit nature park (Walk 6)

island of Cres (see box). The golden eagle (*Aquila chrysaetos*) is occasionally seen in Krka National Park or on Velebit. Another rare species

island of Cres (see box).

BIRD SANCTUARIES

Eko-Centar Caput Insulae, Beli, Cres

The Eco-Centre at Beli (www.supovi.hr, tel: +385 (0) 51 840 525), dedicated to protection of the griffon vulture in Croatia, was established in 1993. It has a sanctuary for injured or poisoned birds, and runs volunteer programs as well as an 'adopt a griffon' program. Open 09.00–20.00 (closed 1 November–1 March), entry 40Kn.

Sokolarski Centar Dubrava, Šibenik

Sokolarski Center Dubrava (www.sokolarskicentar.com, tel: 091 506 7610) is a falconry centre about 7km from Šibenik, near the village of Dubrava. There is a small hospital where sick or injured birds are cared for and rehabilitated, and the Centre runs informative 45-minute presentations on birds of prey, as well as environmental education programs and one- and five-day falconry courses. Open daily 10.00–13.00 and 16.00–19.30, entry 30Kn. Larger groups are asked to call in advance.

---

present in Croatia is Bonelli's eagle (*Hieraaetus fasciatus*). Other birds of prey include the short-toed eagle (*Circaetus gallicus*), buzzard (*Buteo buteo*), peregrine falcon (*Falco peregrinus*), goshawk (*Accipiter gentilis*) and sparrow hawk (*Accipiter nisus*).

Much smaller but no less impressive is the alpine swift (*Alpus melba*), the fastest bird in Europe, which swoops and darts about a number of high peaks at a phenomenal speed. The capercaillie (*Tetrao urogallus*) is found fairly widely including Velebit (and is the symbol of north Velebit national park).

Waders and marsh birds include the grey heron (*Ardea cinerea*), cormorant (*Phalacrocorax carbo*), white stork (*Ciconia ciconia*) and black stork (*Ciconia nigra*). Some of the best places for observing these species are Kopački rit (cormorant), Lonjsko polje (white and black stork), Krka and Plitvička jezera.

Invertebrates

Among the invertebrates found in Croatia are over 180 species of butterfly – including such exotic, localised species as the southern swallowtail (*Papilio alexanor*), blue argus (*Ultraaricia anteros*) and Dalmatian ringlet (*Proterebia afra*) – as well as several species of dragonfly. Freshwater invertebrates include a recently discovered endemic species of subterranean leech, *Croatobranchus mestrovi*, which inhabits the underground caves of Velebit.

Ticks are found in Croatia, and are most common from May to July. Check skin, scalp and clothes after walking through long grass or dense forest cover, particularly if hiking with children (see pages 61–62 for information on removing ticks).

Plants

Croatia's mountain plantlife ranges from mixed coniferous and deciduous forests to sub-alpine scrub and stony grasslands. The Dinaric Alps are more heavily forested in the north, on Velebit and especially Gorski kotar. The islands range from the heavily forested Mljet and Korčula (called Korkyra meliana, 'Black' Korkyra, by the Greeks after its luxuriant, dark vegetation) to the barren and sun-bleached wastes of Pag and Goli otok ('naked island').

Mountain and sub-alpine forest is dominated by beech (*Fagus silvatica*) and Aleppo pine (*Pinus halepensis*). Other typical species include black pine (*Pinus nigra*), Dalmatian black pine (*Pinus nigra dalmatica*), holly or holm oak (*Quercus ilex*), kermes oak (*Quercus coccifera*), downy oak (*Quercus pubescens*), oriental hornbeam (*Carpinus orientalis*), hop hornbeam (*Ostrya carpinifolia*), mountain pine (*Pinus mugus*), juniper (both prickly juniper, *Juniperus oxycedrus*, and Phoenician juniper, *Juniperus phoenicea*, as well as *Juniperus communis* and *Juniperus sabina*), spruce (*Picea excelsa*), sycamore maple (*Acer pseudoplatanus*), silver fir (*Abies alba*), cypress (*Cumpressus sempervirens*) and laurel (*Laurus nobilis*).

Much of the vegetation typically consists of hardy, low shrubs or

Alpine sea holly (Eryngium alpinum), near Premužićeva staza, Northern Velebit (Walk 11)

Water lily (Nymphaea alba), Kopački rit nature park (Walk 6)

maquis, characterised by strawberry tree (*Arbutus unedo*), myrtle (*Myrtis communis*), mastic tree (*Pistacia lentiscus*), turpentine tree (*Pistacia terebinthus*), wild olive (*Olea europaea*), rosemary (*Rosemarinus officinalis*), thyme (*Thymus capitatus*) and rose (*Rosa sempervirens*). In the mountains you will find dense thickets of dwarf mountain pine and juniper (known locally as *planinski bor* and *klekovina*).

Other plant varieties include alpine sea holly (*Eryngium alpinum*), the increasingly rare edelweiss (*Leontopodium alpinum*), known locally as *runolist*, in Velebit and Risnjak, alpine clementis (*Clementis alpina*), and black vanilla orchid (*Nigritella nigra*).

Numerous endemic plant species are to be found (some 485 in Croatia as a whole), particularly on Velebit,

where some 78 have been identified. These include *Degenia velebitica*, *Dianthus velebiticus*, *Saxifraga prenia*, *Gentiana lutea*, *Arbrieta croatica* and *Sibirea croatica*. Endemic species in Biokovo include *Edraianthus pumilo* and *Centaurea cuspidate*.

GETTING TO CROATIA

Arguably the most impressive way to arrive in Croatia is by **train** (www. raileurope.co.uk) – the view on emerging from Zagreb's Glavni kolodvor (main station), followed by a bus ride through the suburbs, certainly being more attractive than anything you can hope for at an airport. However, it's a fairly long journey, and a train ticket from the UK will probably set you back more than a flight – so this may be more of an attractive option for those arriving from cities in neighbouring countries, for example Trieste, Venice, Ljubljana, Budapest, Belgrade or Sarajevo.

Croatia Airlines (www.croatia airlines.com) has **flights** from London (and other European cities including Paris, Brussels and Frankfurt) to Zagreb and all major Croatian cities including Split, Dubrovnik, Zadar and Rijeka. (Note: buying tickets for domestic flights is much cheaper in Croatia itself.) British Airways (www.ba.com) also flies to Split and Dubrovnik, for roughly the same fare as Croatia Airlines. Now that Croatia is firmly back on the tourist trail, flights get heavily booked in the summer – so book as far in advance as possible.

Tram on Ilica, Zagreb

Over the past few years a num-ber of budget airlines have opened routes to Croatia. These include Ryanair (www.ryanair.com, to Zadar, Pula and Osijek), easyJet (www.easyjet.com, to Rijeka and Split), and Wizz Air (www.wizzair.com, to Zagreb). Again, book as far ahead as possible.

Another option is flying to a city in an adjacent country, such as Trieste (Ryanair), Ljubljana (easyJet) or Graz (Ryanair), from where there are direct trains to Zagreb (for train times to Zagreb see www.hzni.hr).

International coach services run from the UK, Germany and other countries in western Europe (see www.eurolines.com) – although the fare from London is not much less than a flight to Zagreb, and certainly more than flying with a budget airline.

There are regular ferry cross-ings (www.jadrolinija.hr, www.splittours,hr, www.snav.it, www.venezialines.com) to Zadar, Split and Dubrovnik, as well as some of the islands, from various ports in Italy (Ancona, Bari, Pescara, Venice).

GETTING AROUND

Croatia is a fairly small country, and getting round on local transport is generally a simple affair. Buses run between most cities; rail services connect Zagreb with Split (via Knin), Rijeka (via Delnice) and towns in Slavonia; and a comprehensive ferry service runs between the coastal cities and the islands.

Of these various options, the **train** (www.hznet.hr) remains the most rea-sonably priced (return fares are gener-ally cheaper than two singles). A seat reservation is recommended, but not essential, on longer journeys, particularly the overnight or the new express train to Split.

Intercity **buses** cover most towns in Croatia (for services from Zagreb see www.akz.hr). They tend to be slightly more expensive than an equivalent train journey, but there are few alternative options along some sections of the coast. Local bus services travel to almost all the villages that lie at the start or finish of the routes in this guide.

The real bargain is the **ferries**, which provide by far the most pleasant means of getting around the coast. Jadrolinija (www.jadrolinija.hr) is a state-run company, and has services (ferries and fast catamarans) to most towns and islands along the coast. A number of private companies also run catamarans on a limited number of routes.

Croatia Airlines has domestic **flights** between Zagreb and most major towns in Croatia including Dubrovnik, Split, Pula, Rijeka and Zadar (note that tickets are much cheaper when purchased in Croatia).

For those travelling around by **car**, Croatia's new motorway system has reduced journey times considerably. Croatia operates a toll system on motorways. Bear in mind that the main road along the coast, known as the *Jadranska magistrala*, gets extremely busy during the summer months, and caution is advised. During the winter months Gorski kotar becomes largely snow-bound, and travel on the old Rijeka–Zagreb road becomes restricted – in some cases cars will not be allowed across

Entrance to Krka national park at Skradin (Walk 14)

without chains. Car rental options include Budget (www.budget.hr) and Sixt (www.e-sixt.com). In the event of a breakdown, you can call the Croatian Automobile Club (www.hak.hr) on 987 (from within Croatia only).

Zagreb's **tram** service covers most parts of the city. Tickets can be bought from newspaper kiosks or (at a slightly higher price) from the driver, and must be stamped in the small machines on the tram to be valid. Thereafter you can use them on any combination of services (including buses), travelling in the same direction, for a period of two hours from when they are first stamped. Day travel cards are also available. As of 2009 tram journeys within central Zagreb are free.

Hitching is an accepted means of transport in the mountains (less so in cities or on some of the busier parts of the coast and islands), and in general getting a ride should not pose too much of a problem. However, bear in mind that in Croatia, as elsewhere, hitching can never be recommended as entirely safe for those travelling alone, particularly women.

Those planning a **cycling** holiday in Croatia should make the most of the excellent 'Bike and Bed' scheme (www.bicikl.hr/bike-bed). Some parts of Croatia are promoting cycling more actively than others – Zagreb County Tourist Office produces an excellent series of free cycle route maps (www.tzzz.hr); Lonjsko polje in Slavonia and the Island of Hvar are two further places developing a good network of cycle routes. For those who want something a little more challenging, there are long routes over the forest roads of Velebit. However the traffic on Croatia's roads is not always particularly cycle friendly – in particular the coast road during summer. For further information on cycling in Croatia see www.pedala.hr.

ACCOMMODATION

Croatia is hardly a budget accommodation destination. Many of the larger **hotels** charge western European prices for less than spectacular rooms and service, while the price of **private rooms** or *sobe* (roughly equivalent to B&B in the UK, but typically without the breakfast) on the coast often runs to rather more than it should for a country trying to attract more visitors. Furthermore, a 30 per cent supplement is charged for guests staying fewer than three nights; and some places simply will not accept guests who wish to stay for less than a week. Still, prices are reasonable for the western visitor. Tarrifs are seasonal, and drop quite considerably outside the high season – although a number of private guesthouses are open only during the summer, or from May to November. In recent years a number of new boutique hotels have opened, making a welcome alternative to some of the enormous places on the coast.

Private rooms are usually booked through an agency. You will pay a commission, but this remains by far the most straightforward way of doing

Hotel Jezero, Plitvička jezera national park (Walk 13)

things. Even if you find a place yourself, if it is officially registered with an agency, you still have to pay the same price as you would through the agency, so you may as well let them do the work for you. There are also plenty of unofficial or unregistered rooms and lodgings, the owners of which congregate around local bus and train stations, and who will certainly approach you if they have anything available. In this case you are advised to go and see the room, which certainly does not bind you to taking it if you find it unacceptable. There are fewer private rooms in Zagreb, where accommodation options are more limited to hotels and to a few hostels (see Appendix C).

Relevant accommodation details are given in the introduction to each walk and in Appendix C. Mountain huts are also plentiful: for details see the 'Walking in Croatia' section below.

FOOD AND DRINK

Croatian cuisine is a blend of influences reflecting its particular geographical position, and is delicious. The boxed list overleaf is far from exhaustive, but should give you an idea of some dishes to track down.

Croatia also produces a fair amount of wine. The main grape-growing regions are the Dalmatian coast and islands (producing predominantly medium to full-bodied reds, and one or two whites) and a number of areas in Slavonia (producing mainly whites). As a general rule, those wines designated *vrhunsko* (from *vrh*, 'top') tend to be much better than those designated *kvalitetno* ('quality'). Dingač and Postup are

47

MENU READER

Grilling carp, Lonjsko polje

Pašticada: Wonderfully opulent Dalmatian speciality, consisting of marinated beef or veal cooked slowly with dried plums, and typically served with home-made *gnocchi* and parmesan cheese.

Sarma: Slavonian speciality. Cabbage leaves stuffed with rice and ground beef.

Mlinci: Baked noodles, typically served with *puretina* (turkey).

Riba: Fish, of which Croatia (not surprisingly) has plenty. Typically either boiled (*kuhano*), topped with olive oil, garlic and parsley, and served with potatoes and *blitva* (Swiss chard); or grilled (*na žaru*).

Brodet: Mixed fish stew, similar to Italian brodetto.

Hobotnica na žaru: Along with *pašticada*, the crème de la crème of Croatian cuisine. Octopus, roasted in the oven in its own juices, with potatoes and onions and olive oil.

Salata od hobotnice: Octopus and potato salad, with parsley, onion, garlic and olive oil.

Punjene lignje: Stuffed squid.

Crni rižoto: 'Black' squid risotto, cooked in its own ink.

Fiš paprikaš: A spicy stew of carp and peppers – another Slavonian speciality.

Ribice: Sprats fried in breadcrumbs – a favourite café snack.

Ćevapčići: Small grilled meatballs, typically served with *ajvar* (roasted pepper and aubergine puree). Not quite as good as those you might find in Sarajevo, perhaps, but still excellent.

Pogača: Pastry filled with anchovies and capers – a speciality of the island of Vis, and similar to Italian calzone.

Grah: A hearty bean stew, sometimes made with *kobasice* (sausages).

Juha: Soup. Particularly good are *juha od povrča* (vegetable soup) and *riblja juha* (fish soup).

Paški sir: Croatia's most celebrated cheese, from the island of Pag.

Pršut: Dalmatian prosciutto.

Kulen: The Slavonian answer to prosciutto – drier, harder, and perfect for hiking.

Palačinke: Pancakes – a favourite Croatian desert.

Kremšnite: A custard dessert, especially good in Samobor.

two small grape-growing regions on the Pelješac peninsula, and are generally considered to produce Croatia's finest red wines, *dingač* and *postup*. *Vugava viška* and *smokvica* are white wines from the islands of Vis and Hvar respectively. *Rajnski rizling*, *traminac* and *graševina* are all produced extensively in Slavonia, with some of the best coming from Ilok and Kutjevo. *Prošek* is a sweet desert wine from the coast.

A number of spirits are also produced, the best-known being the proverbial *rakija*. This comes in a number of guises, all extremely potent, but a really good *domaće* ('home made') is most definitely worth sampling. *Šljivovica* is perhaps the finest and is made from plums; *travarica*, made with herbs, is also good.

Various imported and local beers are available, the best local brews being Ožujsko and Karlovačko, not to mention the rather more elusive (and very good) Velebitsko pivo, brewed in Gospić.

Fruit juices are widely available, and the coffee (*kava*) is excellent.

LANGUAGE

While Croatian may not be the most difficult language in the world to learn, neither is it the easiest. It poses a number of grammatical problems which may be new to the native English speaker, although anyone who has studied a language such as Latin, Russian or German should find no more difficulty with Croatian than with these languages. It is a pleasant-sounding language with an interesting history.

Croatian is a phonetic language – that is, every letter in a word is pronounced, and the pronunciation of a given letter is always the same, making it far more consistent than English or French. Consonant clusters may prove something of a tongue twister to the uninitiated (try *vrt* 'garden'; *trg* 'square'; *krv* 'blood'), but are easy to get used to.

Croatian belongs to the south Slavonic branch of the Indo-European family of languages and is closely related to, but not the same as, Serbian and Bosnian. The relationship between Croatian and Serbian is variously seen as similar to that between British and American English, or as that between two wholly separate and distinct languages, depending on one's point of view. The standardisation of the language during Croatia's inclusion in the Federal Republic of Yugoslavia (1945–91) resulted in the amalgamation of Croatian and Serbian (as the two dominant languages within the Federation), known as Serbo-Croatian or Croato-Serbian. This was written in the Latinised Croatian alphabet in Croatia, and in Cyrillic in Serbia. Since independence, there has been a conscious (sometimes frenzied) effort on both sides of the border to untangle, and in some cases polarise, the two languages. Turkophiles will discover a number of Turkish words, which entered the region during its 500 years under Ottoman rule; while a number of Italian influences are also evident, particularly on the coast.

KEY WORDS FOR WALKERS

brdo	hill
kuk	crag, bare limestone peak
planina	mountain
planinari	hikers
planinarski dom	mountain hut
planinarska kuća	mountain hut (open by arrangement)
planinarska staza	mountain path, trail
put	route
sklonište	shelter
vrh	peak, summit

COMMON ABBREVIATIONS

GSS (*Gorska služba spašavanja*)	Mountain Rescue Service
HPD (*Hrvatsko planinarsko društvo*)	Croatian Mountaineering Association
HPS (*Hrvatski planinarski savez*)	Croatian Mountaineering Committee
KT (*kontrolna točka*)	hiking checkpoint/register
NP (*Nacionalni park*)	national park
PD (*planinarski dom*)	mountain hut
PDS (*Planinarsko društvo sveučališta*)	hiking club

Within Croatia, there are also a number of regional variations, or 'dialects', which typify the language spoken in Zagreb, certain parts of Dalmatia, Slavonia and Zagorje. However, these effectively only differ from one another in a few words and in their accent, and are of little concern to the visitor.

Pronunciation is especially important if you are to be understood, particularly in view of the fact that a number of letters occurring in English are pronounced completely differently in Croatian, most notably 'c' (pronounced 'ts') and 'j' (pronounced 'y'). See Appendix D for further information.

English is widely spoken in Croatia, particularly in Zagreb and major tourist centres, and German and Italian are also common, particularly on the coast. In mountain huts you will frequently find someone who speaks some English, either the warden or local hikers staying there. However, in smaller towns and villages off the main tourist trail you will have to be somewhat more self-reliant.

Appendix D provides an English–Croatian glossary, and a few key words and abbreviations are given above.

VISAS

Visas are unnecessary for visitors from most western countries. For example, a UK passport holder can enter the country for up to three months at a time. After this, it is necessary either to cross over the border into a neighbouring country before returning or to go through the lengthy process of applying for an extended stay permit. Visitors are still officially required to register with the police within 24 hours of arrival, although if you are staying in hotels, private accommodation, mountain huts or official campsites this is automatically done for you when you hand your passport over to the agency, reception or hut warden.

CURRENCY

The Croatian unit of currency is the *kuna* (abbreviated Kn or HRK), 1 *kuna* being comprised of 100 *lipa*. The *kuna* comes in small coin denominations (currently 1, 2 and 5) and larger notes (currently 5 up to 1000). When changing money, try to get a decent supply of smaller notes (20Kn, 50Kn and 100Kn), as the larger notes can be hard to change in smaller shops and supermarkets. The value of the *kuna* has remained relatively stable for a number of years, and at the time of writing £1=7.87Kn, 1Euro = 7.26Kn. You may find a number of prices (particularly accommodation) quoted in Euros, which will then be converted into *kuna* according to the daily rate.

CHANGING MONEY

Changing money in Croatia is very straightforward. *Mjenjačnica* (small exchange booths) are dotted all over the larger towns and cities, and generally give the best rates. Those at bus and train stations tend to give poorer rates. Daily rates are usually posted where you can see them. Changing money in banks usually involves queuing for a long, long time, and you are advised to use the exchange offices. A commission is sometimes charged at exchange offices and is always charged in banks. ATMs are common in major towns and cities. Cash is preferable to traveller's cheques, which you will be able to exchange only in major towns or tourist centres, and which will certainly involve more queuing.

POSTAL SERVICES AND TELECOMMUNICATIONS

The international dialling code for Croatia is 00 385. Area codes include:

- Zagreb (including Samobor) 01
- Rijeka (including Gorski kotar and Cres) 051
- Gospić (including northern Velebit and Plitvička jezera) 053
- Zadar (including southern Velebit and Paklenica) 023
- Šibenik (including Krka) 022
- Split (including Makarska/Biokovo, Brač and Hvar) 021
- Dubrovnik (including Pelješac and Korčula) 020
- Osijek (including Kopački rit) 031

If calling from overseas, omit the initial zero from these area codes. Mobile phones work fine in Croatia, including in mountain areas, but not in areas of heavy forest cover. Those staying for a longer amount of time might consider buying a local SIM card (VIP and T-Mobile are the main service providers), which usually works out at around 150Kn including free minutes.

Call boxes are found in post offices, and are the cheapest way of calling overseas. Otherwise, phone cards are available from newspaper kiosks for use in the blue public card-phones, although these will not last particularly long on an international call. Note that addresses in Croatia are given with the street name preceding the street number.

Mountain Huts and Camping

Mountain **huts** in Croatia are excellent and plentiful, and fall into three categories: a **planinarski dom** (usually abbreviated PD) is a staffed hut open to all, regardless of whether you have made any prior booking (and in most cases you will not need to); a **planinarska kuća** is usually only open by prior arrangement (either with the relevant hiking club or a private organisation), otherwise you will find it locked; a **sklonište** is a small hut or shelter, unmanned and (in most cases) open year round. A *dom* may be open year round, during the summer months, or only at weekends; the availability of a *kuća* may have similar limitations. In many cases huts have a *sklonište* attached to them, which is opened when the rest of the hut locks up for the winter. See Appendix B for a list of huts and relevant organisations.

Prices vary from hut to hut, and there is a reduction for members of an HPS-affiliated club (Hrvatski Planinarski Savez – the Croatian Mountaineering Association); but prices remain extremely reasonable, and it remains unusual for a hut to charge a separate, higher tariff for foreign visitors. There is no fee for staying in a *sklonište*. Many huts offer reasonably priced cooked meals, tea and other drinks, or else provide the use of a kitchen. **Note** Availability of meals varies from hut to hut (and season to season) and cannot be relied upon.

Rossijevo sklonište, Northern Velebit (Walk 11)

Hut staff are in most cases an invaluable source of local information and advice, as are the local walkers and climbers you will doubtless encounter when staying in huts.

Camping is perfectly acceptable in mountain areas, although prohibited within a national park (see below). Camping on the coast is unfortunately restricted to large (and usually extremely busy) campsites. Pitching a tent anywhere else on the coast, and particularly on a beach, will almost certainly result in your being asked to move by the police, and you would do better to find a room, either private accommodation or a hotel.

Equipment

The equipment necessary for the routes in this guide is much the

View northwest from below Motika, Biokovo (Walk 17)

same as it would be for most other European mountain ranges of a similar, or slightly higher altitude.

You should be prepared for rain at any time of year, and a waterproof shell (Gore-Tex or similar) is essential.

Even if you plan to spend all your nights in huts and shelters, you should be aware that solid fuel is scarce and has to be carried up to the mountains by someone: it is therefore prudent to carry a small stove. Camping gas cylinders (*kartuše*) are not always readily available, and a refillable multi-fuel stove is more useful.

A tent is far from essential, but may be useful on some of the longer itineraries. However, bear in mind that camping is prohibited in national park areas, and that water availability is typically restricted to huts.

Boots need to be tough, and able to cope with terrain which is almost

exclusively either jagged limestone or knotted tree roots. Although summer walks on the islands can be undertaken in trainers, these are not recommended for the mountains. Trekking in sandals is an open invitation to snakebite in the mountains.

Beyond these items, what you take will depend on what time of year you visit Croatia. Blistering summer temperatures dictate adequate sun protection – plenty of sunscreen, sunglasses, sun hat – while the shortage (or complete absence) of water between huts on a number of routes makes a supply of water flasks (preferably lightweight aluminium or collapsible plastic, or a combination of the two) essential. A lightweight summer sleeping bag will be sufficient for spring/summer/autumn use in huts. It's worth carrying a sleeping mat, as most *sklonište* don't have mattresses.

During the winter you should be prepared for bitterly cold, frequently sub-zero temperatures in the mountains. A three- to four-season sleeping bag, warm hat and gloves, thermal base layer, and Polartec or similar mid-layer are all mandatory. Walking poles or a long-handled ice axe are recommended, although many local walkers do not use them (but you should not necessarily follow their example!). Crampons may be helpful in a year of heavy snowfall in the Dinaric Alps.

For those in doubt, the following basic checklist may be useful (for multi-day treks in the mountains from Spring to Autumn):

- rucksack (approximately 60–75 litres capacity)
- walking boots, with Vibram soles (wear them in before your trip!)
- other footwear for the coast or in towns (rafting or trekking sandals, such as those made by Teva, are perfect)
- rainproof, breathable shell (Gore-Tex, eVent or similar material)
- warm, preferably windproof fleece (Polartec or similar material) jacket or mid layer
- light thermal base layer
- shorts and long trousers (lightweight, quick-drying material), long-sleeved shirt, T-shirts, underwear
- good quality walking socks (these counter the need to wear two layers of socks or sock-liners)

- warm gloves and hat
- sun hat
- sleeping bag (1–2 season will be fine for all except winter use)
- sleeping mat (closed cell or inflatable)
- water bottles (lightweight aluminium, such as those made by Sigg, and/or collapsible plastic bladders such as those made by Platypus)
- stove (preferably multi-fuel such as MSR) and compatible fuel bottle(s)
- lightweight cooking pot, fork and spoon
- compass and relevant maps (and the knowledge of how to use them)
- torch (headlamps, such as those made by Petzl, are best)
- sunglasses and sunblock
- biodegradable soap (such as that made by Lifeventure)
- small first aid kit
- swiss army knife
- whistle (for attracting attention in an emergency)
- emergency reflective bag or 'space blanket'
- matches (keep them dry in a plastic bag!)
- large plastic rucksack liner
- mosquito repellent
- iodine tablets (unlikely to be needed, but just in case)
- small 2-pin adaptor (same as for most of continental Europe)
- adequate food.

55

You may also wish to add:
- lightweight day pack
- walking poles
- reliable tent (I have used Macpac tents for years).

Maps

Croatia's major mountain areas are covered by a detailed (1:25,000 or 1:30,000) series of maps published by SMAND (www.smand.hr). They give accurate topographical detail (with contour lines drawn to 25m), and mark both paths and huts. Those relevant to the routes in this guide, with their sheet numbers, are:

- Medvednica (01)
- Samoborsko gorje (08)
- Samarske, Bijele stijene, Bjelolasica (11a)
- Bjelolasica (11b)
- Gorski kotar I (11)
- Gorski kotar IV (14)
- Učka (15)
- Sjeverni Velebit (16)
- Srednji Velebit (17)
- Južni Velebit I (18)
- Nacionalni Park Paklenica (19)
- Biokovo (32).

Until recently these were unavailable in the UK, but The Map Shop (www.themapshop.co.uk, tel: 01684 593146) now stocks them, and they can be ordered online. The maps are also readily available from bookshops in Zagreb (see Appendix C), and from hiking clubs and huts, and usually retail at about 55Kn.

Some of the national parks and nature parks produce their own maps, including Plitvička jezera, Paklenica, Lonjsko Polje, Papuk and Medvednica. A new sheet, covering the recently extended boundaries of Risnjak National Park, is also available from PD Snježnik and PD Risnjak, if you are unable to find the relevant SMAND sheet. Also useful for its coverage of the entire Gorski kotar area is the old Gorski kotar planinarska karta (1:100,000), produced in Slovenia, though this may now be hard to find, and a number of the paths shown have now become forest roads. A number of military sheets (1:100,000) are also available through the Croatian Mountaineering Association. However, the SMAND maps remain the preferred choice for walking.

More general maps include the Freytag & Berndt series covering the coast in a number of sheets (1:100,000), but note that while fine for planning trips around the islands, these are not suitable for hiking. These maps do not accurately locate all paths, while the inclusion of huts and springs is frequently misleading, because a number of the huts have been closed for a number of years (or require advance booking if you are to find them open at all), and a number of springs dry up over the summer.

Tourist information offices generally do not carry maps suitable for hiking – a notable exception being the excellent map ('Walking through the countryside of the Pelješac Riviera') available free from the tourist information centre in Orebić.

Finally, a number of Croatian-language hiking guides (see Appendix E) include fairly detailed maps. Recommended even if you are unable to read the text are the following small and inexpensive route guides: *Velebitski planinarski put* (for the entire route from PD Zavižan to Velika Paklenica) and *Mrkopaljski planinarski put* (covering the MPP on Bijele stijene).

Trail Markings

Almost without exception, paths and trails in Croatia are clearly marked with a uniform system of waymarkings (see diagram overleaf). Known locally as *markacija* (markings), and almost always in red and white paint on trees, rocks and any other conspicuous object, the main ones are shown in the diagram.

The first of these signs with a cross through it usually indicates a wrong turn, or disused path. A cross usually indicates a junction. Blue, green and yellow paint are often used to indicate caves, sinkholes and other related features.

Note that the frequent use of forestry markings, typically a number of lines or bands spray-painted on a tree, have absolutely no connection with marked hiking trails and should be comprehensively ignored.

Croatia's mountain areas feature a number of named trails and

Trail markings on Sljeme (Walks 1 and 2)

footpaths. Those covered by the walks in this guide (either in full or in part), in the order in which they occur in the text, are as follows:

- **RT (Riječka transverzala)** A route from the Istrian coast heading inland over Učka (Walk 7).
- **MPP (Mrkopaljski planinarski put)** A route through the impressive limestone scenery of Samarske stijene (Walk 9).
- **KPP (Kapelski planinarski put)** A route over Velika Kapela, including Samarske stijene and Bijele stijene (Walk 9); overlaps with sections of the GPP.
- **Vihoraški put** The most impressive section of the KPP between Ratkovo sklonište and Planinarska kuća na Bijelim stijenama (Walk 9).

Trail Markings

O Simply indicates that you are on a marked trail of some sort. Adjacent signs or names of topographic features (again painted on trees and rocks) let you know exactly *which* path you are following.

|| Indicates that the relevant trail continues straight ahead.

// Indicates a change in direction: not necessarily at a junction.

- **GPP (Goranski planinarski put)** A circular route stretching from the Slovenian border traversing most areas of Gorski kotar, including Risnjak and Snježnik (Walk 8); Bjelolasica, Samarske stijene and Bijele stijene (Walk 9); and Klek (Walk 10).
- **SPP (Spojni planinarski put)** A route linking Velika Kapela with northern Velebit, running from Bijele stijene to Oltare via Kolovratske stijene (ie linking Walks 9 and 11).
- **VPP (Velebitski planinarski put – also marked 'v')** Croatia's most extensive long-distance footpath, traversing northern, central and southern Velebit, from Oltare in

the north to Velika Paklenica in the south (Walks 11 and 12).
- **Premužićeva staza** The section of the VPP covering northern and central Velebit, from near PD Zavižan to Baške Oštarije. It is (at least at its northern end) the most spectacular route in Croatia (Walk 11).
- **BPS (Biokovska planinarska staza)** A route over Biokovo (Walk 17).
- **PEP (Poučni ekološki put)** An alternative route over Biokovo (Walk 17).

Water, Food and Supplies
Dried meats and various cheeses are widely available and, together with

dark bread (*alpski kruh* or *crni kruh*), form the staple of most local walkers on shorter hikes. Packet soups and pasta meals are easy to find in any moderate-sized supermarket, as are powdered drinks such as Cedevita, and dried fruits and nuts.

Instant soup and dried meals requiring less than three minutes' cooking time are more difficult to come by, and it is a good idea to bring a supply of such items from home to augment what is available locally. (A more detailed vocabulary for food items is given in Appendix D, and there is further information in the 'Food and Drink' section above.)

Water is available at most (but not all) huts; springs between these are rare and tend to dry up in the summer. You will therefore need to carry sufficient water for each stage – and, in

some cases, for more than one stage (the availability of water is referred to in the route descriptions).

National Parks

The following areas within Croatia have been designated national parks (*nacionalni park*, usually abbreviated to the prefix NP):

- Brijuni islands
- Kornati islands
- Krka
- Mljet
- Paklenica
- Plitvička jezera
- Risnjak
- Sjeverni Velebit.

An entry fee is payable on entering a national park – either at an entry point (in the case of Plitvička jezera or Paklenica) or at a staffed mountain

Trail on wooden boardwalks, Plitvička jezera national park (Walk 13)

hut (in the case of Risnjak and Sjeverni Velebit). Tickets are available to cover various periods of time – for example 3, 5 or 7 days – so you can buy one to cover the time you plan to stay within the park. Prices are reasonable for the western visitor (less so for locals), for example 30Kn (£4 or €4) for three days in NP Sjeverni Velebit. You should hang on to your ticket to show at subsequent huts. Camping is prohibited in national parks, but may be allowed next to a hut.

A further 11 areas are designated 'nature parks' (*park prirode*, or PP):

- Biokovo
- Kopački rit
- Lastovo islands
- Lonjsko polje
- Medvednica
- Papuk
- Telašćica
- Učka
- Velebit
- Vransko jezero
- Žumberak–Samoborsko gorje

Unlike national parks, these generally carry no entry fee and in general (but not always) have no restriction on camping, although you should obviously show the same consideration for the environment (see 'Leave no trace' box right).

Some areas are UNESCO World Heritage Sites (Plitvička jezera) or UNESCO International Biosphere Reserves (the whole Velebit massif was classified as such in 1978).

LEAVE NO TRACE

Cicerone guide users will hardly need reminding of the following basic guidelines when travelling in the great outdoors, whether a national park or ortherwise.

- Do not leave any litter – carry it out of the mountains and dispose of it in a town or city.
- Never light any open fires, and be aware of the risks of forest fires!
- Close gates behind you.
- Bury toilet waste.
- Do not pick wild flowers.
- Do not disturb wild animals and birds.
- Camp only at designated areas or well off the main trail .

FOREST FIRES

Croatia's hot, dry climate makes forest fires a real danger, both in the Dinaric Alps and on the islands, and visitors should be particularly aware of the threat they pose to the environment. In summer 2003 one such fire consumed much of the lush vegetation below Buljma near Velika Paklenica, and over the years a few mountain huts have also been burnt to the ground. Never light an open fire, and exercise common sense in the use of gas and multi-fuel stoves.

WHAT TO DO IN AN EMERGENCY

In most cases, your best source of advice will be the nearest staffed **mountain hut** (see Appendix B). Otherwise, the **Croatian Mountain Rescue Service (Hrvatska Gorska služba spašavanja, HGSS** or simply **GSS)** can be contacted as follows:
- Delnice (for Gorski kotar) +385 (0) 91 721 0004
- Gospić (for northern and central Velebit)+385 (0) 91 721 0007
- Makarska (for Biokovo) +385 (0) 91 721 0011
- Split (for Mosor) +385 (0) 91 721 0001
- Zadar (for southern Velebit and Paklenica) +385 (0) 91 721 0010
- Zagreb (for Medvednica) +385 (0) 91 721 0002.

These are the full numbers if you are calling from a UK mobile. If calling from a Croatian phone or mobile, omit the +385 and add a zero at the beginning of the number.

The GSS website (www.gss.hr) has contact details of other local offices. Like many such organisations around the world, the GSS provides free mountain rescue but relies on the efforts and bravery of a small group of dedicated volunteers, whose services should not be called upon lightly.

Emergency phone numbers
Police   92
Fire   93
Ambulance   94
Emergency services can also be contacted on **112**.

At present the UK and Croatia have a reciprocal arrangement where emergency state medical treatment is free to citizens of both countries (not including private medical treatment or visits to a GP or dentist). **Missing persons** should be reported to the relevant embassy or consulate (see Appendix C).

In case of **snakebite**, immobilise the limb or affected area and get the victim to a doctor. Antivenoms are available from hospitals and medical centres; sucking the wound and spitting has been shown to be completely ineffective. If possible try to identify the snake in question, but not at the cost of avoid getting bitten yourself.

Ticks should be removed as soon as possible to minimize the risk of infection, by grasping the tick as close as possible to its head (avoid crushing ▶

◄ the abdomen), either with tick tweezers or fingernails, and pulling gently at right angles to the skin. Do not use irritants to dislodge ticks, as this may induce them to regurgitate, increasing the chance of infection. Wash the area afterwards with alcohol or disinfectant.

ABOUT THIS GUIDE

Rating and Arrangement of Routes

A reasonable level of fitness is required for the walks in the Dinaric Alps, while those on the islands are in general very easy. None of the routes requires any climbing skills or equipment: a number do involve a degree of scrambling, although this can frequently be avoided.

Each walk in this guide has been given a rating (very easy, easy, moderate or difficult). In rating the difficulty of a particular route or stage, a number of factors have been taken into consideration: technical difficulty (in particular whether any scrambling, or the use of fixed pegs and steel cables, is involved); terrain; duration; altitude and the total amount of ascent/descent; clarity of the route/trail; availability of water, huts and shelter.

Routes or stages involving the use of fixed pegs or cables have been rated moderate or moderate–difficult, while those involving technically demanding scrambles on poorly marked or unmarked routes have been rated difficult. Otherwise ratings reflect a combination of the above factors.

The guidebook contains both circular and point-to-point routes,

varying in duration from a few hours to a few days. In many (but not all) cases there is scope to shorten or extend routes, bypassing more difficult sections or adding more challenging excursions or alternative routes. Such details are given in the introductions to individual routes.

The routes in this guide fall into eight main sections: walks around Zagreb (1–3), walks in Slavonia (4–6), walks in Istria (7), walks in the coastal ranges or Dinaric Alps (8–10), walks in Velebit (11–12), walks in Plitvička jezera and Krka (13–14), walks in Mosor, Kozjak and Biokovo (15–17) and walks in the Croatian islands (18–26). Within this format, the arrangement of individual routes does not reflect their technical difficulty, duration or attractiveness, but rather follows a roughly north–south arrangement (by range or massif) within the Dinaric Alps, and a south-north arrangement (by island) of the islands. Overall, the more extended, challenging and spectacular routes are those in the Dinaric Alps.

Timings

The timing given in the box preceding the route description refers to an average walking speed, and does not include breaks or stopping time at summits. Excursions not included in the initial route or stage profile are not included in these timings either. Altitudes and distances are given in metres and kilometres throughout.

Spelling and Local Place Names

In general, English spelling has been used throughout this guide for the names of Croatian regions and surrounding countries – thus Dalmatia as opposed to Dalmacija, Slavonia as opposed to Slavonija, Yugoslavia instead of Jugoslavija and so on.

Maps and Sketch Maps

The routes in this guide are all illustrated by sketch maps, except for routes in Appendix A, 'Exploring further', and walks 5, 6, 12, 14 and 19, which are short and simple enough not to need maps. Map references in the information boxes preceding individual routes or stages refer to the relevant SMAND sheet, where available, or reasonable alternative. For the walks around Zagreb and on the islands, a detailed map is hardly necessary (for the latter, there is very little available anyway), and the sketch maps should suffice. However, you would be well advised to purchase the relevant SMAND sheet(s) for routes in the Dinaric Alps (Gorski kotar, Velebit, and Biokovo – there is currently nothing available for Mosor or Kozjak).

Landmines sign, Kopački rit nature park

LANDMINES

Certain areas of Croatia remain heavily mined from the 1991–1995 war. These include the area between Karlovac and Knin, the Bosnian border, certain parts of eastern Slavonia, and even the occasional village not far from Zadar. In these areas, stay on sealed roads, and avoid deserted villages and buildings – they are usually deserted for a reason. Similarly, areas of unused farmland should be avoided. The presence of landmines in the area around Knin means that climbs on Dinara, Croatia's highest mountain, are to be undertaken with caution.

With one exception, none of the routes recommended in this guide passes anywhere near the unsafe areas listed above, and the presence of landmines in these areas should certainly not deter you from visiting the rest of the country. Neither do the above comments on deserted houses and villages apply to those encountered on the routes in this guide, which are typically deserted for economic reasons. The one exception is southern Velebit, certain areas of which are suspected of being mined, and while the paths in this guide are perfectly safe in themselves, adjacent areas are not. A de-mining programme has been initiated in southern Velebit, which will hopefully increase the number of potential walking areas in the future, but at present follow the advice below.

- The area beyond Struge, and the eastern side of the main ridge from Struge to Sveto brdo, is suspected of being mined: do not proceed east of Struge or descend to the eastern side of the main ridge under any circumstances! Do not wander off the main path in this area: if you do not manage to reach a hut and need to camp, pitch your tent on the path.
- The trail to Visošica east of Jelova ruja leads into an area suspected of landmine deployment: make sure you turn south after Jelova ruja.
- The small peak Panos (1261m) south of Šugarska duliba has an abandoned military installation on it: do not approach this peak under any circumstances.
- The strikingly beautiful area around Tulove grede remains similarly out of bounds

Two further areas, Lonjsko polje or Kopački rit in Slavonia, lie close to areas with minefields – make sure you keep to roads and marked trails, and follow local warnings.

64

Mine clearance has been hampered by the fact that, in many cases, there are no precise records of mine deployment, making the process particularly hazardous. Furthermore, the high cost of mine clearance operations (roughly US$50,000 to clear an area the size of a football pitch) and the fact that, as one of the wealthier countries requiring landmine clearance, Croatia has to pay the bill itself, have made progress very slow.

Further information on the efforts to clear landmines in Croatia can be found at the Croatian Mine Action Centre (www.hcr.hr), the International Campaign to Ban Landmines (www.icbl.org) and Adopt-a-Minefield (www.landmines.org).

CROATIA AT A GLANCE

Country name Republika Hrvatska

Capital Zagreb

Language Croatian

Currency *kuna* (Kn or HNK)

Population 4.49 million (estimate, 2009)

Land surface area 56,594km^2

Time zone GMT +1

International telephone code +385

GDP per capita approximately US$15,632 (2009)

Main religion Roman Catholic (87%)

Independence day 25 June

PART 1
AROUND ZAGREB

Zelengaj in winter, Zagreb

INTRODUCTION

Zagreb, Croatia's capital, receives comparatively few foreign visitors, most of whom head directly for the coast. This is a shame, since it is a lovely city, with a completely different atmosphere to Split or Dubrovnik – very much central European, as opposed to Mediterranean. The impressive neo-Baroque and Secessionist architecture of its squares and main thoroughfares, its narrow streets lined with cafés, its large open market overflowing with produce, and main square strewn with flower stalls – all backed by the luxuriant green of Medvednica – combine to make Zagreb a pleasant place to while away a few days before setting off for the karst wilderness of the Dinaric Alps. The majority of Croatian *planinari* (hikers) are from Zagreb, rather than from the coastal cities; and this is where the greatest concentration of climbing clubs is to be found.

Accommodation is somewhat more limited in Zagreb than on the coast. There are fewer private guesthouses, and options are for the most part confined to a choice of hotels and a few hostels (see Appendix C). Tram tickets are available from newspaper kiosks on tram routes or, failing this, from the driver, at a slightly higher price, and

*Medvednica
and Sljeme*

must be stamped in the small machines on the tram to be valid. Thereafter you can use them on any combination of services (including buses), travelling in the same direction, for a period of two hours from when they are first stamped. Day travel cards are also available. As of 2009 tram journeys within central Zagreb are free.

MEDVEDNICA AND SLJEME

Medvednica is the large, forested massif rising directly from the northern suburbs of Zagreb, crowned by a large telecommunications tower at its highest point, Sljeme (1033m). Medvednica is a nature park (www.pp-medvednica.hr) – although any of the bears implied by its name (from *medvjed*, meaning 'bear') were hunted down or disappeared long ago. Locals flock to Sljeme at the weekends, and during the winter an area just below the summit functions as a small ski slope. Various *gostionica* (small restaurants) serve hearty meals, which you can work up an appetite for on the way up. There are numerous routes over Medvednica, together with a road and a cable car (closed for upgrading in 2009) to the top.

WALK 1
Sljeme

Time	4hrs return
Distance	13km
Maximum altitude	1033m
Rating	very easy
Map	SMAND Medvednica (01)
Transport	Take a number 102 bus (either from Britanski trg or Kaptol) to the village of Šestine, and get off just before (or after) the small church with its brightly coloured roof tiles.
Accommodation	See Appendix C for accommodation in Zagreb.
Practical information	The Zagreb City Tourist Office (www.zagreb-touristinfo.hr) is an excellent source of information for all things Zagreb.

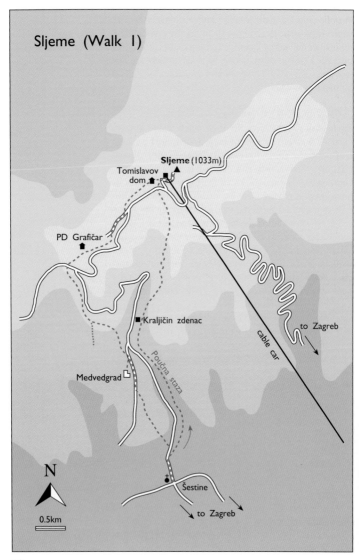

Sljeme (Walk 1)

Sljeme (1033m)

Tomislavov dom

PD Grafičar

Kraljičin zdenac

Medvedgrad

Poučna staza

cable car

to Zagreb

N

0.5km

Šestine

to Zagreb

The following circular route starts and finishes in the small village of Šestine, and forms an easy and straightforward forest walk, with PD Grafičar making a good stopping point for lunch. A visit to Medvedgrad, a 13th-century fortress on the slopes overlooking Zagreb, is included in this itinerary.

Continue uphill from the church in Šestine, passing a cemetery on the left and following the trail markings. After 5mins arrive a car park and a sign reading 'Park prirode Medvednica' (Medvednica Nature Park); just after this pass a small wooden shelter on the right. Here a broad path descends from the road on the right to wind through the shade of tall, ivy-clad *hrast* (oak) and *bukva* (beech), while a small stream is audible trickling through the gully on the right – all in significant contrast to the harsh and waterless Dinaric peaks which await you along the coast. The path, known as Poučna staza ('educational path'), is extensively labelled with details of the surrounding trees and rocks, although the text is all in Croatian.

The path begins climbing slowly, with wooden foot-bridges crossing side-streams, to reach a junction 1hr from Šestine, just above a small café and picnic area by the road – a place known as **Kraljičin zdenac**. ▶

Continue straight ahead, following the signs to Tomislavov dom and ignoring tracks to the left, as the path narrows and enters pine before becoming steeper. After opening out again into a tall stand of beech, the path crosses a side-stream and begins zigzagging up an eroded slope before entering tall pines once more. The path divides and meets again, with occasional markings, crossing a forest road before veering left and zigzagging up to the main road below **Tomislavov dom**, 45mins beyond Kraljičin zdenac. Turn right onto this before ascending past the cable car station to reach the various cafés and *gostionica* at the top of **Sljeme** (1033m) in a few minutes. From here there is a view down over the scattered houses of Gornja Bistra and the forested spurs of northern Medvednica, although PD Grafičar (see below) undoubtedly remains a more pleasant spot to linger.

A short way further up the road there is a rather wonderful sculpture of a bear in grass, moss and lichen.

PD Grafičar, Sljeme

The hut sits at the edge of a grassy clearing, with wooden tables outside, and serves a hearty *grah* (bean stew) and, during the summer, the best *ćevapčići* (grilled meatballs) on Sljeme.

Descend to the cable car station and **Tomislavov dom** before veering right on a marked trail to PD Grafičar. Continue straight ahead, passing a grassy clearing on the left, to join a sealed road along the ridge top by a trail on the right to Gornja Bistra. Follow the road, passing a military base on the left (where a sign points out that photography is prohibited), before turning left onto a path through the trees. This soon descends in switchbacks to **PD Grafičar**, which you reach about 30mins from the summit. ◄

EXTENSION

Just to the SW of PD Grafičar you'll find the Zrinski Mine, one of a number of medieval mines in the area, where gold, silver and other ores were once mined. The Zrinski Mine has interactive displays, and is open to the public Saturdays and Sundays 11am–5pm, tickets 25Kn (adults), 15Kn (children). See www.pp-medvednica.hr for more details.

It is possible to walk to the Veternica Cave and PD Glavica (Walk 2) from PD Grafičar. Allow 3hrs 30mins one way.

To return from PD Grafičar, follow the trail down beside the clearing, descending through the trees to the road; cross the road before continuing along a trail marked 'Lukšić'. Descend on a stony path, passing some paragliding ramps on the right before entering the trees and veering left on a trail marked 'Zdenac' (*not* the path straight ahead to Lukšić). This leads down to the road again, 40mins below the hut.

Medvedgrad is 5mins up the cobbled road to the right. Built in the mid-13th century, it was later abandoned, then restored during the 1990s. ▶

Return to the main road and turn right, following it for 10mins before turning left onto a path marked 'Šestine'. From here it's another 15mins down to the road; continue past the restaurant and car park, and the small wooden shelter, before walking down towards the church in **Šestine**. The bus stop is just beyond the church, by the small newspaper kiosk.

The ruins of another 13th century fort, Susedgrad, lie on the western slopes of Medvednica.

WALK 2
Veternica Cave

Time	1hr 30mins return
Distance	3km
Maximum altitude	420m
Rating	very easy
Map	SMAND Medvednica (01) or Karta Parka Prirode Medvednica
Transport	Take bus 124 from Črnomerec (which is on tram 6 or 11 from Jelačić Square) to Gornji Stenjevec, and get out at the last stop.

A short walk to the Veternica Cave – Croatia's fourth-longest cave, a source of numerous archaeological finds and home to a fairly healthy-sized population of bats – on the southwestern flanks of Medvednica from Gornji Stenjevec. Veternica can only be visited by appointment, with a guide – Saturdays and Sundays from April to November, price (including guide) 25Kn (adults), 15Kn (children). Tours of the cave last around 45mins. To

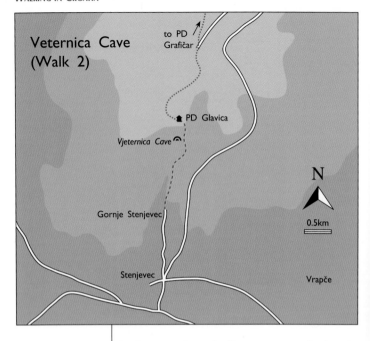

Veternica Cave
(Walk 2)

to PD
Grafičar

PD Glavica

Vjeternica Cave

N

0.5km

Gornje Stenjevec

Stenjevec

Vrapče

book, contact the park office (www.pp-medvednica.hr, tel: +385 (0)1 458 6317).

Walk north from the end of the road in **Gornji Stenjevec**, heading into the forest on the path marked 'špilja veternica'. It's a 30min hike to **Veternica Cave**, climbing gradually.

Veternica is some 2,600m long (that's just the main part – with all the other explored passages, the figure is over 7,100m), of which about 380m are open to the public. Archaeological finds in the form of stone tools and weapons in the cave show that it was used by Neanderthal Man some 40,000 years ago. The cave was found to contain a large number of animal remains, including bones and skulls of the extinct cave bear (*Ursus spelaeus*). Some 14 species of bat have been

recorded in Veternica, including the greater horseshoe bat (*Rhinolophus ferrumequinum*), Mediterranean horseshoe bat (*Rhinolophus euryale*) and Nathusius' pipistrelle (*Pipistrellus nathusii*). The bats hibernate in the cave over the winter – one of the reasons it is closed at that time of year. Although the cave has been protected since 1979, souvenir-hunters had long since removed most of the stalactites from the initial sections. From the cave, continue 10mins up the steep path and steps to reach **PD Glavica**, which does excellent food.

Sign and trail to Veternica cave, Sljeme

EXTENSION

It is possible to walk to PD Grafičar (Walk 1) from PD Glavica. Continue along the forest road from the hut, then take a trail on the left marked 'Grafičar'. Allow 3hrs 30mins one way.

Return to Gornji Stenjevec by the same route.

WALK 3
Samoborsko gorje

Just beyond the small Baroque town of Samobor, a few kilometres west of Zagreb, rise the rolling hills of Samoborsko gorje – lower in altitude than Sljeme, but none the less worthy of a day trip. Samobor itself is an attractive little town, serving some particularly fine *kremšnite* (custard cream dessert), and its hilly environs form part of the Žumberak–Samoborsko gorje nature park (www.pp-zumberak-samoborsko-gorje.hr).

Time	4hrs 30mins return
Distance	15km
Maximum altitude	752m
Rating	very easy
Maps	SMAND covers the area with Samoborsko gorje (8).
Transport	Regular buses travel between Črnomerec (at the end of tram routes 6 and 11) and Samobor, leaving from stops 14 and 15. Of the two services available, take the one travelling via Sveta Nedelja rather than the one travelling via Strmec, which takes considerably longer. Local tram and bus tickets are not valid, and you will have to buy a separate ticket. Get off at the bus station in Samobor – the last stop on the bus route.
Accommodation	See Appendix C for accommodation in Zagreb. For accommodation in Samobor contact the tourist information office (www.tz-samobor.hr, tel: +385 (0) 336 0050), or try the Hotel Lavica (www.lavica-hotel.hr, tel: +385 (0) 336 8000), which has a good restaurant.

An easy day trip, although there is scope for extending the route. A visit to Stari grad, the old fortress on the edge of Samobor, is included.

From the bus station in Samobor, walk south into the main square (Trg kralja Tomislava) and turn right. From

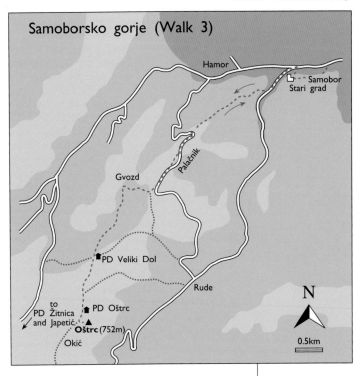

Samoborsko gorje (Walk 3)

Hamor

Samobor
Stari grad

Palačnik

Gvozd

PD Veliki Dol

Rude

to
PD Žitnica
and Japetić

PD Oštrc

Oštrc (752m)

Okić

N

0.5km

beyond the square, turn left over the wooden footbridge, walking through the small park with the stream on your right. Follow the left branch of this path up to the ruined fortress of **Stari grad**, built in several phases between the 13th and the 18th centuries. The walls are crumbling (watch out for falling stones), and the interior is overgrown and littered with broken glass, but the northwest towers are still impressive. Descend by the same route to the playing fields, turning left before crossing the stream once more to return to the road. Take the first road on the left (signposted to Rude), following this for a few minutes past a church and over a small bridge, before turning right on a marked trail to Oštrc.

Follow the unsealed road, turning left as indicated and ascending past some houses, with good views of Stari grad, before veering right and following the track as it narrows, passing orchards and through intermittent forest cover. Pass under a small and rocky bluff before following a clear and well-marked forest trail up through tall beech and oak to reach a minor road, 40mins from the Rude turn-off. Turn left onto the road, following it through Palačnik (and at one point diverging from it briefly to walk through someone's back garden) before turning off to the right and descending slightly towards Gvozd. Here you turn left, following the clear trail as it winds its way to PD Veliki dol. Continue straight ahead past the hut, ignoring the path on the left to Rude, to reach PD Oštrc, approximately 1hr from Palačnik. There are pleasant views southwest towards Japetić from the low peak (752m) just beyond the hut. Return to Samobor by the same route.

EXTENSION

It would be possible to extend this itinerary considerably: either southwest to Japetić (879m) and PD Žitnica (closed in 2009), or south and then east to Okić (499m). However, bus services are less reliable from the roads below these possible destinations, and you may find yourself doing a fair amount of road walking to get back to Samobor.

FURTHER POSSIBILITIES

Japetić

Unless you have your own wheels, Japetić is most easily reached from Šoićeva kuća, on the bus route to Mali Lipovec, a few km SW from Samobor. The trail heads W then SW to Japetić (879m) with its metal viewing tower. Continue past Japetić to PD Žitnica, before returning the way you came or cutting down to the road on the right before Japetić, and then following the road N to Mali Lipovec.

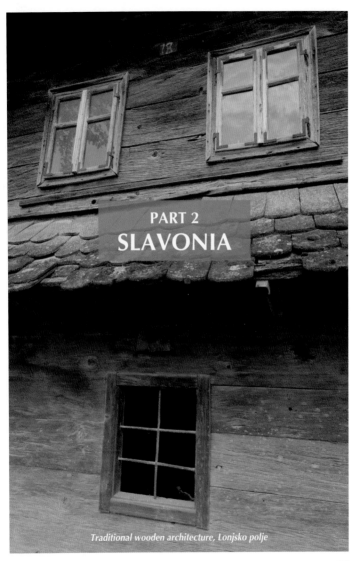

PART 2
SLAVONIA

Traditional wooden architecture, Lonjsko polje

INTRODUCTION

Slavonia is hardly a hillwalker's dream, being mostly flat with the exception of a few relatively small mountainous areas, such as Papuk. Nevertheless it is a lovely part of Croatia, with comparatively few visitors and a genuine feeling of hospitality – all a far cry from the (at times) madding crowds of the coast. There are some fascinating towns with some memorable architecture – not least the wonderfully well preserved baroque heart of Osijek, and the enormous red brick cathedral at Đakovo – and the food is excellent (don't leave without smapling *fiš paprikaš*, a hearty carp and red pepper stew, and *kulen*, the very tasty local dried sausage). There are some outstanding areas for watching birdlife, Lonjsko polje nature park and Kopački rit national park. The area is also home to one of the most poignant reminders of the war of the 1990s – the town of Vukovar, besieged and relentlessly bombarded by artillery, and now rising from the ashes.

PAPUK

Papuk is a relatively compact range of wooded hills, just east of the towns of Kutjevo and Orahovica, on the otherwise resolutely flat Slavonian plain. There are a number of huts, the best being PD Jankovac. Some of its most impressive geological features are towards the western end of the massif, near Rupnica, while a number of endemic plant species are found on the slopes above Velika. Its highest point is Papuk (953m). Its slopes also bear the ruins of nine castles (the most impressive of them Ružica grad). Papuk is a nature park (Park prirode Papuk, www.pp-papuk.hr); entry tickets (assuming you meet someone selling them) are 25Kn.

WALK 4
Ružica grad

Time	45mins return
Distance	2km
Maximum altitude	378m
Rating	very easy
Maps	The park publish a map covering the main areas, and SMAND are due to publish a sheet, Papuk (34).
Transport	There are no buses to the lake from Orahovica.
Accommodation	PD Jankovac is open by arrangement (tel: +385 (0) 98 984 2375).

An easy stroll from the lake and recreation centre above Orahovia to Ružica grad, one of the ruined castles on the lower slopes of Papuk. There's a handy leaflet on the history of the castle available from the nature park office in Velika and Orahovica.

From the bend in the road above the lake, take the trail marked Poučna staza Ružica, up a series of steps then left onto a marked track, ascending roughly SE. Keep straight ahead, passing a path on your right, then turn left onto

Ružica grad, Papuk

a trail which continues up to the ruins of **Ružica grad** (378m). The castle, which is splendidly situated, was built between the end of the 14th and the beginning of the 15th centuries, and once covered an area of some 800m². You can wander through some of the ruins, taking care of loose or falling stones – heading through to the far side gives good views of the remaining features, including the large semicircular bastion. Descend by the same route.

FURTHER POSSIBILITIES

Jankovac–Ivačka glava and Papuk
Head W from the Jankovac hut to **Ivačka glava** (913m) and **Papuk** (953m), before returning by the same route. Allow 3hrs.

Velika–Ivačka glava
From Velika head N, following the ridge of Lapjak to the ski lifts at Nevoljaš, before crossing the road and turning W to **Ivačka glava** (913m). Descend by the same route. Allow 3hrs 30mins.

LONJSKO POLJE

Lonjsko polje nature park (Park prirode Lonjsko polje, www.pp-lonjsko-polje.hr) stretches along the north bank of the river Sava, between the towns of Sisak and Kutina. The area is prone to extensive flooding in the spring and autumn. While walking is fairly limited (and very flat!), this is a beautifully preserved rural part of Croatia, with distinctive traditional wooden architecture (many of the houses date from the 19th century) – and it is simply *the* place in Croatia to see storks (the village of Čigoć is often trumpeted as the 'European stork capital'). Both white and black storks can be seen here, both on the surrounding wetlands, and nesting on the roofs of buildings and specially built wooden platforms. You can also see spoonbills here – not to mention numerous other birds, various species of amphibian and distinctive local breeds of cattle and horse. There is excellent, traditional village accommodation in the villages of Lonja and Čigoć (see below), and cyclists could do a lot worse than basing themselves in one of these and making day trips (see recommended map). There are park offices in Lonja and

White storks (Ciconia ciconia), *Lonjsko polje*

81

Čigoć; entrance tickets are 25Kn. The southeastern areas of the park, near Jasenovac and around the Bosnian border, may still be unsafe following the war of the 1990s; do not wander off the roads in this area.

WALK 5
Lonjsko polje

Time	30mins
Distance	1km
Maximum altitude	150m
Rating	very easy
Maps	The park publish a map covering the main areas, Turistička karta Park prirode Lonjsko polje (1:90,000), which includes suggested itineraries for cycling, though little practical detail for walking.
Transport	There are buses to Lonjsko and Čigoć from Sisak.
Accommodation	In the village of Lonja there is the excellent Usti Lonja (www.ustilonja.hr, tel: +385 (0) 44 710 621, with accommodation in a traditional wooden house, a warm welcome and exceptionally good food (particularly the grilled carp) served on a lovely terrace. Very good value B&B, full and half board. In Čigoć try Tradicije Čigoć (www.tradicije-cigoc.hr, tel: +385 (0) 44 715 124), which is also good.

Simply head over the road from the information centre in **Čigoć**, and follow the marked circular route through the trees. For a slightly longer route, head NE from Čigoć on the marked route ('Posavac Trail') across pastures (subject to flooding), keeping an eye out for storks – as well as on the local cattle.

Horses, Lonjsko polje

KOPAČKI RIT

Kopački rit Nature Park (www.kopacki-rit.com) is an important area of wetland near the confluence of the Danube and Drava, about 10km outside Osijek. There is a huge amount of birdlife, including ferruginous duck, white and black stork, grey heron and a large colony of cormorants. The area is really best explored by boat – a combined ticket which includes a boat trip and a visit to the nearby Tikveš castle costs 70Kn. There are also dedicated ornithological tours in small boats. Entrance to the national park costs 10Kn.

WALK 6
Kopački rit

Maps	The nature park produces a map covering the main areas.
Transport	From Osijek there are buses to Bilje, from where the park is a 3km walk. Alternatively various agencies in Osijek run tours to the national park – contact the tourist information office (www.tzosijek.hr, tel: +385 (0) 31 203 755).
Accommodation	Hotels in Osijek include the excellent Hotel Osijek (www.hotelosijek.hr, tel: +385 (0) 31 230 333) and the Hotel Silver (www.hotel-silver.hr, tel: +385 (0) 1 582 535).

Reed beds, Kopački rit nature park | From the visitor centre follow the marked trail to Sakadaš Lake; return by the same route.

PART 3
ISTRIA

Rovinj, Istria

INTRODUCTION

Named after the Illyrian tribe (Histri) which inhabited the area before the Roman conquest, Istria is the large, wedge-shaped peninsula protruding into the Adriatic between Italy and Slovenia in the north and Rijeka in the south. The rolling, green, fertile interior is dotted with small hill towns; the coastline is more highly developed for tourism, and sports some of the country's most celebrated architectural monuments, including the remarkably well-preserved Roman amphitheatre at Pula and the Euphrasian Basilica at Poreč. Opatija became a popular resort during the 19th century, especially after it had been declared a health resort. The area most interesting to hikers is the mountainous area just inland from Opatija, including Učka and the adjacent Ćićarija.

UČKA

Učka is the highest part of Istria. Its highest peak, Vojak (also sometimes referred to as vrh Učka), rises to 1401m, and is crowned by a large telecommunications tower. However, despite the presence of this and a sealed road leading up to the summit, it remains an impressive peak, with quite spectacular views. Furthermore, these features remain largely obscured by the slightly higher ground of the summit itself, and therefore hidden from view until the last moment, when approaching from Lovran via Suhi vrh (not so when approaching from Poklon dom). Učka is part of a nature park, Park Prirode Učka (www.pp-ucka.hr).

WALK 7
Vrh Učka

Time	5hrs
Distance	11km
Maximum altitude	1401m
Rating	easy
Map	SMAND Učka (15)

Transport	You can reach Lovran easily enough from Rijeka. Jump on a number 32 bus (from the local city bus terminal) and get out at Lovran, where a road ascends to the right (signposted 'Stari grad'). For the return, a bus (number 36) runs between Rijeka and Poklon dom, but (rather frustratingly) only on Sundays. You can try to hitch down the main road via Veprinac (from which there are regular bus services to Opatija).
Accommodation/ practical information	Poklon dom (tel: +385 (0) 51 712 785). For accommodation in Lovran contact the tourist information office (www.tz-lovran.hr, tel: +385 (0) 51 291 740); there's a good pizzeria, Delfino (www.delfino.hr, tel: +385 (0) 51 293 293).

The following, straightforward itinerary begins at just above sea level in the small town of Lovran, and climbs to the peak itself before descending somewhat to the hut (Poklon dom) at 922m, open at weekends (see Appendix B). From Učka it is possible to extend the route by continuing over Ćićarija. Buy supplies in Rijeka or Lovran.

Leave the main road in Lovran at the Stari grad sign, ascending and passing through the small but grandly named Trg slobode ('freedom square') – from which you can turn left to have a look at the old part of town before continuing – to reach a T-junction in a few minutes, where the red-and-white trail markings begin. Turn right, towards Villa Slavija, continuing straight ahead and

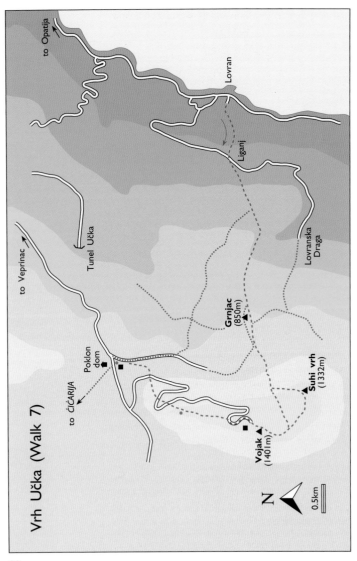

Vrh Učka (Walk 7)

passing a small votive shrine on the right before following the road round to the left. Here a sign to Učka leads up the first of many flights of steep, walled steps, crossing minor roads a number of times and passing through the pretty houses and gardens of **Liganj**, with the sections in between becoming increasingly forested, to reach a junction 1hr from Lovran.

From here there are two possible routes. The trail continuing straight ahead (marked 'Vojak and Grnjac') is undoubtedly the more attractive of the two, and is described here as the main route. However, those short of daylight hours may prefer to follow the alternative, more **direct route** (see below), spending the night at the hut (Poklon dom) before climbing Vojak and descending by following the main trail in reverse. Be warned however that the 'shortcut' is less clear than the main route.

Continue straight ahead, following a rocky path (marked 'RT') which ascends through low trees. On meeting the sealed road one last time, follow this briefly before turning off onto a path marked 'Vojak and Grnjac', opposite a small crucifix. Continue past some walled gardens, ascending on a rocky, winding trail to a forest road. Turn right onto this, then left on a path which leads up and over a ridge, 20mins from the junction.

The path ascends gradually, contouring the side of the valley, with lovely views out over the steep pine slopes to the sea from occasional clearings and rock outcrops. Continue straight ahead, following the RT signs and passing a trail to the small peak of **Grnjac** (850m), which can be reached in about 20mins, on the right. (Those who follow the Grnjac route can continue, rather than returning the same way, to rejoin the main trail just before the forest road.) After passing below scree slopes, the path follows a rocky stream bed and passes another side-trail, this time signposted to the village of Mala Učka. Continue ascending, following the trail marked 'Vojak' and contouring stone walls; pass a trail to Lovranska Draga which joins from the left. A few more minutes brings you to a forest road, just after meeting the path from Grnjac on the right.

Vojak (Vrh Učka)

Continue straight over the forest road to reach a clearing with low trees, wild roses and nettles. From here you get a brief view of the red-and-white antenna on Vojak before re-entering the trees. Almost immediately, you emerge into a second clearing, with a small cottage or hunting lodge on the left. Continue straight across the clearing, re-enter forest cover and ascend to a third clearing, where another route to the village of Mala Učka joins the main trail from the left. Veer right, into the trees, before starting up a relentlessly steep set of switchbacks. These lead to a junction, with a path to Suhi vrh ('dry peak') on the left, and the main trail to Vojak straight ahead.

You have two options here. Turn left, ascending to the top of **Suhi vrh** (1332m) before descending to the saddle below Vojak and rejoining the main trail to the summit. Alternatively, continue through tall beech trees and another clearing choked with nettles and brambles, crossing the forest road twice to emerge on the open saddle between the two peaks, where the path from Suhi vrh descends from the left to rejoin your route, and the imposing white limestone bulk of Vojak towers to the right. (You can leave full packs and ascend the smaller peak in 20mins from this point, before continuing.) Continue up to **Vojak**, ascending steeply, with any trace of roads, car parks and telecommunications towers quite hidden until the last moment, when you gain the summit with its stone lookout tower and the carloads of visitors who have driven up from the coast.

The view from Vojak (1401m) is as huge as it is unexpected. Suhi vrh lies behind you, beyond the open saddle and the forested trail down to Lovran. The land falls away suddenly to the west, where the plains and forests of Istria sprawl below before fading into the distance. Ćićarija extends to the north, while Gorski kotar stretches away to the northeast, and Velebit towers in the distance. Opatija and Rijeka are clearly visible on the coast, as are the islands of Cres, Lošinj and Krk to the southeast.

Continue down to the car park and the road, passing the huge telecommunications tower on the left and following the road for 5mins before branching off to the left on a clearly marked path. Descend alongside a ridge, to reach a tiny trickle of a spring (marked 'Pitka voda', 'drinking water') in 20mins. Continue descending, crossing a broad forest track and the main road a number of times, following the occasional RT or Poklon sign and zigzagging down through mixed beech and pine. A flight of steps brings you round behind **Pansion Učka** to a forest road, where you turn left to reach the main road by a water tap, 30mins below the spring. **Poklon dom** (Planinarska kuća Poklon) is just around the corner, uphill slightly beyond the gutted concrete building ahead. From the hut you can either hitch or catch a bus back down to the coast, or follow one of the two routes described here in reverse. ▸

The large, forested area northwest of Učka (known as Ćićarija) contains a number of trails, by which the walk to Poklon dom can be extended by two further stages – see Further Possibilities, overleaf.

ALTERNATIVE DIRECT ROUTE TO POKLON DOM (2HRS FROM JUNCTION WITH MAIN ROUTE)

At the junction 1hr from Lovran (see above) turn right, crossing a forest road and passing a turn-off to Lužinski Breg on the right before gaining the crest of a ridge and descending slightly to the left. Continue straight ahead, passing another turn-off on the right (this time to Gorica) and crossing the forest road once more, after which the trail becomes increasingly unclear. Take the ▸

◀ left fork, descending before veering off to the right. Turn left onto a broader track, then right again (not straight ahead to Grnjac), following some faint trail markings off to the right, which lead into a clearing.

Veer left on a faint, unlikely looking grassy trail, ascending to another sign to Poklon painted on a tree ahead. Cross another clearing before ascending into forest once more, following a steep path which passes between two rock outcrops. This leads up to a forest road, 1hr 40mins from the junction with the previous route. Turn right along the forest road to arrive at the main road in 15mins, where you can fill up your flask from the tap on the left. **Poklon dom** (922m) is slightly further up the road beyond a large, gutted concrete building, oppsite the old Pansion Učka.

For those heading for the summit of Vojak from Poklon dom, the trail starts from a little way back beyond the water tap, turning right behind Pansion Učka, to gain the RT trail (marked 'vrh Učka, Vojak'). This zigzags up through tall beech (and later mixed beech and pine), crossing the main road a number of times, to reach a tiny trickle of a spring (marked 'Pitka voda', 'drinking water'), 50mins from Poklon. Continue ascending alongside the crest of a ridge, with a cool breeze blowing off the Adriatic, to reach the road again in 15mins, where the large telecommunications tower comes into view. Follow the road to the right, passing the antenna and its fenced enclosure in 10mins and continuing straight ahead up a rocky track from the car park to the circular stone lookout tower on the summit of **Vojak**, with the path down to Lovran continuing on the other side.

FURTHER POSSIBILITIES

Ćićarija

Ćićarija is the large, forested area northwest of Učka, and contains a number of trails. If starting from Poklon Dom (Walk 7), the route leads across Veliki Planik (1272m), Bončić, Griža (1144m), Šija (1234m), Lisina (1185m) and Crni vrh (1031m) before descending either via Zvončev vrh (975m) and Budišin vrh (903m) to Veprinac, or via Beljač (784m) and Orljak (706m) to Bregi and Opatija. There is a hut at Lisina, and a spring near Griža. Allow two days from Poklon Dom. SMAND publish a sheet covering the area, Ćićarija (15a).

Inland Istria

There are numerous short and easy trails to the hilltowns of Istria's otherwise largely flat interior.

PART 4
GORSKI KOTAR

Winter on Risnjak, Gorski kotar

INTRODUCTION

The Dinaric Alps

The Dinaric Alps are simultaneously the longest mountain chain in Croatia and its most spectacular area for walking. Stretching southeast some 700km from the Slovenian border, these mountains run the length of Croatia, through Montenegro and into Albania, from where they continue as the Pindos Mountains in Greece. Their steep western slopes present an almost impenetrable barrier towards the Adriatic, and with only a few exceptions (such as the Krka and the Cetina rivers, which break through the mountains as impressive canyons on their way to the sea) their drainage is almost entirely eastwards into the Danube. They are composed of a series of distinct massifs or ranges, some higher or more extensive than others – from north to south: **Gorski kotar**, **Velebit**, **Mosor** and **Biokovo**, with various smaller areas in between. Behind them, on their eastern side, lies the Lika basin; on their west, the rocky, highly indented coastline for which Croatia has become celebrated. Croatia's islands, which like the mountains run in a general northwest–southeast direction, effectively constitute low-lying outer ranges of the Dinaric Alps, their valleys long ago submerged beneath the waters of the Adriatic.

Gorski kotar

Gorski kotar is the name given to the great crescent-shaped range of mountains stretching down from Slovenia in the north, encompassing Risnjak and Snježnik (both of which lie within Risnjak National Park, www.risnjak.hr), together with Bjelolasica, Bijele stijene and Samarske stijene further south (an area collectively known as Velika Kapela). The terrain consists of rolling, forested hills riddled with limestone dells, and bald, rocky peaks rising to a maximum of 1534m (Kula, on Bjelolasica). In some areas, the limestone formations are outstanding (Bijele stijene and Samarske stijene). As the most heavily forested part of Croatia, Gorski kotar is the area where you are most likely to see brown bear tracks, although you are very unlikely to see the animal itself. The extensive beech and mountain pine also provide a natural habitat for wild pig, roe and red deer. The lynx was hunted to extinction in Risnjak during the 19th century, but has returned in small numbers since the 1970s, after migrating from Slovenia.

The gateway to Gorski kotar is the town of Delnice, which can be reached from either Zagreb or Rijeka by train. Try to get the earliest service from Zagreb (called the 'Rijeka', which leaves around 6am). The bus station, for services to the trailheads for Bjelolasica and Risnjak, is on the main road, opposite the long flight of steps descending from the railway station. There are a few shops in Delnice where you can get most supplies (in particular, left from the bus station, just after the road forks to the left), but you would do better not to rely completely on these and to stock up in Zagreb or on the coast.

Delnice was a major centre of Partisan resistance during the Second World War, an episode of history reflected in such local landmarks as Matić poljana on the route to Bjelolasica.

WALK 8
Risnjak, Snježnik and Hahlić

The following straightforward itinerary takes you via the peaks of Risnjak (1528m) and Snježnik (1506m), each with an excellent *planinarski dom*, although PD Snježnik was closed in 2009, and on to PD Hahlić, from where the route descends to the village of Dražice, 11km from Rijeka. Excursions to adjacent peaks are possible from Snježnik (Guslica, 1490m) and Hahlić (Suhi vrh, 1335m; Fratar, 1353m; Obruč, 1376m) and numerous other points along the way. The route has been broken down into four stages, making the most of the accommodation at Risnjak and Snježnik, although the route could be covered in fewer (if the hut at Snježnik is closed as it was in 2009, you may want to skip the recommended excursion from Snježnik, and either stay at PD Platak or complete the route from PD Risnjak to PD Hahlić in a single day).

Risnjak (from *ris*, 'lynx') and Snježnik (from *snijeg*, 'snow') are two of the most attractive areas of Gorski kotar. The boundary of the national park (Nacionalni park Risnjak, www.risnjak.hr) was recently extended to just west of Snježnik, and you will have to buy a ticket to cover the time you stay in the park. This is easy enough – simply pay for a ticket at the first hut you stay at and hang onto it until you leave the park.

Maps	SMAND covers the area in a single sheet: Gorski kotar IV (14). Also of interest is the new NP Risnjak sheet, covering the areas of Risnjak and Snježnik; this is available from huts in the area if you are unable to find it in Zagreb. The old Gorski kotar *planinarska karta*, produced in Slovenia, gives good coverage of the whole massif at 1:100,000 but is hard to find.
Transport	The traditional approach for Risnjak has always been from the small village of Crni Lug, about 12km northwest from Delnice. However, this can be difficult to reach without your own transport, and the alternative approach from Gornje Jelenje is therefore preferable. From Delnice, take a southbound bus to Gornje Jelenje and jump off at the pass (881m), opposite the turn-off to Crikvenica and Krk. (Note that instead of travelling via this road, a number of southbound buses – including all buses from Zagreb to Rijeka – now follow the new motorway. Buses travelling on the motorway will not take you to Gornje Jelenje.) For those who want to start from Crni Lug (or rather the national park office, which is at Bijela Vodica, just outside Crni Lug) there is an afternoon shuttle bus from Delnice (but check with the national park office for times).
Accommodation	PD Risnjak; at the time of writing (2009) the hut at Snježnik was closed – contact the national park office

for details on when it's scheduled to reopen (tel: +385 (0) 51 836 133); there is a new hut at Hahlić. If you want to stay in Crni Lug, the national park office in has a few rooms available (tel: +385 (0) 51 836 133); for information on accommodation in Delnice, contact the tourist information office (www.tz-delnice.hr, tel: +385 (0) 51 812 156).

STAGE 1
Gornje Jelenje – PD Risnjak

Time	2hrs 20mins
Distance	8.5km
Maximum altitude	1418m
Rating	easy
Map	SMAND Gorski kotar IV (14)

Follow the broad forest road opposite the Crikvenica turn-off, passing a large national park sign ('Nacionalni park Risnjak'), keeping straight ahead and not turning off to the right. The road ascends, winding up through the forest, with intermittent trail markings starting after passing

PD Risnjak and vrh Risnjak, Gorski kotar

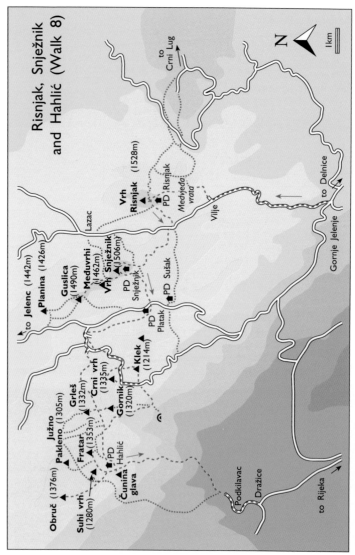

Risnjak, Snježnik and Hahlić (Walk 8)

the turn-off to Platak on the left. Ignore all routes off to the right and left, however tempting they may look, continuing on the main forest road to reach **Vilje** in 1hr 20mins. Here you turn right onto a track clearly marked 'Medvjeđa vrata and Risnjak', taking first one and then another right fork after 10mins. Ascend on a steep, rocky path to reach **Medvjeđa vrata** ('bear pass' or 'gateway of the bears') in a further 20mins. There is a nice, airy view from this point, to which a path leads up through the forest from Crni Lug (if you've walked in from Crni Lug you will arrive here).

Continue along the trail from Medvjeđa vrata, following the signs to PD Risnjak, which comes into view after about 20mins, as you round a final, rocky bluff. Continue, descending briefly before reaching the hut itself in less than 10mins.

> **PD Risnjak**, originally known as Schlosserov dom after the botanist Josip Schlosser (1808–1882), is a picturesque sight, perched upon a grassy saddle and nestled below the dwarf mountain pine- and juniper-clad peak of Risnjak itself, with forested slopes dropping away on either side. There is a well behind the hut, and a *sklonište* (just inside the main door) is open through the winter, when the hut itself is closed.

EXCURSION FROM PD RISNJAK
Vrh Risnjak

Time	30mins return
Distance	0.5km
Maximum altitude	1528m
Rating	easy–moderate
Map	SMAND Gorski kotar IV (14)

Follow the path behind the hut, ascending steeply through dwarf mountain pine and scrambling over rock, with views back down over the hut and saddle, and passing a particularly cavernous doline (sinkhole) on the right, to reach **vrh Risnjak** (1528m) in 15mins. Snježnik is clearly visible to the northwest, and the sea beyond. Descend by the same route.

STAGE 2
PD Risnjak – PD Snježnik via Vrh Snježnik

Time	2hrs 30mins
Distance	7km
Maximum altitude	1506m
Rating	easy–moderate
Map	SMAND Gorski kotar IV (14)

Following the Lazac sign from the hut, descend northwest into the forest on a rocky path to reach a junction in 10mins. Here you continue straight ahead, sign-posted 'Platak' (*not* right to Lazac), winding through beech trees and over rocks and tree roots to reach the forest road in a further 35mins. Turn right onto this, before turning left onto a clearly marked track to Snježnik. Descend through a grassy clearing, then ascend again on a broad forest track, ignoring tracks branching off to the right but turning left as you descend from the crest of a small ridge to reach a T-junction 1hr from the forest road. Turn right, following the signs to Snježnik again, before branching off to the left on a rocky path. This brings you out of the trees and up over a grassy knoll, with views east back to Risnjak and southwest to Platak and the sea. Continue along the ridge, following the path and scrambling up over rock to gain the peak of **Snježnik** (1506m), from where you look directly down onto the roof of the hut, a couple of minutes below you.

> **PD Snježnik** sits on a ledge at 1419m below the western side of the peak, but was closed in 2009. Contact the national park office for details of whether it's open.

Although this is a short day from Risnjak, it is at least another 4hrs 30mins to PD Hahlić, and the terrain in between, not to mention the hut at Platak, is considerably less attractive. You would do better to sit and enjoy the view, or to drop your pack and head off on the recommended excursion.

EXCURSION FROM PD SNJEŽNIK
Guslica (return)

Time	1hr 30mins return
Distance	4km
Maximum altitude	1490m
Rating	easy
Map	SMAND Gorski kotar IV (14)

The route to Guslica follows the ridge northwest from the hut, passing **Međuvrhi** (1462m) and a trail on the right down to Lazac, to reach the peak (1490m) in 45mins. The summit itself is crowned by an old JNA (Yugoslav People's Army) base. For those with more time, it is

Guslica from PD Snježnik, Gorski kotar

possible to extend this route to include **Planina** (1426m) and **Jelenc** (1442m), an additional 2hrs 30mins from the hut. An alternative, full-pack option would be to descend southwest from the ridge between Međuvrhi and Guslica, via Veliko Tešnje, to meet the forest road north of **Platak**, before continuing towards **PD Hahlić**.

EXTENSION

From PD Snježnik it is also possible to continue along the **GPP** (Goranski planinarski put) to Snežnik (note the different spelling), at 1797m, which is over the Slovenian border. It is largely forest walking, at times on forest roads, but provides an alternative onward route for anyone heading for the Slovenian Alps. From **PD Snježnik** head northwest over **Guslica**, **Planina** and Škurina before continuing by road through Lišina and Švedra (both in the area known as Bukova gora), crossing the border at Klanska polica and heading for the hut at Sviščak.

STAGE 3
PD Snježnik – PD Hahlić via Platak

Time	4hrs 30mins
Distance	12–14km
Maximum altitude	1332m (via Grleš) / 1335m (via Crni vrh)
Rating	easy
Map	SMAND Gorski kotar IV (14)

From PD Snježnik, descend steeply into the forest, following the signs to Platak to reach a forest track. Take the left fork of this and arrive at a T-junction, 25mins from the hut. Turn right, then right again onto a forest road before immediately turning off to the left on another path.

Continue down through thick forest, crossing the forest road once more and following the trail markings to reach the road, with PD Platak beyond, 45mins from the hut.

The large and hotel-like **PD Platak** makes a less than attractive place to stay, sitting in the valley at 1111m, on the main road and surrounded by playing fields, and you will almost certainly want to continue to PD Hahlić.

Turn right through the playing fields in front of the hut, keeping parallel to the road and passing a succession of football pitches and ski lifts. Emerge soon into a second open clearing, and continue straight ahead, joining a broad track and entering the forest at the far end of the clearing. This leads to a T-junction in 20mins; turn left (there is a small 'H' for Hahlić) before veering right.

Shortly after this, you reach a path branching off to the left, from where you have two possible options. The first route is the easiest to follow; the second the slightly more direct of the two. The first option, turning left (a route alternately marked '18' and '19'), provides the chance to climb Crni vrh (1335m) and Klek (1214m, not to be confused with the larger and better known Klek near Ogulin), but means sticking to the forest road for rather longer. The second option continues straight ahead (a route marked '15') and quickly takes you off the forest road and through the trees, with a chance to climb Grleš (1332m) and Gornik (1320m), before meeting the first route about 35mins before PD Hahlić. Climbing the peaks on either route will add about 1hr to the total timing given for this stage.

Option 1 – via Crni vrh and Klek
Take the path on the left, which soon rejoins the forest road, followed by a path to the right (marked 'Klek/Hahlić), which again brings you back onto the road. Follow this to the right to reach a crossroads, 35mins beyond the point where the two routes diverge. From here you can climb either (or both) of the two small peaks already mentioned. The path on your right heads up over **Crni vrh** ('black peak') before descending to a small forestry hut, turning

Church in a village in Gorski kotar, near the border with Slovenia

left and rejoining the forest road; that to the left leads over **Klek** and down to the forest road almost opposite the turn-off to Hahlić. If you do not wish to climb either of the peaks, continue straight ahead on the forest road, turning left at a junction in 15mins which brings you after a few more minutes to a path on the right to Hahlić.

Strike out on the Hahlić path, descending through thick undergrowth before emerging into an open, grassy dell. Cut across the side of this, following the now frequent trail markings, to gain the top of a ridge, which is followed to the right. Continue straight ahead, passing a trail on the left to Gogor and a *špilja* (cave), and re-entering low forest cover with the sea visible through the trees to the left. After 15mins emerge onto an open hill slope, which you descend, passing two concrete wells with views of the sea and the island of Krk on the left. Turn right at the bottom of the slope, following the signs to Obruč and Hahlić painted on an old concrete trough. Veer left on the lower of two paths and then turn right to gain a broad, leafy forest track. Follow this, turning left after 5mins and continuing to a junction, 30mins beyond the concrete wells, from where the route via Grleš and Gornik joins from the right (see continuation below).

Option 2 – via Grleš and Gornik
Continue straight ahead on the forest road to the junction, turning left and continuing straight ahead, past

tracks to the left and right, and taking the left fork where the forest road peters out. Continue winding through the trees, passing the odd track on the right, to reach a junction with trails to Grleš and Gornik to the right and left. In both cases, you will have to retrace your steps to the junction before continuing. From here the route continues straight ahead, passing more tracks and crossing a forest road, before veering left to reach the junction with the previous route.

Both options

Turn left (or continue straight ahead if you have arrived from Grleš and Gornik), ignoring the first path on the right but turning onto the second to emerge onto an open, grassy hillside, 15mins from the junction. The prominent peak ahead of you is Obruč. Here you have the choice of either continuing straight to the hut in 20mins, or ascending over **Fratar** (the peak above you on the right) and **Suhi vrh** beyond, to reach PD Hahlić in roughly 90mins. (Note that both peaks can be reached from the hut without carrying a full pack.) Those wishing to follow the latter option should ascend on the path to the right to the top of Fratar before following the recommended excursion (described below) in reverse. Continue straight ahead, descending over a rocky saddle into the trees, and veering left on the clear trail to the hut.

> **PD Hahlić** sits at the edge of the forest at 1097m. If you find it full, there is some flat ground up on the saddle for a tent. The sound of bells is not goats or cattle, as you might expect, but horses, which come to shelter in the forest at night. The wooden barriers around the terrace, therefore, are to keep them out, and not to deter walkers. The name Hahlić comes from the local dialect for *lokva* (meaning 'puddle'), and refers to the old wells in the vicinity of the hut.

You can get a good preliminary view of the surrounding terrain by scrambling up **Čunina glava**, the small peak to the west of the hut, which can be climbed in

5mins. From this surprisingly windy spot there is a full panorama of the Kvarner Gulf, with Opatija and Učka (1401m, Walk 7) towering beyond (SW); the island of Krk and the bridge to it from the mainland (SE); Velika Kapela (SE, Walk 9); Fratar (NE); and the obvious trail leading up the ridge to Obruč (N).

EXCURSION FROM PD HAHLIĆ
Suhi vrh and Fratar (return)

Time	2hrs 15mins return
Distance	4km
Maximum altitude	1353m
Rating	easy–moderate
Map	SMAND Gorski kotar IV (14)

Suhi vrh and Fratar, near PD Hahlić, Gorski kotar

Backtrack through the forest from PD Hahlić (or continue from the base of Čunina glava – the path forms a loop and brings you back round to the hut), initially following the signs to Obruč before turning off to the right on a path to Fratar and Suhi vrh. This leads in 15mins to a track on the

left to **Suhi vrh** ('dry peak'). There is no trail as such, but it is an easy 15mins up to the top (1280m), scrambling over large boulders and loose scree for good views of Obruč and Fratar. Descend by the same route and continue on the main trail towards Fratar ('the friar' or 'the Franciscan'), bearing right and ascending, to emerge on the open, rocky slopes beneath the summit. From here it is 15mins to the top, following a clearly marked trail, with little scree.

The summit of **Fratar** (1353m) commands extensive views, which improve slightly from the high ground beyond the summit record box. Snježnik lies almost due east, with Risnjak just visible behind it; Guslica, with the old JNA base on top of it, lies slightly north of these; and the smaller peaks of Klek and Crni vrh are visible in the heavily forested middle ground. Perhaps the most prominent landmark, however, is the large and steep-sided peak a few degrees west of north. This is Snežnik (note the different spelling), much higher at 1797m and actually in Slovenia.

Descend and return to **PD Hahlić** by the same route; alternatively, vary the return by descending east-south-east to rejoin the main path from Snježnik, and continue from there.

EXTENSION

You could extend the excursion by heading north on a trail between Fratar and Suhi vrh to visit the area known as **Pakleno** ('hell'), with its very impressive karst formations, and in particular **Južno Pakleno** (1305m).

FURTHER POSSIBILITIES

Snežnik
Those wishing to climb Snežnik can do so from Sviščak across the border, either continuing from PD Snježnik and Guslica along the GPP (see extension to the excursion from PD Snježnik at the end of stage 2, above), or by heading for the town of Ilirska Bistrica over the border.

EXCURSION FROM PD HAHLIĆ
Obruč

Time	3hrs return
Distance	5km
Maximum altitude	1376m
Rating	easy
Map	SMAND Gorski kotar IV (14)

A clear trail heads north from below Čunina glava, passing an alternative route down to Podkilavac, and following the ridge crest to reach the summit of **Obruč** (1376m) in 90mins. Descend by the same route.

STAGE 4
PD Hahlić – Dražice

Time	2hrs
Distance	7.5km
Maximum altitude	1097m
Rating	easy
Map	SMAND Gorski kotar IV (14)

Descend over the broad, open slopes below **PD Hahlić**, following the red-and-white-striped poles and the signs to Dražice and Podkilavac. Take the left fork of this trail (signposted 'Podkilavac preko Čeke'), with clear views of Velika Kapela to the southeast. The impressive ridge of exposed rock and forested slopes in the middle ground comprises the peaks Kuk, Hus and Vela Peša. Cross a track before entering sparse, low oak and beech, then join a major track and turn right (again signposted 'Dražice/ Podkilavac'), descending steeply through forest. Cross a forest road before emerging into a clearing, 90mins from the hut, where the path levels.

Following the Podkilavac signs, continue on a broad track, veering right and passing the road from Platak (via Mudna dol). Continue past a large and unsightly rubbish dump before veering left and continuing straight ahead through a junction of various tracks. Cross a small, dry stream bed to reach the sealed road, where you turn left. Follow the trail markings, passing some houses and turning left into a shady lane, before turning right again and passing through the small village of **Podkilavac**. Turn left onto a clearly marked path, soon rejoining the road before crossing over the bridge and following the road around the corner to the village of **Dražice**, which you reach in a few minutes. Buses leave for Rijeka (11km away) from the large 'Dražice' sign before the village.

WALK 9
Bjelolasica, Bijele stijene and Samarske stijene (Velika Kapela)

The following itinerary, covering the area of Gorski kotar known as Velika Kapela ('great chapel'), includes the highest peak in the massif (Kula, 1534m, on Bjelolasica) and the very impressive limestone scenery of Bijele stijene and Samarske stijene. The route follows sections of the MPP (Mrkopaljski planinarski put) and KPP (Kapelski planinarski put), including the section of the latter known as Vihoraški put. Generally straightforward, the section of Vihoraški put between Bijele and Samarske stijene known as Ljuska ('shell' or 'eggshell') does, however, involve some more demanding scrambling with the aid of pegs, cables and ladders. Further scrambling is necessary for vrh Bijele stijene (1334m), and sections of the recommended excursion from Ratkovo sklonište (the MPP, or Mrkopaljski planinarski put). Accommodation is provided by some well-placed *sklonište* and *planinarska kuća*, and Ratkovo sklonište in particular is one of the more attractive in Croatia. The route is divided into four stages, but it could be completed in three. If returning towards Ogulin you may find it more convenient to spend the final night on Klek (Walk 10), which can be reached in 1hr from Bjelsko. Bring all supplies from Zagreb or Delnice.

Maps	SMAND covers the area in a single sheet: Bjelolasica (11b). The new Samarske Bijele stijene Bjelolasica (11a) sheet is excellent for detailed coverage of the MPP and the route across Bijele stijene, though it does not cover the relevant area of Bjelolasica. These two sheets have now largely replaced the older Gorski kotar I (11) sheet. The old Gorski kotar planinarska karta, produced in Slovenia, gives good coverage of the whole massif at 1:100,000, and may still be available from some huts in the area.
Transport	From Delnice, take the Mrkopalj bus from the main bus station (3.15pm, Monday–Friday) or hitch from just outside town on the main road (SW, uphill). From the turn-off to Mrkopalj, which is on the left, it is another 9.5km to the village itself. Mrkopalj is a small village with one or two shops (where you can stock up on a few very basic supplies). Take the road on the right after the Post Office (signposted to Tuk and Matić poljana), then the (main) road left to Tuk, which is a further 3km. The large new hut (Planinarski dom 'Bijele stijene' u Tuku, or simply PD Tuk, 875m) is on the right.
Accommodation	With excellent facilities, hot showers and meals, PD Tuk makes a good place to stop if you've arrived late or if you're following this route in reverse, and have just spent several days slogging across Gorski kotar. Thereafter: Planinarsko sklonište Jakob Mihelčić, Ratkovo sklonište, Planinarska kuća na Bijelim stijenama. For accommodation in Delnice, contact the tourist information office (www.tz-delnice.hr, tel: +385 (0) 51 812 156).

STAGE 1
PD Tuk – Planinarsko sklonište Jakob Mihelčić

Time	3hrs 30mins
Distance	8km
Maximum altitude	1460m
Rating	easy
Map	SMAND Bjelolasica (11b)

Turn right from **PD Tuk**, walking uphill and east on the main road, and then branching right onto a smaller road to rejoin the main road at a bend in 5mins. Follow the trail markings on a telegraph pole which lead up over a grass verge, passing a house on the left. Continue on a clearly marked trail, south-southeast across a grassy slope, to gain a rocky path running along the edge of the trees and then an unsealed road 15mins from the hut. Cross this, following the sign to Matić poljana and gradually ascending to

Standing stones at Matić poljana

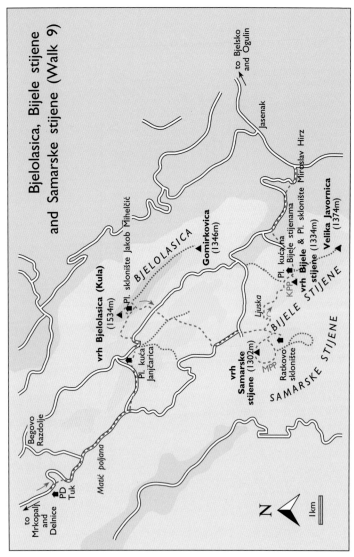

Bjelolasica, Bijele stijene and Samarske stijene (Walk 9)

to Bjelsko and Ogulin

Jasenak

Pl. skloniste Jakob Mihelčič

BJELOLASICA

Gomirkovica (1346m)

vrh Bjelolasica (Kula) (1534m)

Pl. skloniste Miroslav Hirz

Velika Javornica (1374m)

Pl. kuća/na Bijele stijenama

Bijele & Pl. skloniste (1334m)

KPP

vrh Bijele stijene

BIJELE STIJENE

Ljuska

Pl. kuća Janjčarica

vrh Samarske stijene (1302m)

Ratkovo skloniste

MPP

SAMARSKE STIJENE

Begovo Razdolje

Matić poljana

PD Tuk

to Mrkopalj and Delnice

N

1km

emerge into the open onto an unsealed road after 10mins. Take the left fork of this, signposted to Bjelolasica, Bijele stijene and Samarske stijene.

The road leads past level, grassy fields, surrounded by mixed forest and pine and strewn with flowers. This is **Matić poljana** ('Matić fields'), where 24 partisans froze to death one night during the Second World War, an event commemorated by the 24 standing stones which appear on the right after about 5mins. Continue straight ahead, passing a memorial plaque and a road to Begovo Razdolje on the left. About an hour's walking at a leisurely pace brings you to a track on the left at the end of the fields, signposted to Bjelolasica and Janjčarica. Follow this, passing a watchtower used for hunting and baiting bears (regrettably, a popular sport in Croatia), and continuing straight ahead (not left) on a broad, overgrown track. There are no signs at first, but you soon reach arrows and trail markings on various rocks and stones, entering the trees and ascending to rejoin the forest road after 5mins. Turn right onto this, following the signs and ascending gradually, and staying on the road as it switches back to the left. (There is, theoretically, a more direct path up through the trees: however, the newly widened forest road has stripped the signs away, making it more difficult to find.) **Janjčarica kuća** is on the right, opposite the (at this end, clearly visible) path coming up through the trees on the left, about 35mins from the end of Matić poljana.

> **Janjčarica kuća** is a *kuća* rather than a *dom*, so it will be locked unless you've made prior arrangements to stay here (see Appendix B). It is new and well equipped, with cooking facilities. There is also a *sklonište*, but this is rather run-down and best avoided except in emergencies. Still, this makes a fine spot for lunch, with picnic tables and tantalising views almost due east to Bjelolasica from the saddle. There is a well to the left of the *sklonište*.

Descend east following the path at the back of the hut (on the path to Bjelolasica, not the one to Bijele and

Samarske stijene), meeting a track joining from the left and continuing on a broad forest road towards the base of Bjelolasica. Pass an open area of rolling grassland and large limestone boulders on the left, veering left and following the KPP (Kapelski planinarski put) signs. Ignore the first, but take the second turn on the right, following the sign to Bjelolasica, 15mins from Janjčarica. Follow the trail markings, turning left after 5mins onto a broad forest path, then left onto a forest road, and left again onto a rutted track. This narrows and ascends, veering left once more to become a path, before rejoining the forest road. Turn left onto this, then immediately right, again following the sign to Bjelolasica and ascending steeply through the trees. Cross over one more forest track (this one apparently disused) to reach a path on the left to the *vrh* (summit), an hour beyond Janjčarica. Rather than taking your full pack to the summit, continue (right) past this for another 20mins to emerge into a clearing with **Planinarsko sklonište Jakob Mihelčić** nestled below the ridge crest.

In the *sklonište* you will undoubtedly notice the countless sticks and branches plugging any conceivable eyes or gaps in the wooden ceiling: this is an attempt to keep out the resident *puh* (dormouse). It usually finds a way in anyway, so hang all food bags well out of reach.

EXCURSION FROM PLANINARSKO SKLONIŠTE JAKOB MIHELČIĆ
vrh Bjelolasica

Time	40mins return
Distance	1km
Maximum altitude	1534m
Rating	easy
Map	SMAND Bjelolasica (11b)

Leaving full packs at **Planinarsko sklonište Jakob Mihelčić**, ascend behind it to the junction and turn left onto the trail marked 'Bjelolasica', following the clear trail markings and scrambling along the right (north) side of the ridge. On reaching the first high point, you are confronted by the unlikely sight of a football pitch with goal posts in the flat area below you on the right, while Bijele stijene and Samarske stijene are clearly visible to the left. Pass the track coming up from the left (marked 'Tuk') to reach the summit (**vrh Bjelolasica**, 1534m, also called Kula, meaning 'tower' or 'fortress'), 20mins from the *sklonište*.

The impressive rock tower to the northeast is Klek, while to the east the ridge stretches back towards Gomirkovica. Bijele stijene and Samarske stijene are visible to the southeast (Samarske stijene, your next destination, is on the right), although the best view of them is from the first high point on the ridge above the improvised football pitch. Janjčarica nestles in a notch in the ridge to the southwest, while Snježnik and Risnjak are visible in the distance beyond this. Descend to the *sklonište* by the same route.

Bjelolasica

EXTENSION

From the junction above the *sklonište* you might like to continue straight ahead, briefly, on the path marked 'Gomirkovica 2hrs, Staza hrvatskih Himalajaca 5mins'. This is not a comparison with the Himalaya, but a reference to a winter route by which Croatian climbers trained for an Everest expedition, the cables for which still descend over the rocks to the right.

STAGE 2
Planinarsko sklonište Jakob Mihelčić – Ratkovo sklonište

Time	3hrs 30mins
Distance	9km
Maximum altitude	1460m
Rating	easy
Map	SMAND Bjelolasica (11b)

It should be pointed out that there is another route (more interesting looking, at least on paper) via Gomirkovica. However, this in reality takes you through a jungle of low mountain pine and juniper, which makes progress impossibly slow and shreds your legs. Unless the path has been cleared, the route described below remains preferable.

Descend from **Planinarsko sklonište Jakob Mihelčić**, following the clearly marked path at the bottom of the clearing, signposted 'KPP Samarske stijene'. It's 35mins down to the forest road, which you cross onto a rutted track, sometimes overgrown but clearly marked and again signposted 'KPP Samarske stijene'. It leads in a further 25mins to another forest road, where you turn left as signposted. Turn right after 5mins and then descend right on an overgrown path (marked 'Okruglica', if you can find the sign) through a dell. This brings you out into a large, open, grassy clearing which the road you have just followed skirts to the left. Cross the clearing, heading roughly southwest and aiming for the red-and-white marker pole, taking care to avoid the surrounding depressions which disguise sinkholes. The path is faint and ascends at the opposite side of the clearing. ▸

Ascend southwest from the clearing, passing a small shelter on the left and entering the trees. The winding path is overgrown with brambles, but faint trail markings descend alongside a steep gully, veering slightly left at the bottom of this (not straight ahead) to cut across a stream bed and pass through a small clearing. Continue on an open forest track, taking the right fork of this to reach a road 30mins beyond the blueberries. The route here is unclear. Do not continue straight ahead as indicated (a signpost reads 'Ratkovo sklonište and Samarske stijene', but there is no path). Instead, turn left and follow the road for 20mins, turning right at the *rezervat prirode* (nature reserve) sign and following the signpost to Ratkovo sklonište and Samarske stijene.

The surrounding bushes are laden with *borovnice* (blueberries) in the summer, making this an attractive destination for the local brown bear population and for hunters (there is another hunting tower at the end of the track beyond the clearing). Locals collect the blueberries to sell.

Ratkovo sklonište

Ratkovo sklonište was closed for renovation in 2008/9, having been left in an appalling condition by a succession of unscrupulous hikers. It is now open again but please leave it clean and tidy, and don't be part of a reason for reclosure.

Turn left off this after 5mins (marked 'KPP', as opposed to the route ahead marked 'MPP': these abbreviations, sometimes used interchangeably on the same route, can be a little confusing at first). Ascend, sometimes steeply, through the forest, passing a request to carry up some firewood if you're arriving in the winter. About 20mins from the road, pass a path to the left, marked 'Vihoraški put' and 'Ljuska', which marks the onward route from Ratkovo sklonište. Continue straight ahead past this, passing some outcrops of rock and descending briefly as you pass tracks on the right marked 'MPP' and 'Samarske stijene'. Re-ascend over rocky ground, coming round a large rock outcrop to find **Ratkovo sklonište** nestled in a large cave below, 30mins from the road. ◀

Recently rebuilt after the original hut was burnt down a number of years ago, and lovingly maintained by PDS 'Velebit' (Zagreb), **Ratkovo sklonište** is quite possibly the most attractive *sklonište* in Croatia. Like all other *sklonište*, it is free to stay here. However, the number of visitors it attracts (especially at weekends, when it has not been unknown for a whole busload of people from Zagreb to turn up here expecting to stay for free) means that there is now a small charge for staying at weekends. There is a water pump below the balcony and a remarkably fearless local *lisica* (fox), usually game enough to try stealing your food while you eat it. You are advised to keep the door of the hut closed to keep *lisica* out.

EXCURSION FROM RATKOVO SKLONIŠTE

Vrh Samarske stijene and MPP
(Mrkopaljski planinarski put)

Time	3hrs
Distance	4km
Maximum altitude	1302m
Rating	moderate–difficult
Map	SMAND Samarske Bijele stijene Bjelolasica (11a) or SMAND Bjelolasica (11b)

Although this circular route could be completed before continuing to Bijele stijene (see Stage 3) on the same day, most people will find this a pleasant enough trip to occupy the rest of the day (particularly if the route is extended), and will want to spend another night at Ratkovo sklonište.

Retrace your steps as far as the turn-off (now on the left) to Samarske stijene. Follow this path, continuing straight ahead on the route marked 'vrh' (KPP) and passing a track on the left (marked 'MPP') by which you will return. The path ascends steadily, squeezing up through a cleft between two rock outcrops and passing the words 'Još malo!' ('a bit further!') painted on a rock. Scramble straight ahead up the rock beyond this (passing a path on the right marked 'MPP Ratkovo sklonište') to the summit (**vrh Samarske stijene**, 1302m), 40mins from the hut. Bijele stijene is visible to the east, while more of the area's limestone towers crowd the slopes to the southeast, surrounded by pine.

Return to the **MPP** trail, now on the left, a few minutes below the summit. This descends steeply before veering left, where signs mark the route to Ratkovo sklonište. In 15mins a path is reached, which ascends to the right to **Stepenica** (1280m). The route up this appropriately named peak (*stepenica* means 'staircase') spirals

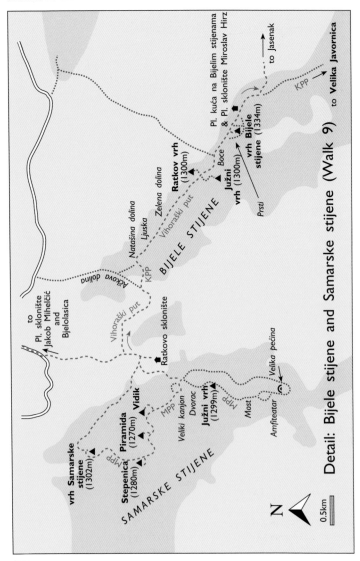

Detail: Bijele stijene and Samarske stijene (Walk 9)

clockwise, via a single peg, to a summit register in 5mins, before the final scramble to the *kapa* ('cap'), which perches, beret-like, atop a limestone tower. This final section to the *kapa* is technically more difficult than anything else on this route, and most walkers may want to content themselves with getting to the summit register.

Descend to the main trail, turn right and continue, following the sign towards Piramida. The path ascends, winding around limestone stacks and towers, to reach **Piramida** (1270m) in 15mins. Technically easier than Stepenica, it has good views back over the terrain you have covered.

Return to the main track, continuing along this and descending into a dell before re-ascending to the right of a large rock outcrop. Descend and re-ascend once more, scrambling to a junction 20mins beyond Piramida, with clear views back to vrh Samarske stijene. A path to the left leads to the top of **Vidik** in 5mins, climbing anticlockwise for good views from the peak. A further 10mins along the main path (signposted *kuća*) is the first of two possible onward routes. The path leading off to the right, marked 'teže' ('more difficult'), goes through **Veliki kanjon** ('great canyon'), while that straight ahead, marked 'lakše' ('easier'), bypasses this.

The canyon is definitely worth seeing; and the more difficult section is confined to its lower reaches. If you find this too much of a hurdle (and it is something of a scramble), return to the main path and continue 5mins to a second path on the right (marked 'Veliki kanjon', and from where you will emerge if you have climbed up from the bottom), which will take you into the top of the canyon. From here you can clamber down for a look, before returning to the main path.

EXTENSION

After a further 5mins there is yet another junction, where by turning right you could extend this itinerary to include a number of other limestone ▶

◀ features. This extended version of the MPP goes via Dvorac, Južni vrh, Most, Amfiteatar, Velika pećina and Medvjeđa dolina before bringing you back to the junction with the main route back to Ratkovo sklonište, and would require an additional 3–4 hours.

Continuing straight ahead, descend through a precariously balanced stone arch before rejoining the track up from Bjelolasica, to reach **Ratkovo sklonište** in 10mins.

STAGE 3
Ratkovo sklonište – Planinarska kuća na Bijelim stijenama, via Vihoraški put, Ljuska, vrh Bijele stijene and the KPP

Time	4hrs
Distance	4km
Maximum altitude	1334m
Rating	moderate–difficult
Map	SMAND Samarske Bijele stijene Bjelolasica (11a) or SMAND Bjelolasica (11b)

Backtrack 10mins along the main path from the *cesta* (road) and Bjelolasica, turning right at the turn-off marked Vihoraški put and Ljuska onto the KPP. This section of the KPP is known as Vihoraški put, from *vihor*, meaning 'strong wind' or 'gale'. The path winds through the trees, over rocks and round a cliff, roughly northeast and veering left where the route becomes less clear. Some 25mins from the turn-off a track appears to the left, which you don't take; it is marked 'Bijele stijene' and 'Ačkova dolina' (although the sign has almost disintegrated). Ignore this and continue straight ahead on a route

marked 'Natašina dolina' and 'Bijele stijene', descending into a limestone dell after 10mins and continuing straight up the other side of this (not left, as signposted, where the old path is blocked by rock-fall). The path is steep as you scramble towards limestone tops and wriggle through a narrow cleft in the rock (a tight fit with a full pack) to reach a junction and pass below impressive blades of rock, 35mins from the last turn-off. The track to the left is that via Ačkova dolina, which would have added at least half an hour to your itinerary.

View from summit of vrh Bijele stijene

Continue straight over the pass, following the trail marked 'Ljuska', descending slightly into Natašina dolina before veering right on the *lakši put* ('easier route') and entering the area known as **Ljuska**. (The 'difficult' route is somewhere off to the left, and should not be considered: in fact, the 'easy' route becomes quite challenging, as you will soon discover.) Steel cables lead round the edge of a steep-sided pit, beyond which you descend a loose, or unbolted, ladder. Ascend a long steel ladder (loose-looking, but bolted at the top) to impressive views of limestone spires. Descend with the aid of steel pegs, keeping right and close to the cliff. Scramble steeply

123

upwards (possibly slippery), ascend over rocks and then descend into forest cover again to reach a clearing 55mins beyond the pass. Here the following words greet you from the rocks on the left: *Kako je lijepa moja zelena dolina* or, more familiarly, 'How beautiful is my green valley'. Continue up over rocks to reach a trail ascending on the right, marked 'vrh', 15mins from the clearing. This is not vrh Bijele stijene, but another peak, known as **Južni vrh** (1300m, not to be confused with the Južni vrh on Samarske stijene), which can be reached after some steep and at times rather awkward scrambling.

Continue on the main trail, following the KPP and kuća ('house') signs, and passing a trail down towards Jasenak (marked 'Begova staza') after 10mins. Walk straight past this, scrambling again and squeezing through another narrow cleft in the rock, and gaining your first view of the impressive limestone spires known as Prsti (literally, 'fingers'), 15mins beyond the Jasenak trail. This is followed by a trail, descending on the right, marked 'kapelica' (chapel) and an alternative route to the summit, also on the right, marked 'vrh'. A few minutes beyond this you arrive at the main summit trail on the right, marked 'na vrh'. Dump your pack here and ascend steeply, with the aid of steel cables and pegs, for 5mins to **vrh Bijele Stijene** (1334m). The views are extensive, with limestone crags to the northwest and, in the distance, Bjelolasica and Klek (northeast, Walk 10). Another trail descends from the summit to link up with the alternative summit route.

Descend to the main trail and continue, as indicated, 'u kuću' ('to the hut'). The path descends, branching left to arrive, with the aid of more steel cables, at the hut (**Planinarska kuća na Bijelim stijenama**, 1300m) in 10mins.

The main hut stands on the edge of a large clearing, with picnic tables and a well (beyond which is an alternative route to the summit). There is also a *sklonište*, **Planinarska sklonište Miroslav Hirtz** (with plenty of beds, and its own *lisica*) on the other side of the clearing.

EXTENSION

It is possible to continue via Velika Javornica and Kolovratske stijene before descending to the coast just south of Novi Vinodolski, or even continue all the way south to **Velebit** (Walk 11), on a route known as the SPP, Spojni planinarski put. While this may sound attractive, it should be added that much of the walking is on roads, and that altogether more spectacular routes await you further south. Furthermore you will doubtless need to get in supplies before an extended walk on Velebit, so would have to head for the coast first anyhow.

STAGE 4
Planinarska kuća na Bijelim stijenama – Jasenak

Time	2hrs 15mins
Distance	7km
Maximum altitude	1300m
Rating	easy
Map	SMAND Samarske Bijele stijene Bjelolasica (11a) or SMAND Bjelolasica (11b)

Of the various ways to descend from Bijele stijene, unfortunately, none is ideal. Certainly none is as impressive as the route which you have followed from Samarske stijene. The one described here is simply the most straightforward, and also the shortest. (A far longer onward itinerary is outlined in the 'Extension' box above.)

Take the Jasenak path, passing the *sklonište* and descending through forest, and then the left fork of this (marked 'Klek, Jasenak') to reach the road and car park in 30mins. Turn left onto the road, descending for 5mins to a bus stop and turning right onto a broad, rutted track. Turn left off this, descending into a gully and following this downhill (northeast). The trail is poorly marked at first, and the gully choked with felled trees, but the path soon broadens and brings you back onto the road. Follow the road down to the right, ignoring turn-offs to the left. Take one more (poorly marked) shortcut on the right, if you can find it (if not, keep following the road down), to arrive at the main road 2hrs from the hut. Turn left onto this, to reach the largely depopulated village of **Jasenak** in 15mins, from where you can hitch or catch a bus (infrequent service, contact Ogulin tourist information office, www.tz-grada-ogulina.hr, tel. +385 (0) 47 532 278 for details) towards Bjelsko and Ogulin. (Alternatively, turn right if you intend to try and hitch down towards the coast.) From Bjelsko, you can walk up to Klek in about 1hr; otherwise, the train from Ogulin will take you back to Delnice and on to Rijeka or back to Zagreb.

WALK 10
Klek

Klek, the easternmost peak of Velika kapela, dominates the skyline as you approach Gorski kotar from the north. An impressive tower of limestone protruding above forested slopes, with the two smaller peaks of Klečice ('little Kleks') below, it is one of the most popular destinations for Croatian climbers, and its southwest face has been described as the 'school' of Croatian alpinists. Appropriately enough, it is the distinctive form of Klek which decorates the logo/blazon of the Croatian Mountaineering Association.

As a *walking* destination, Klek is perhaps not in itself so impressive as some of the other parts of Gorski kotar – although it will certainly be of interest to those equipped with climbing gear. However, those returning from Samarske stijene via Jasenak (Walk 9) will find the hut (located just below the summit), and the route up from Bjelsko, particularly well placed.

This is an easy and straightforward hike from the village of Bjelsko to the hut (1000m) and summit (1182m) of Klek, which can either be spread over two short days or undertaken as a longer day trip. The standard route, from Ogulin (Stage 2), is in fact much longer – although it certainly has the more impressive views – and is here included in reverse, as a descent.

Ogulin has a particular association with witches and fairy tales – there is an annual witches' festival in June, and Croatia's most celebrated writer of fairy tales, Ivana Brlić Mažuranić, lived here.

Maps	Klek is included on the SMAND sheet Bjelolasica (11b) and on the older Gorski kotar I (11).
Transport	Those returning from Bijele and Samarske stijene (Walk 9) will probably hitch, or catch a passing bus, from Jasenak to Bjelsko, and continue by train to either Rijeka or Zagreb from Ogulin. Those coming direct from Zagreb, Rijeka or Delnice will arrive by train at Ogulin, and should follow the second part of the route in reverse.
Accommodation	Practical information Due to its popularity, not to mention its relative proximity to Zagreb and ease of access, PD Klek can get quite crowded at weekends, and you might want to phone and book accommodation in advance (tel: +385 (0) 47 531 206). For accommodation in Ogulin, contact the tourist information office (www.tz-grada-ogulina.hr, tel: +385 (0) 47 532 278). You can rely on the single shop in Bjelsko only for the most very basic of supplies: Ogulin is better stocked.

STAGE 1
Bjelsko – PD Klek

Time	1hr
Distance	2.5km
Maximum altitude	1000m
Rating	easy
Map	SMAND Bjelolasica (11b)

A broad, clear track (marked 'Klek') ascends from opposite the bus stop on the main road in **Bjelsko**, a few metres from the only store. Follow this straight up before branching off to the left on a marked path, which crosses one track and then merges with another from the left. Some 30mins of forest walking brings you to a junction with the trail up from Ogulin on the right. Continue straight ahead,

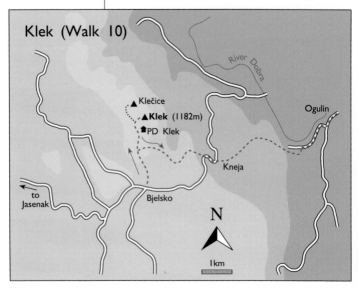

passing notices requesting that visitors carry some firewood up with them in the winter, and noting the occasional well-placed wooden bench, to gain a ridge where a banner greets you with the words: 'Dobro došli u carstvo klečkih vještica' ('welcome to the empire of the witches of Klek') – Klek has long been associated with witches, who according to local legend like to gather on the summit. **PD Klek**, at 1000m, is a few minutes beyond.

EXCURSION FROM PD KLEK
Klek (return)

Time	40mins return
Distance	1km
Maximum altitude	1182m
Rating	easy–moderate
Map	SMAND Bjelolasica (11b)

Continue on the trail past **PD Klek**, ascending gradually and following the occasional sign to Klek and passing a *špilja* (cave) on the right. After 10mins the trail arrives at a junction, from where the path continues straight ahead to **Klečice** (an additional 35mins, for those interested), and from where the trail up to the summit of Klek branches off to the right. Follow the path up below the rock face, ascending more steeply with the occasional scramble (aided by black electrical cable, rather than the more orthodox steel cables). There are good views of Klečice from just below the summit, followed by a concrete helicopter landing pad. Continue along the ridge, passing a rather precarious-looking, roped *kratkica* (shortcut), which is best avoided, to gain the airy summit of **Klek** (1182m), with sheer drops beyond and fine views west to Velika kapela. Descend by the same route to **PD Klek**.

Klek, from the trail to Ogulin

STAGE 2
PD Klek – Ogulin

Time	3hrs
Distance	9.5km
Maximum altitude	1000m
Rating	easy
Map	SMAND Bjelolasica (11b)

Descend 15mins from the hut on the main trail before turning off to the left on the path marked 'Ogulin'. This descends steeply, on a slope which looks as though it would become a mudslide after rain, to reach a clearing in 5mins. Continue roughly east over grassy slopes, with good views back towards Klek, passing a quarried area before gaining a gravel track. This brings you into the trees again, where you continue on a broad, leafy track, veering left before entering a brief clearing with more views of Klek. Turn right on the path marked 'Ogulin', re-enter the trees and veer round to the right, ignoring the path ascending to the left. After skirting the edge of a quarry, the path brings you to the main **Bjelsko–Ogulin road**, 1hr 15mins from the hut.

Turn left onto the main road, following the signs painted on the tarmac before turning off to the right on a marked path after 5mins. Follow this into the trees, then turn right onto a dirt road, which takes you past the large outdoor recreation centre known as **Kneja**. Continue straight ahead, descending and crossing another dirt road, before entering a large, level, grassy clearing, with a wooden hut on the left. Continue NE across this, crossing another dirt road and re-entering the trees before joining a broad forest track. Ignore a succession of tracks off to the left and right until you reach a path on the right leading into the trees, clearly marked 'Ogulin'. This leads onto a dusty track, which splits into two marked trails, 30mins after leaving the main road. Take the right fork, and soon after this a path off to the left, to reach a small lookout point (signposted 'Vidikovac'; from *vidjeti*, 'to see') after about 15mins, from where you'll have your first clear view of Ogulin and the River Dobra.

Continue along the main trail, descending through the trees and passing a sinkhole (in which the bodies of a number of dead Ustaša were apparently buried during the Second World War). This section of the path is known as Ferdina staza, after a popular local figure, Ferdo Uršan. Walk 25mins from the lookout point to emerge from the trees and arrive on a road, between a few houses, where you turn right. From here it is a further 20mins to the main road and a welcome café, where more signs lead left and then right to the station in **Ogulin**, from where you can catch a train to Zagreb or Rijeka.

FURTHER POSSIBILITIES IN GORSKI KOTAR

Skrad
Below the small town of Skrad, about 12km east from Delnice, is a deep canyon known as Vražji prolaz or 'The Devil's Pass' – about 2km long, and in places as little as 2m wide. You can walk down to the canyon entrance (tickets 7Kn) from the train station, then descend a steep trail (often by way of walkways and metal bridges) to the bottom, where there is a waterfall called Zeleni Vir and a car park (it's possible to drive down – allow at least 2hrs 30mins return). Return by the same route. SMAND covers the area on Gorski kotar III (13).

Burnji Bitoraj
From the small mountain town of Fužine, some 12km southwest of Delnice, it is possible to climb Bitoraj (1386m), a peak in the area known as Burni Bitoraj. The route starts from just north of Fužine near Vrata, heading southeast to reach the summit, just below which there's a sklonište, Planinarsko sklonište Bitorajka. Allow 3hrs 30mins each way. SMAND cover the area on Gorski kotar II (12). If you're staying in Fužine there is the excellent Hotel Bitoraj (www.bitoraj.hr, tel: +385 (0) 51 830 005.

Premužičeva staza, Northern Velebit

PART 5
VELEBIT

INTRODUCTION

Velebit is Croatia's most extensive massif, containing some of its highest peaks and its most spectacular scenery, and no hiking trip to Croatia is complete without at least a few days here. In fact, it is possible to spend quite some time on Velebit: a full north–south traverse requires at least 10–12 days, if it includes only some of the various possible excursions.

Boasting domed peaks and jagged crags, brilliantly engineered tracks through some magnificent limestone scenery, brown bears and botanical gardens, sinkholes plummeting some 1392m (that's almost down to sea level) and sheer-sided gorges where until only recently griffon vultures nested above alpine climbing routes, Velebit should have enough to keep most mountain enthusiasts more than busy.

Like its more southerly siblings Mosor and Biokovo, Velebit rises steeply and dramatically from the coast. Perhaps rather appropriately, considering the alarming

Hiker on Premužićeva staza, Northern Velebit

depth of its sinkholes, the ferocity of its winds (the infamous *bura*), and the peculiarity of its light – the glowing pinks and reds of its limestone buttresses before sunset – the 16th-century Croatian writer Petar Zoranić made Paklenica the entrance to Hell in his book *Planine* ('The Mountains', 1569). Zoranić describes the *bura* as a harsh wind blowing from Vražja vrata ('Hell's gate' – hell in modern Croatian being *pakao*, whence Paklenica), and gives a mythical account of its origin – the sighing of a beautiful woman (named Bura) who was confined to the underworld for her excessive vanity.

Less stiflingly hot than Mosor and Biokovo during the summer months, winter brings a whole new character to Velebit, with pine trees springing from its snowbound rocky slopes like something straight out of a painting by Caspar David Friedrich. Despite bitter temperatures, at least one hut remains open throughout the winter (PD Zavižan), when it is possible to look down over the coast and islands from snowbound, icy passes. Those planning a winter trip should note that in a year of heavy snowfall much of the initial section of Premužićeva staza becomes impassable. The *bura* on Velebit can be particularly strong, and the weather full of surprises, even in the summer – so come prepared.

The routes described below cover all of the main parts of northern, central and southern Velebit, from the beautiful area around Zavižan in the north to the limestone gorges of Paklenica in the south; when linked, they form an extended trek through Croatia's finest, as well as some of its highest, mountain scenery. There is no opportunity for restocking supplies along the way, so you will need to carry enough to last the whole trip. Those with only enough time for shorter trips should concentrate on the area around PD Zavižan, followed by Buljma, Vaganski vrh and Paklenica in the south, and finally Bačić kuk in central Velebit – although in each case they would end up marching up and down from almost sea level.

WARNING

Certain parts of Južni Velebit (southern Velebit) remain unsafe following the 1991–1995 war, and walkers continuing south from Baške Oštarije should read the section on landmines at the end of the Introduction (see page 63) and the beginning of the section 'Južni Velebit (southern Velebit) and Paklenica', below.

WALK 11
Sjeverni Velebit (northern Velebit) and Srednji Velebit (central Velebit)

The following itinerary leads from the small village of Gornja Klada on the main coastal highway up to the spectacular scenery around PD Zavižan (1594m), which provides an excellent base for exploring the surrounding area, with its numerous peaks between 1600 and 1699m. The route south follows the brilliantly engineered Premužićeva staza, from which more peaks and ridges can be reached, varying in difficulty from an easy walk to a challenging and demanding scramble. Caving enthusiasts should note that the deepest sinkhole in Croatia (Lukina jama) lies only a short distance from the main route – although it lies within a protected area and is very much off limits unless you can get a permit. A circular route is possible from PD Zavižan (via Veliki Lubenovac, see extension to Stage 3, below), spread over two or three days and bringing you back to the hut; otherwise the main trail continues south from Rossijevo sklonište for another three days, less spectacularly and largely through forest for the second of these, but ending grandly enough with the very impressive limestone crags of Bačić kuk – making a total of six days if you include all the recommended excursions.

From Baške Oštarije the route can be extended into southern Velebit, to reach Buljma and Struge above Paklenica in a further three stages without descending to the coast (see alternative route to southern Velebit at the end of Stage 5). This unbroken itinerary provides the most extensive mountain trek in Croatia, although once again those continuing south of Baške Oštarije are referred to the warnings in the introduction and at the beginning of the alternative route.

Accommodation south of PD Zavižan is provided by a good selection of huts and *sklonište*, and only at the end of the fourth stage is accommodation inconveniently placed, at which point a tent might make things easier.

Northern Velebit, and more specifically the area around PD Zavižan, Rožanski kukovi and Hajdučki kukovi, was recently declared a national park (having previously been classified as simply a 'nature park') and you will need to buy a ticket to cover the period you intend to stay in the area. You can buy your tickets at the Zavižan hut. Ticket prices are 30Kn for three days (15Kn for HPS card holders), and 50Kn for seven days (25Kn for HPS card holders).

Maps	SMAND covers the area on two sheets: Sjeverni Velebit (16) and Srednji Velebit (17). There are also two recommended publications (in Croatian only). The small leaflet and map Sjeverni Velebit – PD Zavižan has a useful list of excursions and their duration (note that the timings are only one way), as well as descriptions of major landmarks. Also highly recommended is the small and very reasonably priced guide by Alan Čaplar, Velebitski planinarski put, which covers the whole route from Zavižan to Paklenica. For those continuing south of Baške Oštarije there is the new SMAND sheet Južni Velebit (18).
Transport	To get to Gornja Klada, take a southbound bus from Rijeka, either to Starigrad (not to be confused with Starigrad-Paklenica) or Karlobag. Make sure you get a bus travelling via the coast, as a number of buses turn inland at the town of Senj. (If you can only get as far as Senj, you should not have too much difficulty hitching the last 20-odd kilometres.) Travelling south, the road to Gornja Klada is on the left, and is signposted, just before a house advertising private rooms (the ▶

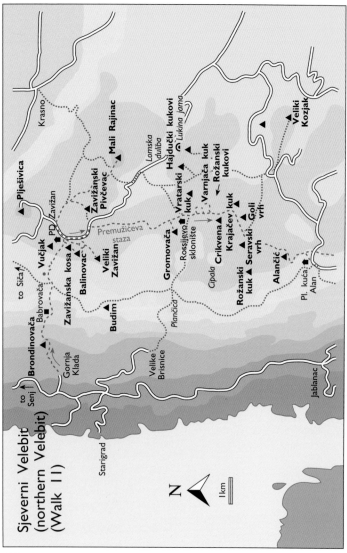

Sjeverni Velebit (northern Velebit) (Walk 11)

Krasno

to Siča

to Senj

Brondinovača

Gornja Klada

Babrovača

Vučjak

PD Zavižan

Zavižanska kosa

Balinovac

Veliki Zavižan

Budim

Plj
ešivica

Zavižanski Pivčevac

Mali Rajinac

Lomska duliba

Hajdučki kukovi

Lukina jama

Vratarski kuk

Varnjača kuk

Rožanski kukovi

Rossijevo sklonište

Gromovača

Crikvena

Krajačev kuk

Rožanski kuk

Seravski vrh

Goli vrh

Alančić

Pl. kuća Alan

Cipala

Plančićd

Veliki Kozjak

Velike Brisnice

Starigrad

Jablanac

N

1 km

◄ ubiquitous *zimmer*, or *sobe* – see below). The village is 5mins up the road.

Accommodation/
Practical information
The house on the main road by the turn-off to Gornja klada has clean, good value rooms (contact Anka Magić, tel: +385 (0) 53 625 343). PD Zavižan (tel: +385 (0) 53 614 209), Rossijevo sklonište Alan (tel: +385 (0) 1 467 4259, mobile: +385 (0) 98 921 8587), Planinarsko sklonište Ograđenica, Kugina kuća (tel: +385 (0) 42 232 377, mobile +385 (0) 98 961 0042), PD Ravni Dabar (tel: +385 (0) 53 633 016, mobile (tel: +385 (0) 98 171 0933), Prpa (tel: +385 (0) 53 674 012), Planinarska kuća Vila Velebita (tel. +385 (0) 53 574 065, mobile: +385 (0) 98 961 0042).

STAGE 1
Gornja Klada – PD Zavižan

Time	4hrs 30mins
Distance	8km
Maximum altitude	1594m
Rating	easy–moderate
Map	SMAND Sjeverni Velebit (16)

Follow the trail markings up through the village to gain a clearly marked, stony track, on which you ascend and veer left. The path drops slightly after 15mins, passing through a gate and veering right onto a stony plateau. Continue across this, winding your way through rock and scrub as the mountains loom ahead, to gain a well-engineered set of switchbacks in 30mins. These lead up, passing a small pool (for watering livestock) on the right and a path joining from the left from below the small peak of Brondinovača (681m) before levelling out again. Ascend gradually, passing through low beech and oak, to gain a second set of switchbacks. These are longer than the previous ones, with a number of shortcuts lead-ing between them. Continue ascending, with views back over the islands of Rab, Goli otok and Pag. The air here is redolent of wild herbs – in contrast to the wild garlic of Gorski kotar. The switchbacks become a broad forest track, which leads round a final corner to a gate and the summer cottage of **Babrovača** beyond, 1hr 45mins from the village. It is just before this point that you will begin to encounter snow if you arrive in the winter.

Continue past the cottage, passing through another gate. Take the left fork and follow the signs to Zavižan, ascending on a rocky path through pine and then mixed forest cover again, and passing a rock outcrop and a small, flat, grassy area on the right. A further 20mins leads to a larger flat area and a rock outcrop with exten-sive views out over the islands, a total of 2hrs 30mins from the village. There is enough room for a few tents here if you have arrived late and don't have enough time to continue up to Zavižan, but there is no water.

Continue up through forest cover, passing a trail to Alan via Velike Brisnice on the right (which you don't take), followed shortly by a path to Siča on the left. ◄ Ignoring these turn-offs and following the signs straight ahead to Zavižan, enter a clearing before ascending on a broad, walled track to reach a second clearing 10mins beyond the Siča path. Here you pass two large, man-made ponds (actually watering pools for livestock) on the left, the sec-ond of which has a small and rather murky-looking *izvor* (spring) just behind it. Continue, following route markings and wading through clover before re-entering forest cover and ascending a broad, steep, leafy track. Some 25mins beyond the ponds, you reach a final set of switchbacks, which lead up through the forest and then left along a last, long stretch to gain the pass in another 30mins. The snow can be knee-deep here during the winter, burying any sign of a path and slowing progress considerably, and you may be glad of a long-handled axe or walking poles if ascend-ing at this time of year.

The view from the pass is breathtaking, particularly if you have arrived in the evening as the sun begins to

It is possible to ascend from the village of Siča to this point, although the route is far less attractive, being largely along forest tracks with not much of a view, and there is little in the way of transport to get you there.

set across the Adriatic. The islands of Rab, Goli otok and Pag are clearly visible. You may be able to make out the much-touted sandy beach at Lopar on the former. Goli otok (literally 'naked island') once housed a high-security prison, whereas Pag is famous for its cheese (*Paški sir*).

PD Zavižan below Vučjak, Northern Velebit

PD Zavižan sits above you on the other side of a deep, bowl-like depression. Continue 15mins, skirting the side of the large doline and following the trail up to the hut. Large and well equipped, with numerous beds and the use of a kitchen (for a nominal fee), it makes an unsurpassed base for exploring the surrounding area. There is a lot to see around PD Zavižan, and you could quite easily spend a few days here. Look out for the *poskok* (nose-horned viper) specimen above the door to the sinks and toilets, a good example of what to avoid standing on during your subsequent travels. The hut is actually a meteorological station (which explains why it is open all year round), and it is this which the helpful Ante Vukušić and his family are officially employed to run, although they effectively end up running the hut as well.

EXCURSION FROM PD ZAVIŽAN
Vučjak

Time	10mins return
Distance	0.2km
Maximum altitude	1645m
Rating	easy–moderate
Map	SMAND Sjeverni Velebit (16)

The small peak of **Vučjak** (1645m), just behind PD Zavižan, is the first place to head for a view of the surrounding area. The path leads straight up from beside the hut. The prominent peak to the northeast, crowned by a telecommunications complex, is Plješivica (1654m). More impressive are Veliki Zavižan (1676m) and Balinovac (1601m), south-southwest above the *botanički vrt* (botanical garden); and Zavižanski Pivčevac (1676m) and Mali Rajinac (1699m) to the southeast, the goal of the trip described below. Framed by these two areas of high ground are the cluttered peaks and crags of Rožanski and Hajdučki kukovi. Descend to **PD Zavižan** by the same route.

EXCURSION FROM PD ZAVIŽAN
Mali Rajinac

Time	4hrs 30mins return
Distance	9km
Maximum altitude	1699m
Rating	easy–moderate
Map	SMAND Sjeverni Velebit (16)

From **PD Zavižan**, follow the path (marked 'Mali Rajinac') for a few minutes down to the road, turning left onto this for 5mins before reaching a path on the right (marked

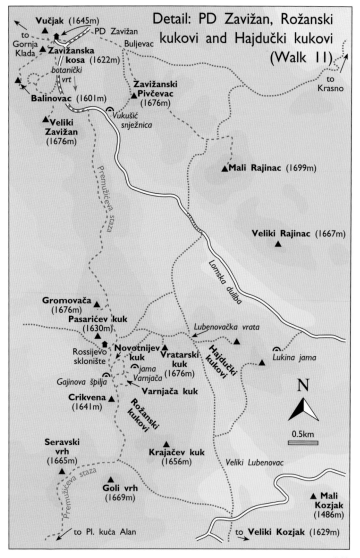

Detail: PD Zavižan, Rožanski kukovi and Hajdučki kukovi (Walk 11)

Vučjak (1645m)

PD Zavižan

to Gornja Klada

Zavižanska kosa (1622m)

Buljevac

botanički vrt

Balinovac (1601m)

Zavižanski Pivčevac (1676m)

to Krasno

Vukušić snježnica

Veliki Zavižan (1676m)

Premužićeva staza

Mali Rajinac (1699m)

Veliki Rajinac (1667m)

Lomska duliba

Gromovača (1676m)

Pasarićev kuk (1630m)

Lubenovačka vrata

Rossijevo sklonište

Novotnijev kuk

Vratarski kuk (1676m)

Hajdučki kukovi

Lukina jama

jama Varnjača

Gajinova špilja

Varnjača kuk

N

Crikvena (1641m)

Rožanski kukovi

0.5km

Seravski vrh (1665m)

Krajačev kuk (1656m)

Veliki Lubenovac

Premužićeva staza

Goli vrh (1669m)

Mali Kozjak (1486m)

to Pl. kuća Alan

to Veliki Kozjak (1629m)

'Mali Rajinac', 'Otočac' and 'Krasno') and following it into the trees. This brings you out into the open again in 25mins, contouring a steep-sided dell to arrive at a junction with a broken sign – an area known as Buljevac. Mali Rajinac is visible to the southeast, and Zavižanski Pivčevac (from *pivac*, the local dialect for capercaillie – which explains the presence of this bird on the national park logo) to the south (beyond the nearer, wooded peak). Turn right on the path to these peaks, leaving the main trail which continues straight ahead to the village of Krasno (meaning 'beautiful'), and then left on the branch to Mali Rajinac, the further of the two peaks. This leads through forest cover before emerging into the open in 10mins, with Pivčevac directly behind you.

A further 30mins of predominantly pine forest, alternating with open, rolling, grassy clearings, leads to another junction, from where it would be possible, by turning right, to continue to Veliki Lubenovac (see page 152). Instead, take the left (Mali Rajinac, Krasno) branch and then, 5mins later, a right fork (marked 'Mali Rajinac'). Ascend through forest and then along the final, rocky path to reach the summit of **Mali Rajinac** in 35mins. ◄ A grand array of high peaks extends to the southwest, with Gromovača (1676m) particularly prominent, almost due southwest. This is Rožanski kukovi, the area through which you will continue from Zavižan, following Premužićeva staza. Veliki Zavižan (1676m) is clearly visible to the northwest. Descend by the same route, returning to the junction at Buljevac in just over 1hr, before continuing on to reach **PD Zavižan** in a further 35mins.

At 1699m Mali Rajinac is the highest peak in northern Velebit.

EXTENSION

This itinerary could be extended from the junction at Buljevac by following the trail up to **Zavižanski Pivčevac** (1676m) in 45mins. From here it would be possible to descend to the road on the other side of Zavižanski Pivčevac before returning along this to the hut, and thus pass **Vukušić snježnica**, a sinkhole (named after the Vukušić family, who used to have a small cottage nearby), where snow remains throughout the year.

EXCURSION FROM PD ZAVIŽAN
Zavižanska kosa, Balinovac and Botanički vrt

Time	3hrs 15mins return
Distance	5.5km
Maximum altitude	1676m
Rating	easy–moderate
Map	SMAND Sjeverni Velebit (16)

Velebit's botanički vrt (botanical garden) sits in a sheltered hollow beneath Balinovac, a short distance from the hut and just beyond the small kapelica (chapel) of Sveti Ante, built just a few years ago. To reach the botanički vrt you can stroll down the road from the hut then branch off to the right, or you can include it, along with Veliki Zavižan (1676m) and Balinovac (1601m), in the following itinerary.

Ascend **Zavižanska kosa** from the saddle below the hut, gaining the summit (1622m) in 10mins, from where there are views of both Balinovac and Veliki Zavižan ahead, and of the hut nestled below Vučjak behind you. Continue beyond the summit on a marked trail, descending steeply to the left for a short distance, before crossing over to the north side of the rocky ridge leading up to **Balinovac**, and finally scrambling up to reach the summit (1601m), 45mins from Zavižanska kosa.

Although Veliki Zavižan can be reached along the ridge from Balinovac, the route involves floundering

145

Zavižan's botanical garden with Balinovac beyond

The botanical garden was established in 1966 by Dr Franjo Kušan, a professor from the University of Zagreb, and contains numerous endemic plant species, as well as the rare runolist (edelweiss).

through some particularly hardy dwarf mountain pine and juniper, and it is far more pleasant (and less damaging) to descend to the **botanički vrt** before continuing from there. The path descends into the trees before meeting the main trail above a steep-sided dell (Modrić dolac) at the head of the open, grassy meadows. ◀

Follow the path around the side of the dell, ascending steeply through the trees from the opposite (southern) side before emerging into another grassy clearing below Veliki Zavižan. Cut across the clearing, from where a trail leads up through the trees, around thickets of dwarf mountain pine, and then scramble steeply up to the summit (1676m), 1hr from the botanical garden. From the top of **Veliki Zavižan** there are clear views south along Rožanski kukovi – your onward route from PD Zavižan – including its highest peak, Gromovača, which is equal to your present altitude. Hajdučki kukovi rises to the southeast, with Veliki Kozjak beyond, and Pivčevac and Mali Rajinac are visible to the east.

Descend by the same route to the botanički vrt, turning right and contouring the slopes above Modrić dolac to the small wooden shelter before continuing to the chapel, the road and **PD Zavižan**.

STAGE 2

*PD Zavižan – Rossijevo sklonište
via Premužićeva staza and Gromovača*

Time	2hrs 40mins
Distance	7.5km
Maximum altitude	1676m
Rating	easy–moderate
Map	SMAND Sjeverni Velebit (16)

From **PD Zavižan** follow the road down to the chapel, turning right off this on the path to the botanički vrt before rejoining the road in a few minutes. Continue along the road as it veers northeast with views back to the hut, before turning right onto the path marked 'Premužićeva staza', 20mins from PD Zavižan.

Premužićeva staza and Rožanski kukovi

Premužićeva staza (and more especially this northern section of it) is a particularly well-engineered track built during the early years of the 1930s at the order of Ante Premužić. A local forestry engineer, Premužić assigned the building work to local labourers, thus ensuring for them a regular income during this period of economic hardship, and providing for the modern-day walker a stunning itinerary. The symbol 'v' is used to mark the course of Premužićeva staza over its entire length.

The path initially passes through trees, but emerges after about 20mins to begin winding around cliffs and bluffs, with spectacular views of limestone rock formations and jagged crags, leading up onto the backbone of **Rožanski kukovi**. 1hr 15mins should be enough to bring you to a path ascending to the right, which leads to the peak of Gromovača. Leave full packs in the trees just off the main trail and scramble up the steep, rocky path, winding your way through dwarf mountain pine to reach the summit of **Gromovača** (1676m) in 10mins. Among those peaks recognisable from the top are: Veliki Zavižan (1676m) to the north, Mali Rajinac (1699m) to the northeast, Crikvena (1641m) to the south and Rožanski kuk (1638m) to the southwest; while the high crags of Rožanski kukovi and Hajdučki kukovi beyond continue to the southeast, and the sea and islands are visible to the west.

The etymology of Gromovača (from *grom*, meaning 'thunder') will become evident from your present location if there are storm clouds in the vicinity, as this peak and the surrounding area attract them like a magnet, sending walkers scurrying back down to the main trail and on to Rossijevo sklonište for shelter. I don't think I have ever seen a darker or more ominously brooding, lowering sky than while clambering over the pass below Crikvena on one of my first visits to the area.

Drop back down to the main trail, collect full packs and continue another 15mins, passing a trail on the left to Lomska duliba, Kozjak, Mali Rajinac and Hajdučki kukovi, to reach the turn-off to Rossijevo sklonište (also known as Rossijeva koliba), which you will find a few minutes away on the path to the right. Those who are staying may enjoy a moderately difficult scrambling route up to **Pasarićev kuk** (1630m), directly behind the hut, or the excursion detailed below.

Rossijevo sklonište sits in a lovely spot, perched on a ledge at 1580m. Although rather small to rely on during the summer months, it is certainly worth spending some time here if you get the chance. The well beside it is fouled, and you will need to purify water taken from here. There is a small wood stove, although anyone carrying their own stove would be more considerate to use this and leave the wood for locals.

ALTERNATIVE

For those who require a direct route down to the coast, a trail descends to Velike Brisnice, Modrići and Starigrad, via Plančica (1229m) – although it should be added that it is not a particularly interesting route, and is rather longer than it looks.

EXCURSION FROM ROSSIJEVO SKLONIŠTE
Rossijevo sklonište – Varnjača kuk

Time	2hrs 15mins return
Distance	1.5km
Maximum altitude	1634m
Rating	difficult
Map	SMAND Sjeverni Velebit (16)

The following excursion is a difficult and challenging ridge walk, which (whether or not you choose to stay the night at Rossijevo sklonište) is better undertaken without the burden of a full pack. The route is mostly unmarked and overgrown, and requires some exposed scrambling. Furthermore the conservation status of Varnjača kuk is slightly ambiguous at present – there has been talk of banning walks and climbs on the ridge. Ask at PD Zavižan or Rossijevo sklonište for the latest information.

Continue south on the route to Alan (see Stage 3, below) for a few minutes before picking up the beginning of the faint trail off to the left, marked 'Rossijev kuk', 'Novotnijev kuk' and 'Varnjača'. The Croatian sign at the bottom means: 'Experienced walkers only'. It is 10mins up to the first of these peaks, from where the route continues via Novotnijev kuk (from where it is possible to reach Vratarski kuk) and passes a sinkhole (Varnjača jama) in 1hr.

You can continue by scrambling along **Varnjača kuk**, an airy ridge some 400m long, and in places less than 1m wide, picking a way around its three peaks (Sjeverni, Srednji and Južni vrh) before returning to Premužićeva staza (either from Južni vrh or Sjeverni vrh), making a total excursion of a little over 2hrs. Those not continuing south to Alan (see Stage 3) should take this opportunity of climbing Crikvena, which is just a little way south

Varnjača kuk, in Rožanski kukovi, Northern Velebit

along the main trail. Return to **Rossijevo sklonište** along Premužićeva staza.

STAGE 3
Rossijevo sklonište – Planinarska kuća Alan

Time	2hrs 30mins
Distance	7km
Maximum altitude	1641m
Rating	easy–moderate
Map	SMAND Sjeverni Velebit (16)

Continue on the main trail from **Rossijevo sklonište**, following the signs to Alan and passing a trail to Velike Brisnice (which links up with the route up from Gornja Klada to PD Zavižan, see Stage 1) on the right. Just around the corner a faint trail leads up to the left, which marks the beginning of the Varnjača kuk excursion described above. Continue straight ahead, passing some particularly impressive limestone scenery and the other end of the Varnjača kuk excursion on the left as you head up towards the pass. The path drops down fairly steeply on the other side of this, from which point (leaving full packs) there is an easy scramble up a marked route to **Crikvena** (1641m; from *crkva*, meaning 'church'). There are good views of the surrounding area from the summit.

Premužićeva staza is unfortunately somewhat less spectacular beyond this point, and does not regain its grandeur until the section around Bačić kuk, a day and a half beyond Alan. From the base of the pass, continue through forest cover with occasional glimpses out over limestone formations, passing one track to the left up to Krajačev kuk (1656m), which can be reached in about 30mins, and a second, also on the left, to Veliki Lubenovac.

EXTENSION

Veliki Lubenovac is a level, grassy clearing at 1265m, below Rožanski kukovi, Hajdučki kukovi and Veliki Kozjak. It would be possible, by following this path on the left (see above), to descend to Veliki Lubenovac in 1hr, from where you could climb **Veliki Kozjak** (1629m). There used to be a *sklonište* at Veliki Lubenovac, but it burned down a few years ago.

To the north of Veliki Lubenovac lies **Hajdučki kukovi**, an area under special protection. **Lukina jama**, the deepest sinkhole in Croatia (and among the ten deepest in the world), is on the opposite (northeast) side of Hajdučki kukovi, and is usually reached from the road as it passes through Lomska duliba – though it is strictly out of bounds unless you manage to obtain a permit. Plummeting some 1392m into the bowels of Velebit, Lukina jama was discovered only in 1992, and is named after Ozren Lukić, a climbing and caving enthusiast who joined the local volunteer unit (a mountain division) during the 1991–95 war and was killed by a sniper in 1992.

There are a number of other caves and sinkholes in the area. In 2003 a Croatian caving team discovered another sinkhole, near Crikvena, which is suspected of being even deeper than Lukina jama. Another sinkhole in Rožanski kukovi, called Slovačka jama, has a depth of 1017m; while Patkov gušt, discovered in 1997, contains a single vertical drop of over 500m.

A marked trail leads back to **PD Zavižan** from Veliki Lubenovac, heading north between Hajdučki kukovi and Rožanski kukovi and climbing to a pass (Lubenovačka vrata) below Vratarski kuk, before crossing the road and continuing to meet the trail from PD Zavižan at the base of Mali Rajinac (see page 143). This circular route would require a further one or two days to complete, depending on how many daylight hours you have remaining and whether you choose to visit Veliki Kozjak, with a night at Veliki Lubenovac (assuming the *sklonište* here gets rebuilt).

Continue straight ahead past the Lubenovac turn-off, and the main trail soon emerges onto open grassland with views behind you back to the high peaks of northern Velebit. A trail on the right up to **Seravski vrh** (1665m), which can be reached in 15mins, is followed by another to Alančić (1611m, also on the right) 40mins later. Some 10mins beyond this, the sea comes into view on the left before a sudden switchback forces you, rather confusingly, to walk north rather than south. Re-enter the trees, to arrive at a path on the right (marked 'Alan sklonište') in 5mins, which leads down to the hut in a further 10mins.

Planinarska kuća Alan is open, with use of the kitchen, from June to the end of September; outside these months, when these facilities remain closed, it is open as a *sklonište*, providing mattresses and shelter. It makes a convenient place to stop for the night, although it is not in quite such an attractive spot as PD Zavižan or Rossijevo sklonište.

ALTERNATIVE

There is a route leading down to Jablanac from Alan for those who need to descend to the coast; it follows the road in its initial stages but soon diverges from it, emerging onto the coast near the attractive channel, or cove, called Zavratnica. There is a very basic hut here, **Pl. kuća Miroslav Hirtz**, open during the summer.

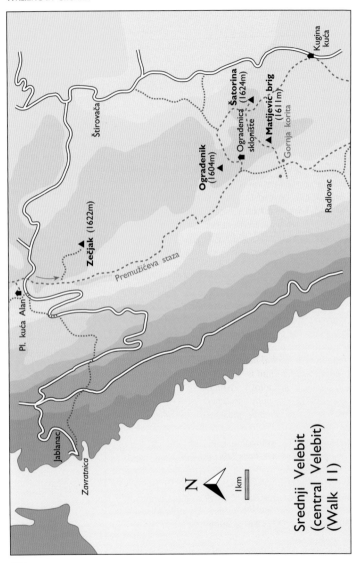

Kugina
kuća

Šatorina
(1624m)

▲Matijević brig
(1611m)

Štirovača

Ograđenica ■
sklonište

Gornja korita

Ograđenik
(1604m) ▼

Radlovac

Zečjak (1622m) ▲

Premužićeva staza

Pl. kuća Alan ■

Jablanac

Zavratnica

N

1km

Srednji Velebit
(central Velebit)
(Walk 11)

STAGE 4
Planinarska kuća Alan – Kugina kuća

Time	6hrs 45mins
Distance	20km
Maximum altitude	1624m
Rating	easy–moderate
Map	SMAND Srednji Velebit (17)

Accommodation on this section of the route is rather less conveniently placed than on others. Those intending to climb Šatorina (at 1624m the highest peak in central Velebit, but less spectacular than its northern siblings) can fix their sights on either the sklonište at Ograđenica, just off the trail as it climbs between Ograđenik and Šatorina, or Kugina kuća, further to the SE. The former is closer to the main trail, but is very small (sleeps 4) and would make a very short day from Alan (there's no water, so you'll need to carry enough to last until the following day if staying here); the latter is more attractive, but needs to be booked in advance (see Appendix B) otherwise you will probably find it locked (as a last resort, there is a small sklonište in the woods behind it), and the route from Kugina kuća back to the main trail is far from clear. Furthermore, the old sklonište at Radlovac (which was way off the main trail anyway, and fairly run down) is now closed. Those not planning to climb Šatorina are likely find Kugina kuća an inconvenient and unnecessary detour – in which case, those with a discreet tent and some extra water will find themselves in a more favourable position.

From **Planinarska kuća Alan** follow the path back up through the forest to regain the main trail, turning right onto this to emerge from the trees 15mins from the junction. Cross the road (leading up from Alan and on to Štirovača), passing a monument to the Partisans of the Second World War (specifically the Alan Division,

155

A track just beyond this leads up to Mali Vidik ('little viewpoint'), with not much of a view and some particularly ugly pylons.

The trail to the left leads to Zečjak at 1622m the second highest peak in central Velebit, in about 1hr.

formed in 1943) on the opposite side. ◄ Continue straight ahead, following the signs to Kugina kuća and Baške Oštarije, through trees at first but soon emerging with a view down across open, rolling grassland to the left, criss-crossed by the dry, uncemented stone walls known as *suhozid* (from *suho*, meaning 'dry', and *zid*, 'wall'). Just beyond this, you arrive at a junction, where you can follow the path up to the right to Buljma, with good views of Rab and Pag – although the views are just as good further along the main trail. ◄ Continue straight ahead, walking parallel to the coast with clear views out over the islands, and passing a track on the left to Štokić duliba in 15mins. All views are soon lost as the path re-enters the forest, continuing a further 90mins to a junction (from which two onward routes are possible – see alternative route via Premužićeva staza, below), 3hrs 30mins from the hut.

Turn left and follow the trail as it spirals up around Šatorina (from *šator*, meaning 'tent'). The route takes you up over a saddle below Ograđenik (1604m), and **Ograđenica sklonište**. Those who wish to stop here can do so – although it makes a rather short day from Alan (about 4hrs) and a longer day tomorrow (9hrs 30mins), and the nearest water is at Gornja Korita, back down on Premužićeva staza.

Continue along the main trail from the saddle, passing a turn-off to Štirovača on the left, from where a further 50mins brings you to the summit trail, which branches off to the left. It's 10mins up this to the top of **Šatorina** (1622m), with clear views north to Veliki Kozjak and south towards Bačić kuk from the summit.

From the base of the summit trail a path descends via Matijević brig (1611m) to rejoin Premužićeva staza at **Gornja korita** in 1hr (korita means 'water-trough', and refers to the water-trough downhill a short way from the main trail). For those who've spent the previous night at Ograđenica sklonište, this is the way to proceed, before continuing along Premužićeva staza, passing two trails on the right to Radlovac (the old *sklonište* there is now closed) and a faint trail on the left to Kugina kuća marked

'Težekovac' (a poorly marked route which is more difficult than that described in Stage 5). Follow the signs straight ahead to Skorpovac, passing a clearing with suhozid and a small cottage below on the right, and skirting the rocky hillside to reach a junction in a small, relatively level clearing, just over 1hr beyond the first Radlovac turn-off, where the trail from Kugina kuća (see Stage 5, below) joins Premužićeva staza on your left.

Otherwise, for those intending to stay at Kugina kuća a second path, not always very clear, leads down from the junction just below the summit of Šatorina to reach this hut in 1hr 30mins.

Kugina kuća is usually open at weekends during the summer, or by arrangement (see Appendix B). Water is available from the well outside, and there's a small *sklonište* behind the hut.

ALTERNATIVE ROUTE VIA PREMUŽIĆEVA STAZA

It is possible to take a more direct route S without climbing Šatorina, although now that the *sklonište* at Radlovac has closed this is only really feasible if you're carrying a tent. Veer right at the junction below Šatorina and Ograđenik, following the signs to Radlovac and Baške Oštarije and continuing a further 45mins to a point where the path zigzags down the hillside slightly before continuing in the same direction. Just beyond this is the small spring known as Gornja korita (there's a water-trough down a path to the right – fill up here), and the trail on the left leading up to Šatorina via Matijević brig (see main route, above). Continue straight ahead along Premužićeva staza as described in the main route, to reach the small clearing and the trail to Kugina kuća, a little over 1hr beyond Gornja korita. Those with a tent may want to pitch it in the clearing, although there's no water. From the clearing it is also possible to reach Kugina kuća (1hr 20mins), but this would involve a considerable detour, and make little sense if you've come this way instead of over Šatorina.

STAGE 5
Kugina kuća – Prpa

Time	8hrs
Distance	16km
Maximum altitude	1317m
Rating	easy–moderate
Map	SMAND Srednji Velebit (17)

If starting from **Ograđenica sklonište**, continue via Šatorina, Gornja korita and Premužićeva staza as described above.

From **Kugina kuća**, cross the road and cut up into the forest on the trail marked 'Ravni Dabar' and 'Bačić kuk', before turning right onto the forest road and following this for a little way. The most direct route from Kugina kuća to Skorpovac used to be along a trail marked 'Šturo', however this has been largely obliterated by the new forest road. Instead, turn right off the road to traverse open, rocky slopes (where I saw more snakes than anywhere else in Croatia) and then descend through the trees to rejoin **Premužićeva staza** at the clearing described in Stage 4, about 1hr 20mins from Kugina kuća (another more direct trail branches off to join Premužićeva staza at Skorpovac, but the point at which it diverges from the route described above is very unclear).

Low clouds on Bačić kuk, Central Velebit

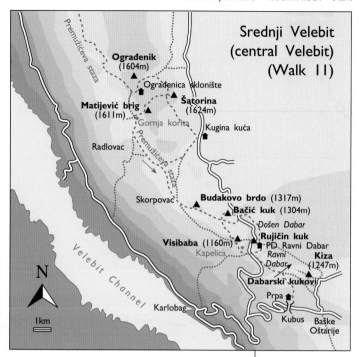

Srednji Velebit (central Velebit) (Walk 11)

From the clearing, continue along Premužićeva staza, passing a turn-off to Pejakuša on the right, to arrive at the ruined and deserted village of **Skorpovac** in just under 1hr. Immediately before the ruins, another path (see above) to the left branches off to Kugina kuća. ▶ Continue straight ahead, and a further 15mins brings you to a turn-off, on the left, for Budakovo brdo and Bačić kuk. Follow this path, ascending through tall beech forest to emerge into a clearing in under 1hr.

There is a well on the right but the quality of the water from here is questionable.

From just above the tree line, follow a path up to the left, which leads to the top of **Budakovo brdo** (1317m) in 10mins. From Budakovo brdo continue southeast along the grassy ridge, with unobstructed and increasingly impressive views of the limestone crags of Bačić kuk, descending slightly before reaching a four-way junction, with the beginning of the trail up to the summit on the left. Follow this to reach **Bačić kuk** (1304m) in 40mins, with spectacular views southeast along the spine of Dabarski kukovi.

Return to the four-way junction referred to above, from where you have two options.

Option 1

Turn left onto the main trail and continue over a grassy knoll before descending to the road in 40mins, beyond which a saddle is gained, and then descend another 30mins to Došen Dabar. From here the route continues for another 30mins, passing between Čelina and Rujičin kuk to reach **PD Ravni Dabar** (723m), from where a steep trail climbs to Premužićeva staza and the road described at the end of Option 2. Descending all the way to Ravni Dabar only really makes sense if you plan to stay there; those continuing to Prpa or short of time should follow Option 2.

EXTENSION

Those who have descended all the way to Ravni Dabar may wish to follow an alternative route to **Kiza** (1247m), via Crni Dabar, after which they would have to double back slightly on Premužićeva staza before branching off to Prpa.

Option 2

The path straight ahead at the junction re-enters the forest and descends to Premužićeva staza in about 30mins – and is the route of preference in case of poor weather.

ALTERNATIVE

Yet a further trail branches off to the left before you reach Premužićeva staza, to **Visibaba** (1160m, meaning 'snowdrop'), from where you can either

> descend to Premužićeva staza or continue east to
> meet the road at Rujičin kuk, above Ravni Dabar.

Turn left onto Premužićeva staza, following the signs to
Baške Oštarije, and passing a trail on your left to Bačić
kosa and Visibaba after 50mins. Continue straight ahead,
passing a spring (marked *voda*, 'water', and known
as *Kapelica*, 'chapel') up over the rocks on the left in
10mins. Beyond this you have fine views to the left of
Dabarski kukovi; follow the open ridge to reach the road
in 25mins, just before which you pass a trail descending
on the right to Karlobag. From the road you have a magnificent view down over **Ravni Dabar**, the hut and Čelina
behind it, and of the southern slopes of Bačić kuk. You
should be able to pick out the course of the direct route
down from Bačić kuk (see Option 1), crossing the road
on the way down.

From the road overlooking Ravni Dabar, continue
along the trail to Baške Oštarije, passing a trail on the left
to Butinovača (about 45mins away) and re-entering the
forest to arrive at a path on the right to Prpa in 20mins.
Although there are places to stay in Baške Oštarije, they
tend to be large and relatively expensive, and the small
wooden chalets at Prpa are in every sense preferable. Turn
right and ascend through the forest to gain a saddle in
25mins. Veer left through a clearing with more *suhozid*,
descending over open slopes towards the houses and a
farm track, from which there are good views of Dabarski
kukovi to the left. Turn right onto the farm track, passing
under the pylons before turning right, ascending and following the wooden telegraph poles towards the pines.
Just 5mins should be enough to bring you to the Alpine
style wooden chalets among the trees at **Prpa**.

> The **chalets** at Prpa come equipped with fridge, stove
> and toilet; the shower is piping hot, and you can even
> arrange to have meals provided for you, with a little
> advance notice.

For those heading down to Karlobag (about 20km), there are buses from Oštarije – simply continue on the farm track to reach the Oštarije–Karlobag road. Note the large stone cube (known as Kubus) above the tunnel on the right, which was carved in 1846 when the Karlobag–Gospić road was under construction. There was once a Roman road here, too; and the name Oštarije seems to be of Roman origin. From Karlobag, buses head north and south on the main coastal highway.

ALTERNATIVE ROUTE TO SOUTHERN VELEBIT VIA ŠUGARSKA DULIBA, STAP AND VELIKO RUJNO

Those wishing to continue into southern Velebit on foot, rather than descending to the coast and then climbing all the way back up to Veliki Rujno, can do so from Baške Oštarije. From here it would require a further three stages (with two overnight stops, at Šugarska duliba and Stap, each of which has a *sklonište*) to reach Struge, situated above Paklenica.

From **Baške Oštarije** (927m), the route heads south to Sladovača brdo and past Sadikovac to the *sklonište* at **Šugarska duliba** (1212m, 6hrs); the water from the tank here has been known to run out during summer, and should be purified in any case. From here it continues past Mali Stolac (1131m) before veering left to Jelova ruja (*not* straight ahead to Panos – this small peak (1261m) has an abandoned military installation on it: do not approach Panos under any circumstances). The water at Jelova ruja is fouled. The route then turns right (*not* straight ahead – the trail to Visošica east of Jelova ruja leads into an area suspected of landmine deployment: make sure you turn south after Jelova ruja) towards Debeli kuk (1269m) and the *sklonište* at **Stap** (960m), with drinking water available from a cave about 30m from the shelter (5hrs). Stap is a flat, grassy area surrounded by limestone crags; the peak itself is about 40mins away.

From Stap the route continues to Malo and **Veliko Rujno**, where it links up with the Južni Velebit and Paklenica route (see Walk 12, Stage 2), and continues to **Struge** (7hrs).

It is essential that anyone considering this route should arm themself with a decent, post 1991–95 conflict map. SMAND cover the area with a fairly new sheet, Južni Velebit (18).

Despite ongoing protests by environmental groups and walkers, **roads** continue to carve their way into Velebit, destroying huge numbers of trees and damaging the natural habitat of numerous animal species. In central and southern Velebit, they threaten the integrity of Premužiceva staza and the VPP (Velebitski planinarski put), Croatia's most extensive long-distance footpath.

You can show your support for those trying to oppose this destruction, by writing to Velebit.Planine. Org (www.velebit.planine.org; see the 'Support our Campaign/Write your Comment' section), and HPD Zagreb-Matica (www.zagreb-matica.hr), Croatia's oldest Mountaineering Society, which has been particularly active in opposing these developments.

WALK 12
Južni Velebit (southern Velebit) and Paklenica

Southern Velebit contains some outstanding scenery, not to mention two of Croatia's highest mountains (Vaganski vrh and Sveto brdo) and the limestone gorges of Velika and Mala Paklenica. The following itinerary ascends to Bojinac (1110m) and Veliko Rujno before following the main ridge over Vaganski vrh (1757m) and on to Sveto brdo (1751m), and descending to PD Paklenica. When linked to the route over northern and central Velebit (see Walk 11, alternative route to southern Velebit, above), it provides the most extended mountain trek in Croatia; otherwise, it can be completed in four days. A number of shorter itineraries are also possible (see Further Possibilities, below).

Although most visitors enter the national park through Velika Paklenica, and begin and end walks at PD Paklenica, it is much more rewarding to start a little further north, and include the twisted limestone crags of Bojinac (1110m). This also allows more of a sense of continuity from the route over northern and central Velebit (Walk 11), and joins the southern extension of this (see alternative route to southern Velebit box above) at Veliko Rujno.

Although not quite the roof of Croatia, the rugged area around Vaganski vrh is far more attractive than Croatia's two slightly higher peaks, Dinara and Sveti Jure, and Velika Paklenica itself contains numerous climbing routes just beyond the car park and the national park entrance.

WARNING!

Certain areas of southern Velebit remain heavily mined from the 1991–1995 war. Although the paths followed in this itinerary are perfectly safe, adjacent areas are not always so. In particular, the area beyond Struge, and the eastern side of the main ridge from Struge to Sveto brdo, are suspected of being mined: do not proceed east of Struge or descend to the eastern side of the main ridge under any circumstances! Do not wander off the main path in this area: if you do not manage to reach a hut and need to camp, pitch your tent on the path. See the section on Landmines on page 63.

Maps	SMAND covers the area in one sheet: Nacionalni park Paklenica (19). For those continuing south from Baške Oštarije there is the new SMAND sheet Južni Velebit (18). Also highly recommended (for those familiar with Croatian) is the small and very reasonably priced guide by Alan Čaplar, *Velebitski planinarski put*, which covers the whole route from Zavižan to Paklenica.
Transport	Starigrad-Paklenica lies on the main road south from Karlobag. The turn-off to Velika Paklenica is just to the south of the town beyond the Hotel Alan; it's 2 or 3km up the road to the national park entrance.
Accommodation	Practical information Accommodation is provided by three *sklonište*, at either end of the main ridge, a tiny cave beneath the northern flanks of Bojin kuk, and by a large hut (PD Paklenica) at the head of the gorge below. Many locals come to the church at Veliki Rujno on Assumption Day (15th August), and huts in the vicinity tend to be full at this time. For accommodation in Starigrad-Paklenica, try Hotel Rajna (www.hotel-rajna.com, tel: +385 (0) 23 359 121). Buy supplies at Starigrad-Paklenica.

STAGE 1
Milovci – Bojinac

Time	4hrs
Distance	6km
Maximum altitude	1000m
Rating	moderate
Map	SMAND Nacionalni park Paklenica (19)

Although there are two tiny springs on Bojinac, these cannot be relied on and you should bring enough water to last you until Veliko Rujno on Stage 2. The sklonište at the end of stage 1 is just a small cave; you may prefer to carry a tent and continue slightly beyond Bojinac towards Veliko Rujno and camp.

From the small car park in **Milovci** follow the signs to Veliko Rujno, before turning left on a path with faint trail markings and the occasional cairn. Cross a plateau, then follow the trail as it zig–zags up. Continue alongside a dry stone wall (not over it), following cairns and passing a ruined stone house on your left. Contour the hillside on a well engineered track with views back over the sea, and of a peak on your right. Follow the trail as it zig–zags up again, passing alongside another dry stone wall (which again you don't cross). Pass a trail on your right, keeping straight ahead up the slope, to reach a **pass**, 1hr 30mins from Milovci. There is a small devotional shrine here, and views back across the Velebit Channel.

Continue, descending slightly, then ascend again on a rocky path through dry grass and low bushes, to reach a trail on your left to Bojinac in 15mins. The path is unclear at first, following a wall before clear trail markings appear, and then climbing steeply with views back towards vrh Ercegov. Just after a grassy clearing, you reach a junction, where a trail on the left leads to a viewpoint in 5mins (but

Southern Velebit and Paklenica, seen across the Velebit Channel from the village of Vinjerac

the 'view' really isn't worth it – better views lie ahead). Keep straight ahead on the trail marked Bojinac, to gain the edge of a rocky dell in 30mins. Descend into this then veer right (look out for cairns), passing a prominent and distinctly phallic rock formation (Jagin kuk), with the polished limestone cliffs of Bojin kuk beyond. Continue, passing a trail on the left, then scrambling up and turning right then left. Pass a trail to Veliko Rujno on your right to reach the **sklonište** in a few minutes.

Planinarsko sklonište pećina (also known as **Planinarsko sklonište na Bojincu**) is nothing more than a small rock cave, which can sleep up to about four people at a squeeze. If you decide this isn't for you (and it can be rather claustrophobic) and you have a tent, continue a short distance along the Veliko Rujno trail (see Stage 2, below), where there are some reasonably level, grassy slopes suitable for camping, just on the edge of the national park boundary, or camp at Veliko Rujno itself

(Bojin kuk and the dell below it are part of Paklenica national park, so camping is prohibited there). There are two tiny springs in the vicinity (one back in the dell, the other on the excursion detailed below), but (assuming you've brought enough as advised) you'd do better to wait until Veliko Rujno.

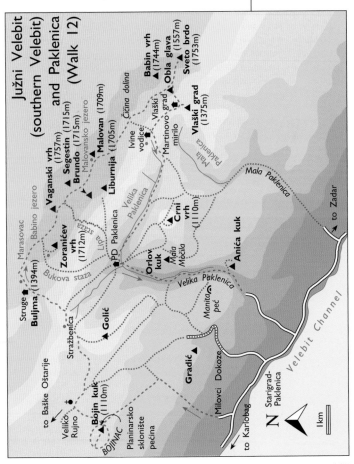

Južni Velebit (southern Velebit) and Paklenica (Walk 12)

ALTERNATIVE ROUTE TO VELIKO RUJNO
FROM DOKOZE (2HRS 30MINS)

It is also possible to reach Veliko Rujno from the village of Dokoze, which is about 2km up a small road behind Starigrad-Paklenica – making it easy to reach Struge in one stage (5hrs 15mins) rather than two. From **Dokoze**, ascend on the jeep track (passing a path on the right to Manita peć in Velika Paklenica, followed by some particularly impressive rock formations on the left, **Gradić** and **vrh Ercegov**) to the car park in 1hr. Descend briefly from the car park on a stony path before steadily ascending, following the occasional arrows painted on rocks and passing a house where the path joins from Milovci (see Stage 1, above) – an area known as **Veliki Vaganac**. Approximately 90mins from the car park the ground levels out, and after passing various odd huts and shelters you arrive at a junction with the route from Bojinac (see Stage 1) and main north–south Velebit trail (the VPP, or Velebitski planinarski put). The church at **Veliko Rujno** is a short distance along the path to the left.

EXCURSION FROM
PLANINARSKO SKLONIŠTE PEĆINA
Bojin kuk

Time	3hrs
Distance	2.5km
Maximum altitude	1110m
Rating	moderate
Map	SMAND Nacionalni park Paklenica (19)

There are two routes up Bojin kuk – a steep, exposed via ferrata from the south, and a more moderate, rocky scramble up a gully from the west. If you want to try the former, ascend that way and descend via the easier route. The following itinerary ascends and descends by the easier route, and continues by making a short circuit of Bojin kuk. You should have plenty of time to complete the excursion and continue to Struge (Stage 2) the same day.

Retrace your steps from the sklonište, leaving full packs at the junction with the onward trail to Veliko Rujno, then keeping right rather than descending all the way into the dell, and following the trail marked 'Zliba'. Ascend steeply over limestone formations, to gain a shoulder with fantastic views (the best spot for breakfast). The more difficult and exposed via ferrata route to Bojin kuk starts from just above this. Continue, following the *voda* (water) signs and passing trails on your left, one of which leads to a sinkhole. 10mins brings you to a tiny, rather dirty spring a little way up the cliff on your right. Pass this to reach a sheltered, grassy clearing, where you turn right on the trail to Babin kuk. A sign at the bottom reads 'Bablji smjer', which translates, rather mischeviously, as 'granny route' – just so you know you've picked the easier of the two possible ascents. A degree of caution is still advised however: the trail passes a deep sinkhole (on your right; nearby rocks are marked *pazi*, danger, and *ponor*, abyss), and as you scramble up the rocky gully, watch out for snakes. It's less than 30mins to the summit of **Bojin kuk** (1110m), with excellent views. The more difficult route descends on the other side (not recommended). Instead, retrace your steps

Hiker on Bojinac, Southern Velebit

back down to the main trail, and turn right, to gain a small saddle in 20mins. Continue beyond this, keeping right and ignoring a trail on the left to Veliko Rujno, to reach the sklonište in another 20mins. Collect full packs and continue to Veliko Rujno as described in Stage 2.

STAGE 2
Bojinac – Struge

Time	3hrs
Distance	6km
Maximum altitude	1400m
Rating	easy–moderate
Map	SMAND Nacionalni park Paklenica (19)

Descend a short distance from the sklonište, and turn left on the trail marked Veliko Rujno. Ascend slightly before descending steeply and entering forest. 30mins from the *sklonište* you emerge into a clearing with a water cistern on your left, where a trail marks Stap as 3hrs distant. Head right then left across the clearing, to reach the main north–south Velebit trail (the VPP) and **Veliko Rujno** – a large, grassy clearing at 850m. The church, where there is a water tank, is a short distance along the path to the left. Numerous people flock to the church (Gospa od Rujna) on 15th August for Velika Gospa (Assumption Day).

Strike south on the main trail before turning left towards Stražbenica after 10mins. (The path straight ahead leads down into Velika Paklenica in 3hrs.) Follow a broad track through pines before veering right and ascending, the pine trees gradually being replaced by beech, to reach a trail to Golić on the right in 35mins. Turn right along this before immediately turning off to the left and continuing to a small pass with a viewpoint just up to the left (signposted 'Vidikovac'; from *vidjeti* 'to see'). Descend a few minutes to **Stražbenica**, a junction near which there is a small

Rock formations on Bojinac, Southern Velebit

izvor (spring), and from which a path leads down to PD Paklenica in 90mins. Ignoring this path, continue straight ahead, ascending at first then temporarily descending, with good views down over Velika Paklenica. Pass a small spring on the left and then two more paths down to the hut on the right before ascending the final, steep switchbacks to the pass (1394m), which you should reach 35mins beyond Stražbenica. The pass, called **Buljma**, commands impressive views down over Velika Paklenica, and out over the Velebit Channel and the island of Pag.

Before proceeding any further, read the section on landmines at the beginning of this section and in the Introduction. The paths are perfectly safe, but some of the surrounding areas are not. As a sign on a rock 5mins beyond the pass declares, 'Forward you go your own responsibility [sic]'.

Continue to the junction 5mins beyond the pass (from where a route leads directly up to the main ridge, joining Bukova staza near Babino jezero), then straight ahead a further 10mins to **Struge**.

Struge is a tall, A-frame *sklonište* at 1400m; there is now a small charge for staying here during summer. Water is available from the well at Marasovac, 15mins away. Do not take any shortcuts to the well, and do not go in the dark without a torch.

STAGE 3
Struge – Vlaški grad via Vaganski vrh and Sveto brdo

Time	6hrs 30mins
Distance	14.5km
Maximum altitude	1757m
Rating	moderate
Map	SMAND Nacionalni park Paklenica (19)

This is a fairly long day, with some outstanding views – start early, as you can't afford to be caught out in the dark on the ridge.

Continue from **Struge** along a clear path. Do not wander off into the forest to the left under any circumstances. The path soon veers to the right, around the side of a basin – do not follow the path straight ahead beside the trees, and do not take a short cut through the basin. Pass a track on the right (leading to the trail from the junction just beyond Buljma, referred to above in Stage 2) to reach the well, known as **Marasovac voda**, 15mins from Struge. Do not continue N of Marasovac.

From **Marasovac**, ascend right (roughly S) on the path to Vaganski vrh, passing a small bunker in a group of trees and climbing steadily, to reach a large cairn, with views out over Lika and back towards central Velebit. Continue past the cairn, the path levelling before bringing you to a junction, 45mins from Marasovac, from where **Bukova staza** ('beech path') descends to PD Paklenica via **Babino jezero** on the right. A trail branching off this path before the lake leads up to the top of **Zoranićev vrh** (1712m), named after the 16th-century Croatian writer Petar Zoranić, whose *Planine* ('The Mountains') attempted to imbue the area with mythical history and legend. Continue straight ahead on the main trail, ascending slightly through juniper and dwarf mountain pine, thistles and raspberries, with views of folded cliffs on your left. The path gradually veers left and then right, ascending to the grassy summit of **Vaganski vrh**, 45mins beyond Bukova staza.

At 1757m, Vaganski vrh is the highest peak in Velebit and the third highest in Croatia. However, it is a far more attractive peak than either of its slightly loftier siblings – Sveti Jure on Biokovo (1762m) is surmounted by an enormous red-and-white TV antenna and has a road leading to the summit, and Dinara (1831m) is a rather more barren area, which still has landmine deployment. It offers a lovely view of the surrounding area – providing, of course, that cloud has not brewed up in the east and swallowed the entire ridge, as it is prone to do, in which case you will see very little at all.

From the summit, descend southeast on a steep and rocky path, over tufts of grass to a junction in 10mins. For those short of time, it is possible to descend from here directly to PD Paklenica (see direct route box, below, a total of 4hrs 30mins from Struge) instead of continuing along the ridge to Sveto brdo and Ivine vodice.

DIRECT ROUTE TO PD PAKLENICA VIA LIPA STAZA

The direct route carries the alluringly titled *Lipa staza* ('beautiful path'). However, *lipa* it most certainly is not, involving a steep, knee-jarring descent over some quite horrendous scree followed by an equally steep and seemingly endless descent through the forest. It is generally accepted that nobody would choose to come up this route.

From the junction below **Vaganski vrh** (see above) descend a steep path, before ascending to gain a ridge in 20mins. From this point, the descent is relentlessly steep over unconsolidated scree, redeemed only by spectacular views before entering forest cover and losing even these. Continue the steep, rocky descent, passing a path down from **Liburnija** and **Babin kuk** on the ▶

left before reaching the junction with Bukova staza, 1hr 50mins below the ridge. Continue beyond this to a further junction just above a small settlement, where you veer left, descending through mossy forest cover to reach the large PD Paklenica in 40mins. Water is available beside the hut. For the route from PD Paklenica, see Stage 5.

For those continuing to Sveto brdo, continue straight ahead from the junction, passing a trail to **Brundo** and **Liburnija** on your right, and then **Malovan** (1709m) and the small lake, **Malovansko jezero**, both on your left. Climbs on the peak itself are to be strongly discouraged. Continue, passing a large cairn, and through thick mountain pine, to emerge suddenly on the coastal side of the ridge, with views down over Paklenica and the bridge at the end of the Velebit Channel. Old bunkers are visible on both peaks on your left. Contour scree slopes, to reach **Čičina dolina**, where a path descends on your right to Ivine vodice (40mins) and PD Paklenica (3hrs). Instead, continue straight ahead, winding your way over **Obla glava** (1557m) and below **Babin vrh** (1744m)

Main Velebit ridge above Paklenica, near Vaganski vrh

before reaching another trail on your right, to Vlaški grad. Continue past this, leaving full packs and ascending over grassy slopes to reach the summit of **Sveto brdo** (1753m) in 1hr, with its large metal cross. Sveto brdo ('Holy Mountain') is the distinctive 'bump' which marks the southern point of the main Velebit ridge, when viewing the range from the coast (see photo page 23) – and the views, not surprisingly, are spectacular.

Return to the Vlaški grad turn-off on the main trail, turning left and descending to **Vlaški grad sklonište**, just below the peak of the same name, which you reach in 1hr 15mins from Sveto brdo.

The hut here was rebuilt a few years ago, the old one having burned down. There's a water tank beside the hut (empty on my last visit); the old water source is behind the hut. (Alternatively, if you find the hut here full, continue to the *sklonište* at Ivine vodice, just under 1hr away following the route in Stage 4.) The peak **Vlaški grad** (1375m) can be climbed – a trail heads up from just above the hut.

STAGE 4
Vlaški grad – PD Paklenica

Time	3hrs 15mins
Distance	7.5km
Maximum altitude	1280m
Rating	easy
Map	SMAND Nacionalni park Paklenica (19)

From **Vlaški grad sklonište** follow the trail roughly NW through the forest, descending and reascending again before reaching the **Ivine vodice sklonište** in just under 1hr.

The hut itself is in a rather poor state of repair, but the nearby well provides a reliable water source. Note that you cannot camp at Ivine vodice – apart from the fact that you're in a national park, the flat grassy area here is a helipad!

Descend on the main trail 45mins to **Martinovo mirilo** (914m), which takes its name from the stone mirilo of local burial customs. While a body was being carried the considerable distance to the cemetery for burial, the bearers were permitted to stop and rest – and place the body on the ground – at one designated point only, roughly half way. The length of the body would be recorded, and a stone *mirilo* placed here later. It was to this *mirilo*, rather than to the actual grave located in a distant cemetery, that relatives and mourners would come to pay their respects. The custom died out in the 1950s.

Pass two trails on your left to Velika Močila and **Mala Paklenica**, keeping straight ahead and then crossing to the true right bank of the Velika Paklenica stream. Continue through the tiny settlement of Parići, descending between two walled gardens then straight ahead behind a walled padock, to join the combined Lipa staza and Bukova staza trails coming down on your right. Turn left, to arrive at **PD Paklenica** in 5mins.

PD Paklenica is a large hut at 480m (marked 550m on SMAND). Water is available from the tap outside.

STAGE 5
PD Paklenica – Starigrad via Velika Paklenica

Time	2hrs 30mins
Distance	9km
Maximum altitude	480m
Rating	easy
Map	SMAND Nacionalni park Paklenica (19)

From **PD Paklenica**, cross the bridge and descend, passing the path up to Sveto brdo on the left and following the broad, stone track alongside the river. Pass a track on the left to **Mala Močila** (see alternative route below), to arrive at a foresters' hut and an old mill, 35mins from PD Paklenica. Cross over to the true right bank and continue, passing trails up to Veliko Rujno and to **Manita peć** on the right, and a spring on the left. After 45mins, with increasingly good views of **Anića kuk** (712m), you reach a track off to Jurasova glavica and Mala Paklenica on the left, and a further 10mins brings you to a track on the left to Anića kuk itself. An impressive rock face some 400m in height, it was first climbed by Dragutin Brahm in 1940. There is a map of climbing routes on the right a little further along the main trail. For hiking routes to Manita peć and Anića kuk, see further possibilites, below. Continue, re-crossing the stream and descending, as the route becomes increasingly gorge-like, to the rock walls and climbing routes and the **car park** beyond. The last of the griffin vultures which once nested at the top of these crags were poisoned a few years ago.

Walk or hitch (or if you're lucky catch the occasional passing minibus) the last 2km or 3km down to **Starigrad-Paklenica**.

Anića kuk in Velika Paklenica

ALTERNATIVE ROUTE:
PD PAKLENICA – STARIGRAD VIA MALA PAKLENICA

Those who entered the national park through Velika Paklenica may prefer to vary their route out by leaving through Mala Paklenica – but bear in mind that the path crosses the stream bed a number of times and may be impassable during the winter, while in the summer you will probably meet quite a few snakes.

From **PD Paklenica**, cross the bridge before taking the path on the left to Mala Močila and continuing on the PPP (Paklenica planinarski put), via **Velika Močila**, to another Stražbenica, and descending through the gorge of **Mala Paklenica** to reach the coast road at **Seline**. **Starigrad** is about 3km along on the coast road to your right.

FURTHER POSSIBILITIES

Anića kuk
From Velika Paklenica, a short walk above the car park (or 90mins if descending from PD Paklenica), a route branches off to the right (E) towards the enormous sheer face of Anića kuk. The hiking route heads up below and beside the face, then a final, slightly exposed scramble brings you to the summit (712m).

Manita peć
The trail to Manita peć heads left (W) from Velika Paklenica, climbing first to the cave and then on to the plateau above the canyon and the villages of Ramići and Marasovići. Either descend to Velika Paklenica from here, or head along to PD Paklenica.

PART 6
PLITVIČKA JEZERA AND KRKA

Plitvička jezera national park

INTRODUCTION

The spectacular series of emerald lakes and travertine falls of Plitvièka jezera ('Plitvice lakes') were declared a national park – Croatia's first – in 1949 and named a UNESCO World Heritage Site in 1979. Set amid lush vegetation and beech forest, there are 16 lakes in total, the largest of which are Kozjak and Prošèansko jezero. The travertine beds are formed through the precipitation of calcium carbonate onto mosses, leading to the formation of a highly porous sedimentary rock. The falls range from the impressive Sastavci (where the final lake plunges some 70m into the Korana) and the nearby Veliki slap (76m), to numerous smaller cascades; in winter, many of the smaller waterfalls freeze, becoming picturesque castles of ice. Local legend tells that the lakes were formed when locals pleaded for rain to the infamous Crna kraljica ('black queen') during a terrible drought; she replied by unleashing such a deluge that the whole area was flooded and the present lakes formed.

There are bears here – although count yourself special indeed if you actually see one. The national park also has the unhappy distinction of being the site of the first deaths (both Croat and Serb) during the 1991–1995 war, following the occupation of the park headquarters by Serb militia and the ensuing clash with Croatian police.

Plitvička jezera (www.np-plitvicka-jezera.hr) is perhaps the most heavily promoted national park in Croatia – an emphasis reflected in the entrance fee, a hefty 110Kn. There are two entrances, one near the Lička kuća restaurant (Ulaz 1) and the other near Hotel Jezero (Ulaz 2).

The well-marked network of trails and wooden boardwalks makes walking in the national park very easy. Bear in mind that the park gets extremely busy, and you'll be sharing the boardwalks with an awful lot of people – aim to start walking as early as possible, before the park gets too crowded.

WALK 13
Plitvička jezera

Time	2hrs 30mins
Distance	3km
Maximum altitude	620m
Rating	very easy
Map	The national park office produce a sheet, available from shops and ticket offices in the park: Nacionalni park Plitvička jezera Tourist Map (1:50,000)
Transport	Buses run to the park from Zagreb, Zadar, Split and other towns. Getting a bus *from* the park can sometimes be a problem, since they're often full and don't always stop to pick passengers up here. There are shuttle buses (or 'trains') and boats in the park itself, running every 15–20mins.
Accommodation/ Practical information	There are several large hotels at the various entrances to the park, all rather characterless but (unless you've got your own wheels) the most convenient option by far. Hotel Jezera is the best of the bunch; there's also a campsite at Korana, 8kms from Ulaz 1 (you can't camp in the park). Those with their own transport might consider staying in the small village of Rastoke, with its old mills and waterfalls. There is a small shop at Ulaz 1, but aim to buy any food you want in Zagreb or on the coast. Lička kuća is a good (though often fairly busy) restaurant, also at Ulaz 1.

This is just a short route to some of the better-known sites in the park – there's plenty of scope for further exploration and longer itineraries.

From Hotel Jezera descend to the ticket office, then down to the water, where a boat will ferry you over to the other side. Follow the boardwalks, keeping to the route marked R C G2, and passing a succession of picturesque

181

pools and falls. Take the shuttle bus back from Galovac or Okrugljak veliko (marked ST3 and ST4 on maps) to Milanovac (ST1). From the viewpoint turn right and descend through the large hole in the rock, then head right along boardwalks beside the falls, passing boardwalks on your right (marked 'parking', which lead up to Ulaz 1) before descending further to the base of Veliki slap. Return along the same route and take the shuttle bus back to the ticket office and Hotel Jezera at Ulaz 2, or follow the trail around Milanovac and take the boat across Kozjak jezero, and return to Hotel Jezera from there.

KRKA

Rising at the foot of Dinara near Knin, the River Krka carves an impressive gorge on its way down to sea level, tumbling over seven main groups of travertine falls on the way. The area was declared a national park in 1985 (Nacionalni park Krka, www.npkrka.hr). The most impressive of the numerous waterfalls is Roški slap, which plunges more than 25m in a single step; and the main step of Manojlovački slapovi, which falls more than 30m;

A typical waterfall in Krka national park

while Skradinski buk and Manojlovački slapovi fall in various steps and stages more than 45m and almost 60m respectively. The national park is on the migration route of numerous birds, and is also a home to that most singular of amphibians, the olm. There is a Franciscan monastery on Visovac, an island on a lake of the same name.

There are two main entrances to the park, one at Lozovac and another at the village of Skradin. Shuttle buses run from the ticket office and car park at Lozovac down to a point from which the footpaths and wooden walkways begin, near Skradinski buk; boats run every hour from the waterfront at Skradin, up into the national park near Skradinski buk, from where you can start walking, and back. Trails in the park are well-marked and mostly on wooden boardwalks, so detailed route description is really hardly necessary.

Entrance is 95Kn. In order to visit Visovac you will have to buy a separate boat ticket to take you to the island, which may make it more economical to book an all-inclusive boat tour from Šibenik, which includes a visit to the monastery.

WALK 14
Krka

Time	1hr
Distance	1.5km
Maximum altitude	150m
Rating	very easy
Map	The national park produce a sheet, Nacionalni park Krka.
Transport	There are several buses a day from Šibenik to Skradin and Lozovac, and boat trips head up river from Šibenik to Skradin, and from there into the national park; otherwise for those arriving by car the most convenient entrance is Lozovac.

Accommodation/ Practical information	There is a good national park information centre in Skradin; if you want to stay in Skradin, try the Hotel Skradinski Buk (www.skradinskibuk.hr, tel: +385 (0) 22 771 771).

From either entrance, follow the network of boardwalks around **Skradinski buk**. There are boat trips up to **Visovac**, as well as further up the Krka to Roški slap, where there are more wooden boardwalks.

PART 7
MOSOR, KOZJAK AND BIOKOVO

Sveti Ilija from peak near Sedmina, Biokovo

INTRODUCTION

The harsh uplands of these more southerly ranges in the Dinaric Alps – pock-marked with karst formations and covered with only a scattering of hardy, stunted vegetation – are traversed by some spectacular hiking trails. These areas are naturally well-known to local hikers, but (with the exception of the area of Biokovo directly above Makarska) see even fewer foreign visitors than Velebit and Gorski kotar further north.

MOSOR

An impressive ridge stretching from the ancient fortress of Klis in the north to the gorge of the River Cetina in the south, the main blade of Mosor rises like a dorsal fin above Split, reaching its highest point at Veliki Kabal (1339m). It is a harsh and desiccated landscape, having suffered particularly severe deforestation over the course of history, and what limited vegetation there is consists primarily of stunted maquis and garrigue. The heat during the summer is considerable, and there is little or nothing in the way of surface water. Nevertheless it is an attractive area, with some breathtaking views.

Mosor forms a natural barrier, and due to its geographical isolation an independent republic, known as the Poljička kneževina, had developed around Poljica (the area behind Mosor) by the 11th century. Later the Glagolitic priests of Poljica, having fled the Ottomans during the 16th century, settled on the island of Brač, where they founded the hermitage at Blaca. Split itself is justifiably famous for its Roman ruins, first and foremost among these being the palace of Diocletian.

The main entry points for walks on Mosor are Klis, Kućine and Gornje Sitno. The latter is the most convenient for day trips up to the main ridge and Veliki Kabal. However, Kućine is preferable for a full traverse, as described below, with a trail from Grlo near Klis meeting this route on Debelo brdo.

WALK 15
Mosor traverse

The following flexible itinerary covers the main peaks of the Mosor ridge, including its highest points, Vickov stup (1325m), vrh Mosor (1329m), Veliki Kabal (1339m) and the more distant Kozik (1319m).

Mosor suffers from an acute shortage of water during the summer, and unless you visit at the weekend when the hut is open you will have to carry enough for the whole trip. Alternatively, it would be possible to descend to the village of Gornje Sitno for water before plodding back up. Note that there is no water outside the huts, and there is unlikely to be any water at the *sklonište* (Kontejner-Ljuto kame), either.

It would be possible to complete the whole route in two days, starting early, with a night at PD Umberto Girometta or a bivouac on the main ridge. Otherwise, the walk should be spread over three days, with two nights at PD Umberto Girometta and a day trip sandwiched in between. There is the potential to extend the route beyond Kozik to include Lišnica (950m), and more technical routes lead from the main ridge over Jabuka. Buy all supplies in Split.

Maps	At the time of writing there was no detailed map available of Mosor, although SMAND is due to publish one at some point in the future (sheet 31). Note that the Freytag & Berndt sheet, Middle Dalmatian Coast 3, does *not* give accurate coverage of the routes on Mosor.
Transport	Buses for Kućine (number 32) leave from Split's local bus station (on the corner of Domovinskog rata and Gundulićeva; the same one as for buses to Trogir) every hour or so. The journey takes about 20mins.
Accommodation/ Practical information	Accommodation on Mosor is far from ideal, as the one *planinarski dom* (PD Umberto Girometta) is open ▶

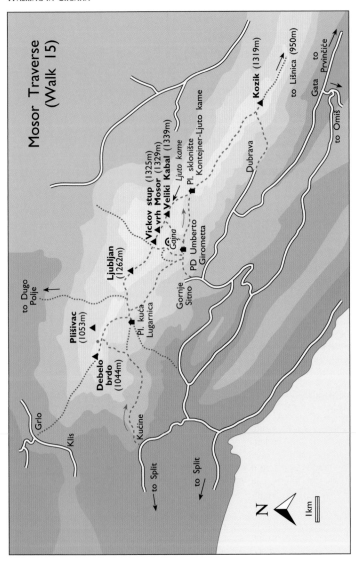

Mosor Traverse
(Walk 15)

to Prvinčiće
Kozik (1319m)
to Lišnica (950m)
Gata
to Omiš
Pl. sklonište
Kontejner-Ljuto kame
Dubrava
Ljuto kame
Vickov stup (1325m)
vrh Mosor (1329m)
Veliki Kabal (1339m)
Gajina
PD Umberto
Girometta
Ljubljan (1262m)
Gornje
Sitno
to Dugo
Polje
Pl. kuća
Lugarnica
Plišivac (1053m)
Debelo
brdo (1044m)
Kučine
Grlo
Klis
to Split
to Split

N

1km

◄ only at the weekend, while the other hut (Planinarska kuća Lugarnica) needs to be booked if you are not to find it locked. There is also a very basic *sklonište* (Kontejner-Ljuto kame). In view of the above, if you arrive mid-week you are advised to bring a tent. In Split, try the excellent and very good value Apartments Simoni (www.apartments-simoni.com, tel: +385 (0) 21 488 780), down behind the railway station. Buy all supplies in Split.

STAGE 1
Kućine – PD Umberto Girometta
via Debelo brdo and Ljubljan

Time	5hrs 30mins (direct route) – 7hrs 30mins (via Ljubljan)
Distance	13–14km
Maximum altitude	approx. 1315m (via Ljubljan)/1044m (direct route)
Rating	easy–moderate (direct route)/ moderate–difficult (via Ljubljan)
Map	none available – see sketch map

Get off the bus at the last stop in Kućine and walk up the road from the small café, following the signs to Lugarnica. Take the marked shortcut on the right, continue up the road, and then turn left just before a small church dated 1871, ascending a steep track between houses towards the pines. Already, at this altitude, Split sprawls below you in a cloud of exhaust fumes.

Ascend diagonally (ENE) on a well-marked trail, through scrub and trees blackened by recent fires, doing your best to ignore the unsightly quarry to the right. There is nothing in the way of shade, and the heat is intense in the summer. Walk under the pylons, heading

189

The main Mosor ridge from Debelo brdo

for the obvious notch in the cliffs above, to gain the pass, 45mins from the church. Here you can shelter briefly from the sun under a lone, shady tree – although the stagnant little pond makes this spot less attractive than it might otherwise be.

Continue past the pond, veering right on a rocky path leading towards the main ridge. In 15mins reach a relatively flat area with a small shepherd's hut. Continue over dry grass and scrub, walking parallel to the low cliffs on the left as the sea comes into view on the right. Heading almost due E now, the path goes straight over a stone wall, with Kozik visible at the far end of the main ridge, before winding through stunted holm oak, where a Lugarnica sign painted on a rock confirms that this is the right track. Zigzag up before scrambling over low cliffs, heading for the small hut visible just below the skyline and taking the left fork (marked 'Lugarnica') to arrive at a junction, just over an hour beyond the pond.

Instead of continuing directly to Lugarnica, turn left here and ascend towards the tiny spring (called Živca) and Debelo brdo (literally, 'fat hill'). The path is sometimes unclear but continues straight up to arrive at a further junction in 40mins. Turn left here (marked 'voda' and Debelo brdo) to arrive at a small *izvor* (spring) in 15mins – little more than a stagnant pool in the rock, which hopefully you won't need to rely on. Leave full packs in the vicinity, continue and turn left at the next junction, about 20mins to the summit of **Debelo brdo** (1044m), where there are good views out over Split and ESE along the main ridge. A path beyond the summit descends to Grlo, another possible starting point for this itinerary.

Return to the spring to collect your pack and continue straight ahead, passing the trail by which you came up on the right, together with a faint (but unconfirmed) trail to Ljubljan and a path to Plišivac, both on the left. By following the latter trail it would be possible to reach Plišivac (1053m) in 30mins. The path descends slightly before you take the right fork to Lugarnica to arrive at a T-junction 25mins below the peak. Turning right here would take you down to **Planinarska kuća Lugarnica** (872m), just a few minutes away. However, you will find this locked unless you have made prior arrangements to stay here, and there is no water outside the hut. Instead, then, turn left on the track marked 'Planinarski dom' and 'S. Gornje' (Gornje Sitno) and continue 10mins to a junction, from where there are two possible onward routes. The path to the right (marked 'S. Gornje, Pl. dom') follows the more direct, and fairly level route to PD Umberto Girometta (see 'Direct Route', below) and takes about 90mins. That to the left (marked 'Dugo Polje, Ljubljan, Pl. dom') leads up onto the main ridge and on to PD Umberto Girometta, via Ljubljan and Vickov stup (with some scrambling), and takes about 2hrs longer. This is undoubtedly the more interesting and challenging of the two routes; it is also the less clearly marked. However, you may be forced to follow the former by a lack of daylight hours.

Ascend left on the clearly marked trail, passing a path on the left to Dugo Polje, to reach **Ljubljan** (1262m) in 1hr 30mins, with more views of the main ridge, Vickov stup and Veliki Kabal. From the summit, the route leads along the ridge, scrambling for much of the time, towards the red shelter on Vickov stup. Just before reaching this, you arrive at a junction, with a route down to Dugo Polje on the left, and the trail descending to PD Umberto Girometta on the right. You almost certainly won't have enough time to explore the rest of the main ridge, but will have to climb back up from the hut tomorrow. Descend steeply to the right, then, crossing a small valley before climbing slightly to a pass and descending over rocky slopes to the hut.

PD Umberto Girometta is a large hut at 868m, open at weekends during the summer but with no water available outside the hut, and named after Professor Umberto Girometta (1883–1939), considered by many the founding father of alpinism in Dalmatia. There is no *sklonište* as such, although the small stone building beyond the hut will provide emergency shelter if not beds or mattresses; it also has its own resident *puh* (dormouse). There is a level area below the hut suitable for pitching a tent, which is reached by descending through the trees. If you arrive mid-week and are low on water, you will have to descend to the village of Gornje Sitno to fill up there. It's an easy 30mins straight down the *prilaz* (meaning 'approach') trail; a steep 45mins back up to the hut. The path descends through trees before veering right, then roughly follows the course of the telegraph poles. There is a shop with a water tap outside, just round the main bend beyond the café.

ALTERNATIVE DIRECT ROUTE TO PD UMBERTO GIROMETTA

To continue directly to the hut without climbing Ljubljan, continue from the junction (see above) on the right-hand (S. Gornje) path for 20mins before taking a right fork (marked 'S. Gornje' again) and passing through some ruined stone cottages. A further 20mins brings you to another junction where you take the right (unsignposted, but still clearly marked) trail for 5mins before continuing straight ahead (marked 'Dom', rather than right, marked 'Sitno').

Scramble up a rocky path, at times overgrown and only faintly marked, contouring the steep side of the valley and following the *dom* signs (first right and then veering left and ascending) to arrive at a junction with a large red sign in 30mins. The path to the left leads off to join the main trail to Vickov stup, Ljubljan and the main ridge; that to the right joins the main trail down to Gornje Sitno. Continue straight ahead on the trail marked 'dom', heading SE into the pine trees and passing a cave on the left, to arrive at the main trail up from Gornje Sitno (marked 'prilaz', meaning 'approach'), where the word 'zdravo' (the old Serbo-Croatian form of greeting, literally meaning 'healthy') greets you from a rock. Turn left to reach **PD Umberto Girometta** in 5mins.

EXCURSION FROM PD UMBERTO GIROMETTA

Vickov stup and Veliki Kabal (return)

Time	3hrs 30mins return
Distance	5km
Maximum altitude	1339m
Rating	moderate
Map	none available – see sketch map

Ascend from **PD Umberto Girometta** on the Vickov stup trail, passing a side-trail to Istarska glavica (the small peak on the right), to gain a small pass in 25mins, with the main ridge directly ahead across a small valley. Descend into the valley, passing a path to the sinkhole called Gajna on the right, followed by one to Gornje Sitno on the left. Continue straight ahead, ascending through *šipak* (rosehip) and wild roses on a progressively steep and thorny path to reach a junction just below the crest of the main ridge, a little under 1hr from the first pass. Scrambling left along the top of the ridge from here would bring you to Ljubljan. Turn right and follow the ridge southeast to arrive at the small red shelter on top of **Vickov stup** (1325m) in 10mins (stup means 'pillar' in Croatian, and refers in this case to the narrow shelter).

Vickov stup, Veliki Kabal, Kozik

The views from the ridge crest are, as you might expect, expansive, with Kozik particularly impressive further to the SE. Continue along the airy ridge another 5mins to **vrh Mosor** (with the rather precisely calculated altitude of 1329.63m).

A further 5mins brings you to a junction, by way of a few steel cables, from where a technical route on the left (marked 'Planinarska staza') continues to Jabukovac. Descend slightly to the right, before continuing along the line of the ridge and ascending the final section to **Veliki Kabal** (1339m), 30mins from Vickov stup.

Those not returning to the hut can continue along the ridge from Veliki Kabal to Ljuto kame, descending from there to rejoin the main Kozik trail beyond the *sklonište* (**Kontejner-Luto kame**). Otherwise, drop back down on the steep path to the hut and the Gajna sinkhole, paying particular attention to the loose steel cables on the way, to regain the valley floor in 20mins. Gajna, which is 170m deep, is reached along a path to the right. Otherwise, continue straight ahead to reach the main Kozik trail in 20mins, turning right onto this to reach **PD Umberto Girometta** in 5mins.

STAGE 2
PD Umberto Girometta – Dubrava via Kozik

Time	5hrs
Distance	12km
Maximum altitude	1319m
Rating	moderate
Map	none available – see sketch map

Leave PD Umberto Girometta on the main Kozik trail, passing the route up to Veliki Kabal on the left after 5mins and continuing straight ahead, with views out over Brač to the right, to reach a *sklonište* (1055m) in 30mins. Aptly known as Kontejner-Ljuto kame (remember, 'j' is pronounced 'y'), this *sklonište* is just that: a large container with a few mattresses and a large plastic water tank (empty on my last visit). Continue straight ahead, passing first one and then another trail up to

Mosor from Kaštel Stari

Ljuto kame (also known as Ljuti kamen) on the left, and picking your way along an overgrown path, which ascends slightly to the left. ◄

It doesn't make much sense to ascend Ljuto kame from this point. It is better to include this area on a descent from Veliki Kabal, as mentioned at the end of the excursion above.

Rather than ascending directly to the high ground to the right as you might expect, the path leads first to a saddle to the left (N) of this, 35mins beyond the *sklonište*. From here, ascend right a further 10mins to gain the main ridge, and follow this for 10mins to the point where the sea and islands come into view. Kozik is now clearly visible ahead, as you continue along the ridge and then, rather annoyingly, are forced to drop down to the left, losing some altitude and the sea view in exchange for a mossy forest trail.

In another 25mins the path re-emerges into the open, and leads back onto the ridge top, with impressive views of the ridge beyond Kozik and of Biokovo towering in the distance. In a further 25mins the path arrives at a junction, from where the route to Dubrava descends to the right. Leave full packs here (unless you plan to continue to Lišnica, in which case you will not return to this point), bearing in mind that Kozik is the most spectacular spot for lunch on the entire route, and is also exposed and likely to be quite windy. Continue straight ahead up the final pyramid, scrambling over rock to reach Kozik (1319m) in less than 30mins.

The views from Kozik are breathtaking; and, although slightly lower than Veliki Kabal, it feels a lot higher. The ground falls away in sheer cliffs to the SW, while the full length of the main Mosor ridge extends to the NW – a great blade of rock, with the shelter on Vickov stup reduced to a red dot, and Kozjak beyond. Split sprawls below this, and Biokovo looms up beyond the chasm-like gorge of the River Cetina to the south. Alpine swifts (*Alpus melba*, the fastest bird in Europe) dart and dive about the summit at an incredible speed, while dark flocks of birds detach themselves silently from the cliffs below to rise against the blue of the Adriatic. The islands of Brač and Hvar are clearly visible. The stone ruins are those of the small chapel of Sveti Jure.

EXTENSION

From Kozik it would be possible to continue along the ridge to **Lišnica** (950m), initially following the trail marked 'Skočibe', before descending to **Prvinčići** and continuing by road to Gata and Omiš.

To return to Dubrava, retrace your steps to the junction below the summit pyramid, and descend steeply to a level trail leading to a broad farm track in just under 1hr. Turn right on this to reach **Dubrava** in a further 20mins. From the bus stop just beyond the car park on the main road you can catch a bus back to Split, passing through Gornje Sitno on the way.

KOZJAK

The long, rocky ridge of Kozjak stretches above Kašteli, the area between Trogir and Split, for about 16km. Although not as high or nearly as spectacular as Mosor, it is equally

Kozjak

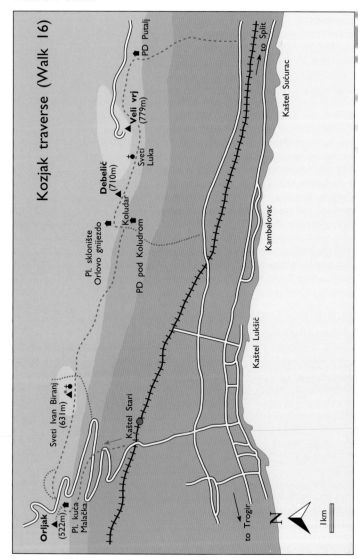

Kozjak traverse (Walk 16)

PD Putalj

Veli vrj
(779m)

Sveti
Luka

Debelić
(710m)

Koludar

PD Putalj

Pl. sklonište
Orlovo gnijezdo

PD pod Koludrom

Sveti Ivan Biranj
(631m)

Kaštel Stari

Orljak
(522m)

Pl. kuća
Malačka

Kaštel Lukšić

Kambelovac

Kaštel Sućurac

to Split

to Trogir

N

1km

prominent from Split, and well worth a day trip for those with some extra time in the area. Due to the intense heat, summer really is not the best time to visit Kozjak.

WALK 16
Kozjak traverse

Time	6hrs
Distance	13km
Maximum altitude	779m
Rating	moderate
Map	There is currently no detailed map available of Kozjak, though SMAND plans to release one in the future (sheet 30). See sketch map.
Transport	The most convenient starting point is the railway station at Kaštel Stari, on the main railway line from Split. Otherwise, take the Trogir bus (number 37) from Split's local bus station and get out at the stop, by a Kaštel Stari sign, at the point where one of Kaštel's bell towers is just coming into view on the left. Just beyond this and opposite a signpost to Trogir and the airport (*Zračna luka*), a road turns off to the right with the now familiar red-and-white trail marking painted on the corner. Following these will bring you to Kaštel Stari station in about 20mins.

A straightforward and fairly flexible day trip, climbing to the ridge from Kaštel Stari before following it SE via the small church at Biranj (631m). The route descends somewhat to PD pod Koludrom (325m), then re-ascends to Koludar, Debelić (710m) and Veli vrj (779m) before descending to the coast road again at Kaštel Sućurac. The section beyond Debelić, known as Pejšin put, is more demanding than the rest of the route, and involves crossing a rocky shelf with the aid of steel pegs and

View of Split from Kozjak

cables – hence the 'moderate' rating for a route which is otherwise fairly easy. There are a number of huts along the route (see Appendix B) for those who would prefer to break the trip into two stages, and alternative routes down to the coast for those who want a shorter day trip.

From the railway station at **Kaštel Stari** cross the railway line, veer right, then continue straight ahead (not right to Sveti Ivan and Sveti Juraj), following the 'dom' signs. Ascend a broad, rather grubby track, which eventually narrows, crossing the road twice before contouring the hillside. The path soon veers to the right, leading up the slope to reach the hut (**Planinarska kuća Malačka**, 477m), 50mins from the railway station.

> As is the rule with most planinarska kuća, you will probably find this one locked, and there is no water outside. **Orljak** (522m) is less than 15mins away to the left.

Continue along the ridge on the trail marked 'izvor' (spring), crossing the road and then taking the right fork towards Biranj, passing a number of stone shelters dug into the ground and another hut, and continuing along the cliff top. About 40mins from Malačka the trail arrives at the small church of **Sveti Ivan Biranj** (631m), which sits perched on the crest of the ridge, surrounded by picnic tables and shady trees. ▶

Continue past an unsightly rubbish dump on the left and a ruined stone hut, and descend to the point where an unsealed road crosses the ridge. Descending to the right from here will bring you back to the main road and the railway station; the track to the left descends to a sinkhole, some 90mins away. Otherwise, continue straight ahead, following the ridge before descending somewhat to reach **Planinarski dom pod Koludrom** (325m) in another 90mins, which sits on the slopes below **Koludar**, the prominent cliff above. From here a trail leads back down to **Kambelovac**, for those who have had enough.

Ascend steeply from the hut, following the trail to the left of Koludar to gain the top of the ridge in 40mins. Here you will find the small and aptly named **Orlovo gnijezdo** (meaning 'eagle's nest'), a *sklonište* at 598m. Continue along the ridge for 15mins to **Debelić** (710m) for more views, before descending on the other side to the section of the route known as Pejšin put, which follows a rocky shelf across the cliff with the aid of steel pegs and cables. Beyond this the route follows the ridge top again, passing the small chapel of **Sveti Luka** (690m) to reach the highest point on Kozjak, **Veli vrj** (779m), 20mins beyond the chapel. The peak itself is fenced off. Continue to **PD Putalj**, a huge hut at 460m, which is open all year – a total of 4hrs from Malačka. From the hut a clear trail leads down to **Kaštel Sućurac**, and the bus route between Trogir and Split, in 1hr.

There is a water tap on the wall of the small café, although – as the sign states – its supply its limited (*ima malo* – 'there is little').

BIOKOVO

Rising almost sheer from the narrow strip of coastal settlements and towering over the picturesque town of Makarska, Biokovo is one of the most dramatic sections of the Dinaric Alps. The terrain consists primarily of bare karst tops riddled with limestone pits and dells, with scattered low beech and mountain pine. These saucer- or funnel-shaped depressions, or dolina, are known in Croatian as *vrtača* (*vrt* meaning 'garden') – and as the word implies they often have walled gardens at the bottom, where fertile soil has accumulated, and crops such as potatoes are grown despite the tendency of the depressions to become flooded. Together with the larger dells and depressions, they are typically drained by some alarmingly deep and cavernous sinkholes, in a number of which water remains frozen throughout the year. There are a number of endemic plant species in the area, and large numbers of mouflon, or wild mountain sheep (*Ovis aries musimon*), wander freely below the crags. At 1762m, Sveti Jure is Croatia's second highest peak. Unfortunately, it is crowned by a huge TV antenna and has a road (known as Biokovska cesta) leading up to the summit, making it one of the least inspiring peaks in the area to climb.

There are three main points of access: from Gornja Brela to the north; from Makarska itself; and from the village of Bast – arguably the most impressive approach, and the one taken in the following itinerary. (Note that the trail from Gornja Brela is very poorly marked.)

WALK 17
Biokovo traverse

Maps	SMAND covers the area on a single sheet: Biokovo – Park prirode (32).
Transport	To reach Bast from the north, take a southbound bus from Split's main bus station (next to the railway station and ferry port) – there are almost hourly services to Makarska. (Avoid taking a bus going to Šestanovac, which would turn inland before Baška Voda, unless you want to start from Gornja Brela.) Ask to be let out just after Baška Voda on the main road, at the turn-off to Bast on the left, from where the now familiar red-and-white trail markings begin. It's about 30mins up to the village (unless you're lucky enough to hitch a lift), veering right on the main (sealed) branch and ascending towards the church.
Accommodation/ Practical information	There is a shortage of places to stay on Biokovo, the few huts in the area being privately owned or requiring some prior arrangement with the relevant organisation in Makarska (see Appendix B) if you are not to find them all locked; so, despite the fact that camping is officially prohibited on Biokovo, you might want to carry a tent – just in case.

This steep though spectacular route runs from the village of Bast (about 300m) to the pass below Motika (1400m) and the peaks of Sveti Ilija (1642m) and Sveti Jure (1762m), before descending from Vošac (1425m) to the town of Makarska on the coast. As on Mosor to the north, there is an acute shortage of reliable water sources on Biokovo, so bring enough to last the whole route. A two-day traverse is recommended if you are to do the area justice, although day trips are quite feasible. Bring all supplies from Split, as there's almost nothing in Bast itself.

STAGE 1
*Bast – Lokva via Motika, Sveti Ilija
and the Biokovska planinarska staza (BPS)*

Time	7hrs
Distance	12km
Maximum altitude	1642m
Rating	moderate
Map	SMAND Biokovo – Park prirode (32)

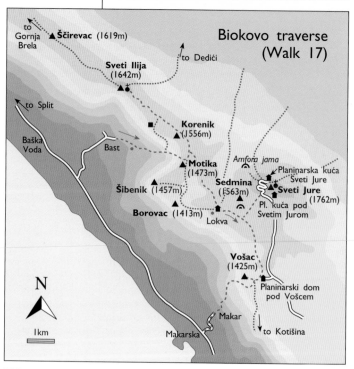

Continue past the church in **Bast** until you arrive at a water fountain on the left and a walled track (leading to a second, smaller church). Follow this walled track behind the fountain (ie not to the church itself), ascending concrete steps to some houses and turning right between these, before veering left up an unmarked walled track, 10mins to the bottom of the scree. From this point turn right and continue straight along a level path across the scree, 5mins to a junction. Here you will find a sign to Sveti Ilija on a rock, and have a good view out over Brač. (Alternatively, continue straight past the fountain to the end of the asphalt, ascend left between the last houses by way of some steps, to reach a trail with route markings on rocks and trees, which leads up to the same junction.) From here the route heads up the scree slopes towards that notch in the cliffs far above.

From the junction, ascend over rock and scree, following clear trail markings, to reach a spring (located on the right, a little below the path) just after a small devotional shrine, about 20mins from the junction. ▶

Continue ascending, over increasingly steep scree, passing a sign to Motika painted on a rock. The view up the steeply inclined couloir above is stunning. The path zigzags and gradually veers to the right, leading off the scree and, for the time being, onto more stable ground. (Continuing up the scree would bring you to Osićine, a small hunting lodge nestled under the cliffs, from where a path continues up to join the main trail between Korenik and Sveti Ilija. However, the route via Motika remains the most attractive approach.)

About an hour from the spring you gain a saddle, from where you ascend, following minimal trail markings and keeping slightly below the crest of the ridge on its other (south) side, and aim for the needle-like point of **Motika**. A final, narrow gully with steep stone steps leads up to a grassy area at the top of the cliffs, a total of 2hrs from the spring. At 1400m this makes a fine spot for lunch, sheltered behind a protruding outcrop of rock, with spectacular views out over the islands and north towards Sveti Ilija, and with Motika (meaning 'hoe') just above at 1473m. ▶

Take the opportunity to fill up all available water flasks: this is the last reliable water source until Makarska.

A small plaque just below the cleft in the rock (from which there is a sheer drop at the far end) reads: *Uvijek gledah na liticu od koje se otcijepih* ('I always looked on the cliff from which I broke away').

View northwest from below Motika, Biokovo

There are two trails from here: left to Sveti Ilija and the Biokovska planinarska staza (BPS) to Lokva and Sveti Jure; and right to Šibenik (1457m, not to be confused with the town of the same name) and Borovac (1413m), a route marked 'PPP', which passes a large, walled enclosure followed by a gaping sinkhole on the right.

Take the left (northernmost) path from Motika (avoiding what looks like a partially filled sinkhole between the two trails), contouring the rim of a doline and passing a trail to Sveti Jure (marked 'BPS') on the right, to arrive at a cluster of ruined cottages in less than 5mins. You can leave full packs in the vicinity, as you'll have to return the same way. If you're short of daylight hours and don't think you'll have time to continue as far as Lokva, this is the last level spot to discreetly pitch a tent, bearing in mind that camping is officially prohibited on Biokovo.

Ascend left over the slope behind the ruins, following the occasional faint trail mark and some cairns, to gain the top of the main ridge. Follow the back of this, bearing roughly NW. The trail is faint, with the occasional cairn, sometimes running along the crest of the ridge itself and sometimes contouring the slopes of *vrtača*, deep funnel-shaped depressions with stone-walled gardens at the bottom. These features, so characteristic of Biokovo and the other karst areas, are particularly impressive in this area. Sveti Jure, crowned with a huge red-and-white antenna, dominates the skyline to the right, appearing much closer than it actually is. The trail continues past Korenik (1556m), and the trail up from the hunting lodge, to reach **Sveti Ilija** (1642m), with its small chapel and extensive views in all directions, a total of 90mins from Motika. ▶

Retrace your steps to the ruined cottages, and then continue back slightly further to the trail, now on the left, to Sveti Jure. This immediately ascends, taking you scrambling over a succession of tops and crests, and past the fringes of the occasional stand of low beech and oak. After about 30mins the words 'Lokva BPS' painted on the rock confirm that you are on the right trail; and a further 30mins of walking and scrambling should bring you to **Lokva**, with its hut (**Planinarska kuća Slobodan Ravlić**), a total of 7hrs from Bast. As an indication of the appalling weather conditions which can unleash themselves upon the unsuspecting hiker in the Dinaric Alps, this hut is named after a local walker, Slobodan Ravlić, who was killed in 1980 during a monstrous hailstorm on Biokovo.

From here a trail continues NW to **Ščirevac** (1619m), and on to **Gornja Brela**, while one heading E leads down to the village of **Dedići** on the Šestanovac–Vrgorac road.

Unless you have arranged to collect the key from Makarska, you will find this **Planinarska kuća Slobodan Ravlić** locked. Worse, the only water available is the rather unpleasant-looking pond from which the area derives its name (*lokva*, meaning 'puddle'). You need to have brought water with you (as advised above); and, although camping is officially prohibited on Biokovo, it may be the only form of accommodation here.

ALTERNATIVE

There is a trail back to Borovac (1hr) and Šibenik (1hr 30mins) for those who wish to return to Bast and don't mind missing some lovely scenery.

STAGE 2
Lokva – Makarska via Sveti Jure and Vošac

Time	7hrs
Distance	11km
Maximum altitude	1762m
Rating	moderate
Map	SMAND Biokovo – Park prirode (32)

Leave **Lokva** on the trail marked 'Vošac and Sveti Jure' from beside the hut. Clearly marked and well maintained, this section has clear views back (N) along the main ridge to Sveti Ilija and (SSE) to Vošac, with its small shelter perched on top. After about 15mins you pass a particularly deep depression with a massive cave on the left, below **Sedmina** (1563m) and Ćavlenovaća.

A further 5mins beyond this arrive at a junction, with Vošac marked a further 45mins straight ahead, and Sveti Jure marked 1hr to the left. Take this latter (left) fork regardless of whether you intend to climb Sveti Jure itself, as there are some particularly good views on the way. Full packs can be left a little way off the main trail. The path leads up through intermittent beech and over limestone tops, with Sveti Jure disappearing for a while before looming back into view above and ahead.

A road leads to the summit, and the trail joins it just beyond **Planinarska kuća pod Svetim Jurom** – which, like the previous *kuća*, is likely to be locked unless you have made prior arrangements. It's all a rather uninspiring sight after the more unspoilt trail from Bast. However, at 1762m Sveti Jure is Croatia's second highest peak, and since you are here you may just as well climb it. Before arriving at the road itself, note the series of small peaks off to the left, their tops marked by short red and white poles. Scrambling up to these gives superlative views N to Sveti Ilija and beyond, with Omiška Dinara and Mosor in the distance.

The most direct route to the summit of **Sveti Jure** leads from the hut (Planinarska kuća pod Svetim Jurom) and follows steel cables to gain the summit (1762m) in 30mins. With its TV antenna and small chapel of the same name, Sveti Jure commands unobstructed and panoramic views. On a particularly clear day, it is reputedly possible to see the Apennines in Italy. The chapel originally stood on the highest point, but was moved to its present location to make way for the TV antenna.

A trail to the deepest sinkhole in the area, **Amfora jama**, 614m deep, begins a little way down the road.

Return the way you came and arrive at the junction of the Sveti Jure trail. Turn left towards Vošac, passing through the occasional stand of trees and arriving at a further junction, 35mins from the Sveti Jure turn-off. Here you turn right towards **Planinarski dom pod Vošcem** (ie turning off what at this point appears to be the main trail straight ahead), following clear trail markings and descending to the road. The large hut is just beyond the car park, but this has been closed for some time. A sign marks Makar, the small village above Makarska, as 2hrs 30mins away.

Sveti Ilija, Biokovo

> There is a **well** here, although when I passed this way there was, rather frustratingly, no bucket to reach the water with. However, the water is not particularly clean, and it should be purified – assuming that you manage to reach it at all.

Follow the Škrbine trail, which drops slightly before ascending in long switchbacks, with a number of short-cuts between these. It is about 20mins up to top of **Vošac** (1425m), passing Škrbine (the lookout point, *pogled*, and the beginning of the descent to Makarska) about half way and off to the left. The shelter here (PD Vošac) is usually locked. The view, however, is quite magnificent – the land falling away in great cliffs down to the red-tiled roofs and beaches of Makarska.

Drop back down to Škrbine (1388m), passing a trail to Kotišina on the left and turning right onto the path down to Makarska. The descent is far less gruelling than might be expected, following long and easy switchbacks below the cliffs. Scattered beech gradually give way to pine and cypress, while wild mountain sheep bound over the rocks above. About 75mins should bring you to a small but unreliable well and, in a further 30mins, to the upper houses of **Makar**. Follow the road down, with the occasional shortcut, to **Makarska** itself, crossing a bridge over the main coastal road and continuing straight down past the market to the church of sveti Marko in the main square and to the sea beyond.

PART 8
THE ISLANDS

Sveti Nikola, Hvar (Walk 21)

INTRODUCTION

The islands of the Croatian archipelago, hugely popular with local and foreign holidaymakers, may seem an unlikely place to find secluded walking trails. Nevertheless, along with the exquisite architecture and the crystal-clear waters of the Adriatic, it is possible to find rocky peaks, national parks and forest trails.

PELJEŠAC

The long, slender Pelješac peninsula runs some 70km from Ston in the south, almost touching the island of Korčula in the north, and is mountainous for much of its length. The northernmost area, inland from Orebić and a short ferry ride from the town of Korčula, is particularly impressive, rising up to the high point of Sveti Ilija (not to be confused with the Sveti Ilija on Biokovo) at 961m. As a peninsula it should not really be included in this section. However, owing to the proximity of the above area to Korčula, rather than to the mainland, and following the logic that a peninsula (*poluotok*) is half an island anyway (from *pol*, 'half,' and *otok*, 'island'), it appears here.

Illyrian presence on the peninsula is attested by graves and ruins at Ston, while Greek and Roman settlements existed at Orebić, Viganj and Trpanj. Pelješac came under Byzantine rule before being absorbed by the Republic of Dubrivnik, at which time Orebić was the seat of the local duke. From the 17th century wealthy merchants and sea captains built numerous villas on the peninsula, many of which survive. Pelješac is also the home of two of Croatia's most celebrated wine-producing areas, Dingač and Postup – which, rather conveniently, are only a few kilometres from Orebić. The walled town of Korčula, just across the Pelješac Channel from Orebić, has reasonably priced boat trips to the island of Mljet.

WALK 18
Sveti Ilija (Pelješac)

Time	6hrs return
Distance	13.5km
Maximum altitude	961m
Rating	easy–moderate

Maps An excellent local map ('Pješice krajolicima pelješke rivijere', 'Walking through the countryside of the Pelješac Riviera'), with contour lines and text in Croatian, English, German and Italian, is available free from the tourist information centre in Orebić.

Transport There are regular (hourly, in summer) passenger ferries to Orebić from Korčula, leaving from near the tourist information office (the car ferry is less convenient as it leaves from about 3km outside the town itself). If you are approaching from the south, there are buses from Dubrovnik – although this is something of a long haul.

There is a fast catamaran service to Korčula from Split (www.krilo.hr), and Jadrolinija's 'Marko Polo' and 'Liburnija' ferries (www.jadrolinija.hr) call at Korčula on their route between Rijeka, Split and Dubrovnik. There is also a catamaran and ferry (both Jadrolinija) between Split and the town of Vela Luka, at the other end of the island, from where there are buses to Korčula itself.

Alternatively, some ferries (such as Jadrolinija's 'Marko Polo' and 'Liburnija') travel between Dubrovnik and Korčula on their way to Rijeka. If you're arriving from Split, there are two fast catamaran services to Korčula, as well as a ferry to the town of Vela Luka at the other end of the island, from where there are buses to Korčula itself.

Accommodation/ Practical information Private accommodation can be found in Orebić itself (www.tz-orebic.com, tel: +385 (0) 20 713 718), while, less conveniently, there are campsites at Viganj and Trstenica, a few kilometres to the north and south. ▶

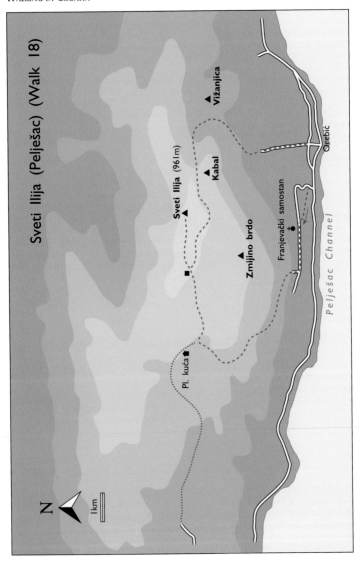

Sveti Ilija (Pelješac) (Walk 18)

N

1 km

Vižanjica

Sveti Ilija (961 m)

Kabal

Zmijino brdo

Franjevački samostan

Pl. kuća

Orebić

Pelješac Channel

◄ Alternatively, you might prefer to stay within
the medieval walls of Korčula, supposed home of a
certain Marco Polo, just across the channel – one of the
loveliest towns on the Croatian coast. People with rooms
available regularly patrol the bus station, or a room can
be booked through a number of agencies (try Kantun
Tours, tel: +385 (0) 20 715 622, www.kantun-tours.com,
see Walk 19). There is a good supermarket in the old
town where you can buy more than enough for a short
trip such as the one described below.

*One of the most impressive day trips on the Croatian
coast, this is a straightforward circular route over Sveti
Ilija (961m), starting and finishing at sea level in the small
town of Orebić. Take enough water, as there is none on
the main trail, and that off the main trail needs purifying.*

Head north along the main road from the harbour at
Orebić until you reach the Hotel Bellvue and its adjacent tennis courts on the left. A forest road opposite
these (on your right) has the now familiar red-and-white
trail markings and a sign to Sveti Ilija. Follow this, and
almost immediately turn left onto a clearly marked trail,
which zigzags up through the trees to reach a minor
road in 10mins. Turning left onto this will bring you to
the **Franjevački samostan** (Franciscan monastery) and
church (Gospa od Anđela, 'Our Lady of the Archangels').

Continue N along the road from the monastery,
reaching an unsealed road on the right in 15mins, which
is signposted to Sveti Ilija. Follow this, then continue up
a fairly steep marked trail, bearing left. This contours the
hillside and ascends gradually, passing a trail coming
up from the small chapel of Sveti Lovrinac after about
10mins and, soon afterwards, a dry well at just over
300m. About 40mins later the path begins to veer right
and inland, arriving at a wooden gate in a further 15mins.
Beyond this the path continues through pine trees, arriving at a junction in 5mins.

The Pelješac peninsula and Sveti Ilija, from Korčula

The left fork, marked 'aqua', would take you to a **planinarska kuća** in about 5mins. However, the keys for this are in Orebić, and unless you have made prior arrangements you are likely find it locked. In any case, it does seem rather unnecessary to carry full packs up here when you can be based in Orebić or Korčula. You are advised to leave the water (which needs purifying) for the benefit of those who do want to stay up here. As the view is restricted by the surrounding woodland, wait until reaching Sveti Ilija itself for a lunch break, where there are far more impressive, panoramic views.

On the way take the opportunity to have a look at a deep, yawning jama *(sinkhole) which is reached from a junction on the left after about 5mins, and is a only a couple of minutes from this point.*

Take the right fork, marked 'Sveti Ilija', ascending fairly steeply again for 35mins to reach a small hunting lodge (again locked, with no water), from where a trail branches left to the *vrh* (summit). It's about 20mins up to the top, following a clear trail and scrambling over rocks and boulders. ◄ The view from the summit of **Sveti Ilija** (961m) is spectacular, west over Korčula and south along the ridge towards southern Pelješac. A path is just visible at the far end of this ridge, which runs up from Orebić; however, reaching it would involve an extended scramble of uncertain technical difficulty, over an unmarked route.

Descend to the hunting lodge and the main trail. The next section is the only part of this route which is at all unclear, as forest fires have removed most of the trail markings and any sign of a path. Follow the Orebić trail down through the trees, but not too far: avoid veering too far right or descending all the way to the paddocks, beyond which is a field of particularly jagged rock followed by a sheer drop halfway down to sea level. The trick is to stay roughly on a level, heading for the base of the small cliff below the upper slopes of Sveti Ilija, steering a route through the trees and ascending slightly to a point where the path once more becomes clear. (If you descend too far, skirt the edge of the rock field, ascending left towards the base of the low cliff already mentioned).

Once back on a clear trail, you soon regain the view along Pelješac and down over Orebić, crossing scree above steep cliffs and then descending through forest. The cliffs below Kabal are now visible on the right, falling in sheer crags from the field of jagged rocks, which hopefully you avoided straying into. The path once more emerges into the open, becoming a well-engineered trail below **Vižanjica**, just above 300m. Orebić soon comes into view, and the trail narrows to become a thorny track. In 1hr 15mins from the hut, you should arrive at the first houses, and a sign back to Sveti Ilija (marked as 2hrs 45mins). Continue straight ahead down a four-wheel drive track, veering left then right through olive groves and more houses to reach the main road in **Orebić** after a further 15mins. Cross over, and continue straight down past the church to the waterfront.

KORČULA

Korčula must be counted one of the loveliest islands on the Adriatic – slightly further from Split than Hvar and Bol (and therefore slightly less crowded than these), yet still very easy to get to. The town of Korčula itself is, along with Dubrovnik, one of the finest medieval walled cities on the Mediterranean – although it sees a fraction of the number of visitors. Just across the channel is Sveti Ilija (Walk 18) at the tip of the Pelješac peninsula, and it is easy to make day trips to Mljet and Dubrovnik from the town of Korčula. Korčula is famous for its spectacular sword dance, the Moreška – a distant relation of Morris

Dancing, but you'd never guess – which is performed regularly in the summer. It is also celebrated as the (possible) former home of Marco Polo, and you can visit his house (if indeed it was his house), or what's left of it. The town of Korčula is a criss-crossed by a herringbone pattern of tiny alleys, and dominated by the lovely cathedral, or technically church, of St Mark (Sveto Marko).

WALK 19
Kula (Korčula)

Time	40mins
Distance	1.5km
Maximum Altitude	100m
Rating	very easy
Maps	Not necessary – see sketch map.
Transport	There is a fast catamaran service to Korčula from Split (www.krilo.hr), and Jadrolinija's 'Marko Polo' and 'Liburnija' ferries (www.jadrolinija.hr) call at Korčula on their route between Rijeka, Split and Dubrovnik. There is also a catamaran and ferry (both Jadrolinija) between Split and the town of Vela Luka, at the other end of the island, from where there are buses to Korčula itself. There are buses to Korčula from Dubrovnik.
Accommodation/ Practical information	There is a tourist information office on the waterfront (www.visitkorcula.net, tel: +385 (0) 20 715 701). There are quite a few (mainly large) hotels in Korčula, though you'd do better with private accommodation, of which there is plenty (try Kantun Tours www.kantun-tours.com, tel: +385 (0) 20 715 622; or www.apartment-korcula.com). You can also rent mountain bikes from Kantun Tours and other agencies. Restaurants include the excellent Konoba Gajeta (on Šetalište Petra Kanevelića) and a nice pizzeria, Caenazzo (on the square in front of Sveto Marko). There is a good Konzum supermarket by the old town.

A very easy stroll up to the Kula (tower) above the town of Korčula.

From **Korčula's** old town begin to walk NW along the waterfront (Put Sv Nikola) then turn left and begin ascending the right-hand branch of two flights of stone steps (Ulica Bernarda Bernardi). This leads up through houses, crossing the road twice before entering forest and ascending past a radio antenna to the old **Kula**. Descend by the same route, or head left along the second road you cross, which will take you down to Put Sv Nikola, where you turn right, passing the monastery before arriving back at Korčula's old town.

MLJET

An elongated and largely forested island south of the Pelješac peninsula, Mljet has some of the tallest and thickest maquis anywhere on the Mediterranean, with some particularly impressive stands of Aleppo pine. Mljet also used to host a sizeable population of snakes, until the mongoose was introduced in the 19th century to control them. Needless to say, the mongooses thrived (they're still here).

Legend tells that it was to Mljet that Odysseus was blown by the winds of Poseidon. Mljet was settled by the Greeks (who called the island Melita) and by the Romans, who built a palace at Polače, the ground plan of which survives. The northwest corner of the island, including the two lakes, Malo jezero and Veliko jezero, was declared a national park in 1960 (Nacionalni park Mljet, www.np-mljet.hr). The Benedictine monastery on the island of Sveta Marija on Veliko jezero dates to the 12th century. Veliko jezero opens into the sea, and is connected to Malo jezero by a small channel spanned by a footbridge (Mali most).

The amount of time you spend on Mljet, unless you are staying on the island of course, will be conditioned by the amount of time the boat stays here – which is usually not that long (but enough for the itinerary below).

WALK 20
*Malo jezero, Veliko jezero
and Veliki Gradac (Mljet)*

Time	3hrs (not including boat trip to monastery)
Distance	6km
Maximum Altitude	160m
Rating	easy
Maps	The national park have a sheet, though it's not really necessary for the route described here – see sketch map.
Transport	There are numerous boat trips to Mljet from Korčula; alternatively there is a ferry service between Sobra and Dubrovnik.
Accommodation/ Practical information	There is a tourist information office at Polače, a national park office at Pomena, and an information centre at the point where the boat leaves for the monastery. Accommodation on the island is limited to the Hotel Odisej (www.hotelodisej.hr) and some private accommodation (see www.mljet.hr).

After buying your national park entry ticket at the national park office in **Pomena**, follow the road inland behind this, then take a path on the right marked Malo jezero. This brings you down through the trees to the shore of **Malo jezero** in 10mins. You can walk in either direction around the lake. Turning left (the shorter route) will bring you to Mali most in about 10mins; following the lake around to the right (marked *kružni put*, 'circular route') to Mali most will take around 30mins. **Mali most** is the small bridge dividing Malo jezero and Veliko jezero. There's a small national park kiosk here, as well as a small beach and picnic area. It's also possible to hire bicycles and canoes at Mali most.

Continue, following the asphalt road along the N shore of Veliko jezero, passing a few houses and cafés before heading away from the lake briefly (there's very

little shade here) to reach a junction. There is an information office here, and the departure point for the boat out to the monastery on the island of **Sveta Marija** is down to the

Veliko jezero

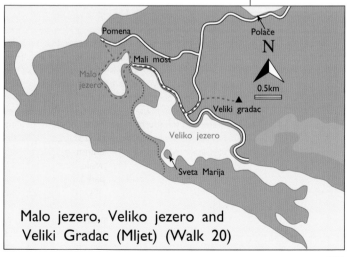

Malo jezero, Veliko jezero and Veliki Gradac (Mljet) (Walk 20)

right. The boat trip is included in the national park entry, but assuming you're here on a day trip, you might not have time to visit the monastery as well as Veliki Gradac.

Follow the road on the left up to the picnic area (marked *ambulante*), then turn right onto a track passing the *groblje* (cemetery). Turn right onto the footpath marked Veliki gradac, ascending with increasingly fine views and passing a trail marked *polje* (fields) before reaching the modest summit of **Veliki gradac** (160m), 90mins from Pomena. There are good views out over Veliko jezero. Return to **Pomena** by the same route.

FURTHER POSSIBILITIES

Montokuc

Montokuc (250m) is accessible from Veliko jezero, from a marked trail on the road a short distance E of where the boat leaves for the monastery. Zakamenica is a fine viewpoint which can be reached by following the S shore of Veliko jezero from Mali most, then heading S over the ridge behind Sveta Marija.

HVAR

The island of Hvar, supreme favourite among Croatia's jet-set crowd and regularly touted as having more hours of sunshine than anywhere else on the Adriatic, nevertheless has one of the nicest walks on the islands (Sveti Nikola), and a good network of cycling routes. Hvar was a centre of the Danilo culture around 4500BC and a Greek colony from the 4th century BC (Paros, modern Stari Grad), and there are some beautiful old towns and villages scattered across the island, not least the town of Hvar itself.

WALK 21
Sveti Nikola (Hvar)

Time	4hrs
Distance	15km
Maximum Altitude	628m
Rating	easy
Maps	None available – see sketch map
Transport	Jadrolinija (www.jadrolinija.hr) runs a catamaran between Split and Hvar (on the route to Vela Luka on the island of Korčula, and on to the island of Lastovo; and another on the route to Vis), a ferry between Split and Stari Grad, and a catamaran between Split and Jelsa (via Bol, on the island of Brač). Krilo (www.krilo.hr) also runs a catamaran between Split, Hvar and Korčula. A number of agencies in Bol run boat trips to the island of Hvar. Local buses run to Vrbanj from Stari Grad, Hvar and Jelsa.
Accommodation	There are plenty of hotels and private rooms in Hvar (www.tzhvar.hr), Stari Grad (www.stari-grad-faros.hr) and Jelsa (www.tzjelsa.hr) – or for something a little more low key, Vrboska is a pleasant little fishing village.

An easy walk with stupendous views, which can be extended to Sveta Nedjelja, or to Dol and on to Stari Grad.

From the bus stop in **Vrbanj**, by the post office and church, follow trail markings up to the village square and then left following the sign to Svirče (the route to the right is marked Dol; see alternative return route, below). Bear left following markings through houses then ascending on a broad, clear track. Follow the markings to the right (not the road on the left), then descend through the village of **Svirče** after 20mins. At the road junction, a sign marks Sveti Nikola to the right – but it's worth making a quick detour to the prominent, domed church of Sveta Magdalena on the left, surrounded by cypresses and

223

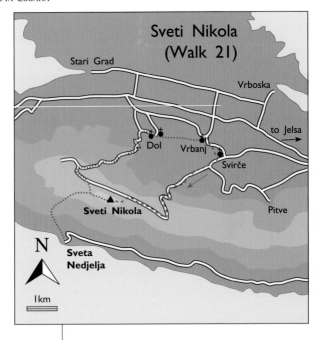

Sveti Nikola
(Walk 21)

Stari Grad

Vrboska

to Jelsa

Dol   Vrbanj

Svirče

Sveti Nikola

Pitve

N

Sveta
Nedjelja

1km

palm trees. The church dates from the 20th century, and
was built on the site of an earlier church, from which the
original bell tower survives.

Follow the Sveti Nikola signs, turning right and passing a small devotional shrine on your left. Pass some
burnt trees and another devotional shrine on your left,
then round a bend and immediately turn right onto a
marked path. The path crosses and recrosses the road a
number of times while ascending, passing a small chapel and joining the road again as it passes between low
hills. Take one more shortcut (right) off the road before
rejoining it, then turn right at the crest of the ridge onto
a marked path, with the peak, church and cross visible
straight ahead. Follow the unsealed road past vineyards
and houses, to reach a marked path on the left, 90mins
from Svirče. The initially walled path heads uphill to a

junction with another trail from your left, just below ridge crest. Turn right, with amazing views and steep crags falling sheer almost all the way down to Sveti Nedjelja, to reach the summit of **Sveti Nikola** (628m). There is a small church (originally built in 1459, but damaged by lightning and rebuilt many times since), and a large cross.

The view is immense – from the Pelješac peninsula and the islands of Šćedro and Korčula to the SE, with Lastovo just visible beyond, to Vis in the SW – and, on a clear day (and Hvar does have all that sunny weather), a distant Palagružia and beyond, the heel of Italy.

The shortest way back to **Vrbanj** is to return by the same route, following the signs to Svirče. However you can vary your return by following a route down via Dol (although much of this is on a forest road, with not much of a view) – see below. You could also descend all the way to Sveta Nedjelja (undoubtedly the most scenic option), however you would then be reliant on an infrequent bus service back to the opposite side of the island (the road goes through a tunnel, so you can't walk it), or would have to hike all the way back up to Sveti Nikola again.

Sveti Nikola

ALTERNATIVE ROUTE VIA DOL

Follow the path along the ridge, following the signs to Dol and passing the small meteorological and radio hut. Pass a trail on the left marked Gospa od Zdravlja, which leads all the way down to Sveta Nedjelja, and an unsealed road on the right to Svirče. At a junction, turn right following signs to Dol, Purkin kuk and the Faros cycle route. Pass a trail on your left to Purkin kuk, continuing along the forest road to reach the church in **Dol**, 1hr 20mins from Sveti Nikola.

Follow the trail markings down the steps opposite the church, turning right onto a sealed road then left and descending on a marked path behind a church. The stone path zigzags down through the pines, to join the road where you turn right (near a road sign for Dol). Keep straight ahead, passing a church on your left and ignoring roads to right and left, then ascending through some houses. Veer left at a fork in the road, then left again onto an unsealed road, which you follow to the right (not the track left up into the trees). Keep straight ahead on a narrow path over the crest of a ridge, then head down the stony track into **Vrbanj**. Follow trail markings to the right onto a path up through houses to meet a sealed road, then head right, down past the Svirče route to the church.

FURTHER POSSIBILITIES

Grapčeva špilja

Grapčeva špilja, a cave on the western coast of Hvar, has been the source of a number of imprtant archeological finds – but you will almost certainly find it locked. The easiest approach is from the village of Humac (take any bus east along the narrow 'tail' of the island towards Gdinj or Mlaska, then walk up to Humac on your right), which (I should also mention) has one of the least friendly or helpful restaurants (Konoba Humac) I've encountered anywhere in Croatia. Pass the houses and *konoba*, veering right, then turn left by a single-storey concrete building onto a clear but unmarked walled path, down towards the sea. There's a bit of a steep scramble at the end, before you reach the cave itself in 20mins (allow 1hr return to the cave from the main road).

It is possible to return to Jelsa via the unsealed road running along the ridge from Humac, via vrh and Tor, but waymarkings are poor. If you are interested, continue along the main ridge with Hum (604m) ahead, passing a small chapel and unsealed road on your left. An unmarked route begins on the right near here (if you miss it you will end up on a leg-shredding cross country route through thorny bushes and a maze of dry stone walls), later becoming a clear stone track, which descends past the ruins of a Tor and a church before arriving in **Jelsa**.

BRAČ

The island of Brač (the name probably derives from the Illyrian *brentos*, 'deer') is one of the most popular summer destinations in the Croatian archipelago, so it may come as a surprise that it also has a number of attractive hiking routes. Moreover, the ever-popular town of Bol with its adjacent, much-photographed beach (Zlatni rat) is a fine example of how to make the most of an area's potential for tourism without ruining it in the process. The name Zlatni rat does not refer to war or battle (*rat* meaning 'war' in Croatian), but comes from an old dialect in which the modern Croatian word *rt* (meaning 'cape' or 'point') was simply pronounced longer, with a vowel – thus 'Golden Cape'. One of the finest buildings

Zlatni rat

on Brač is Pustinja Blaca, the very impressive hermitage founded in 1551 by Glagolitic priests from Poljica (the area behind Mosor) who had fled the Ottoman advance.

Accommodation in Bol, as in many other favourite spots on the islands, becomes completely booked up during the summer, and booking accommodation well in advance is essential. The two best agencies to contact are Bol Tours and Adria Tours (see below). You can also rent mountain bikes from them and book boat trips along the coast to Pustinja Blaca and to the island of Hvar. There are also a number of large, well-serviced campsites, mostly on the slopes just above the town. However, these will put you in rather close proximity to the huge 'Faces' disco. Looking like something from War of the Worlds descending furiously upon the town from the crags of Vidova gora, this pounds away until six in the morning, and all those who wish to sleep are advised to camp a safe distance away.

WALK 22
Vidova gora (Brač)

Time	4hrs return
Distance	8km
Maximum altitude	780m
Rating	easy
Maps	None available – see sketch map.
Transport	The fastest and most straightforward way to get to Bol is by catamaran. Jadrolinija has a service running from gat Sveti Nikola in Split, the jetty by the airport bus stop (not the main ferry dock), where you can also purchase tickets from the small kiosk. This leaves in the afternoon and continues to Jelsa on the island of Hvar, before returning early the following morning. A private company also runs a service to Bol (from the same departure point in Split), but it is slightly more expensive. Brač can also be reached

	by ferry, either: Split–Supetar, followed by a local bus to Bol, or Makarska–Sumartin, although this is much less convenient if you are heading for Bol.
Accommodation	For accommodation in Bol contact Bol Tours (www. boltours.com, tel: +385 (0) 21 635 693) or www.bol.hr.

Vidova gora (780m) is the highest point on Brač. The following route climbs from just above sea level, following a steep-sided valley up around and behind Veliko koštilo (610m) to gain the cliffs above Bol. There is little in the way of shade on this route and, despite its short length, you are advised to take a hat and plenty of water, particularly in the heat of summer. A small konoba (restaurant) at the top provides much needed refreshment, lunch and a cooling breeze.

From **Bol**, follow the main Supetar road up past the disco and the supermarket. Turn left after these, following a sealed road and the new Vidova gora signs to a gate and the well-maintained, rocky track beyond. This ascends above terraces, vegetable gardens and *suhozid* (dry stone walls), the air redolent of wild rosemary and with the cliffs of Veliki koštilo above you to the left. Pass through more gates (making sure you close them behind you), the path zigzagging upwards at an easy gradient as a particularly impressive crag, like something out of Albrecht Dürer's Alpine sketchbook, comes into view on the left. Continue ascending, passing a narrow sinkhole on the left (and noting the huge spiders' webs stretched between the branches of trees adjacent to the path) to gain a plateau at the top of the cliffs, about 90mins beyond the first gate. Turn left just before you reach a fence with a gate in it, at a point where a path joins from the right. Continue under telegraph poles almost to the cliff edge, then follow this towards the large telecommunications towers, with magnificent views down over Bol and Zlatni rat below you and across to the island of Hvar. The path

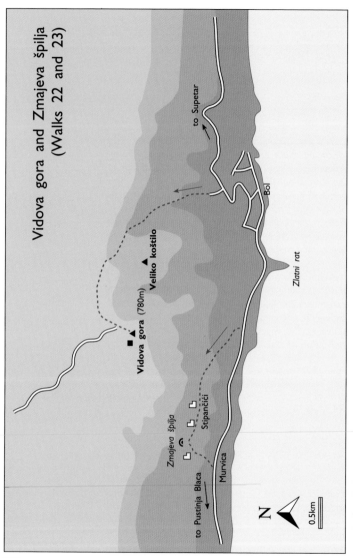

Vidova gora and Zmajeva špilja
(Walks 22 and 23)

to Supetar

Bol

Zlatni rat

Veliko koštilo

Vidova gora (780m)

Zmajeva špilja

Škripančići

Pustinja Blaca

Murvica

to Pustinja Blaca

N

0.5km

joins the road and continues up, through the gate then left along the cliff edge again, to bring you to **Vidova gora** (780m), with its small but very welcome *konoba* (restaurant) beyond the telecommunications towers. Descend by the same route.

WALK 23
Zmajeva špilja (Brač)

An easy walk to Zmajeva špilja ('dragon's cave'), with its intriguing stone carvings of cultic images, religious figures, gargoyles and monstrosities, via the abandoned houses of Stipančići, and finishing in the small village of Murvica. Note that the cave itself is locked, and to get inside you need to contact a guide/key-holder (details available from Bol Tourist Information Office, see Appendix C), who will meet you at the restaurant in Murvica and lead you up and down by the same route (that which descends from the cave in the following itinerary). The main rock carvings can be seen quite clearly from the gate, but if you want to explore the interior more thoroughly, you could always go up with the guide, and then make your own way back to Bol, following the route described here in reverse.

Time	2hrs
Distance	4km
Maximum altitude	300m
Rating	very easy
Map	none available – see sketch map for Walk 22
Transport/ Accommodation	See Walk 22.

Continue along the promenade from **Bol**, past Zlatni rat to the car park, passing the main Bol–Supetar road on the right, and continuing straight ahead along the unsealed road towards Murvica. About 10mins along this, arrive at a path on the right marked 'grotte'. Ascend this to arrive

231

at a level track in 5mins, turning left onto this and then right through a gate (marked 'ZŠ'), ascending gradually on a rocky, overgrown path. Pass through more gates, the path becoming unclear at one point and dividing, only to rejoin a few minutes later. Rock buttresses loom above on the right, and the first cluster of ruined houses comes into view. Beyond these, the cave should be visible above a large, double-headed cypress tree.

Pass through a second cluster of ruined stone houses, 40mins from the road, continuing straight ahead and descending slightly to a junction just after the large cypress. Ascend to the right to reach the cave in 1min. **Zmajeva špilja** dates from the 16th century, and was the first settlement on the island of the Glagolitic priests from Poljica (the area behind Mosor), who then went on to build the hermitage of Pustinja Blaca.

Descend to the main track and continue to the top of a scree slope, just before another group of ruined stone houses. Descend this (there are no signs) as far as you can, then continue straight down a faint path through scrub and pine before turning right above a dirt track and continuing into the village of **Murvica**, where you

Zmajeva špilja

descend between houses to the road from Bol and a rather well-placed restaurant. From Murvica, turn back along the unsealed road to Bol.

FURTHER POSSIBILITIES

Pustinja Blaca
The easiest way to visit Pustinja Blaca is to take one of the various boat trips from Bol. These take you to a small bay, from which you can hike up to the monastery. Alternatively, you could hire bikes and follow the (unsealed) coast road west from Bol, past Murvica, to the point where the road zigzags steeply up the hillside and heads inland. Pass a road on your left, which you don't take, then a short distance further on at another road on the left (still unsealed), this time signposted to Pustinja Blaca (continuing straight ahead here would bring you to Nerežišća). Turn left onto this, which takes you west then south, to the point where a stony track zigzags down to the monastery. Return to Bol by the same route. Check opening times with the tourist office in Bol before you set off (tel: +385 (0) 21 635 638; www.bol.hr).

CRES AND LOŠINJ
The islands of Cres and Lošinj almost meet at the small town of Osor, where they are separated by a small channel only a few metres wide and joined by a bridge. Both islands were inhabited during the Neolithic period and settled by the Illyrian Liburni before falling to Rome. Briefly part of the medieval kingdom of Croatia, they fell under the rule of a succession of foreign powers: Byzantium, Venice, Napoleon, Austria and Italy, before becoming a part of Croatia again after the Second World War. One of the most celebrated artefacts on Cres is the Valun tablet (kept in the church at Valun), with its 11th-century Glagolitic inscription; while at Beli on the northeast of the island there is a griffon vulture sanctuary (see page 41).

The most convenient place to stay for the route on the island of **Lošinj** (Walk 24), is the town of Nerezine. There are plenty of places to stay in the town, and a popular beach lies below the packed campground.

Alternatively, you could base yourself in the lively little town of **Cres**, for this walk and those on Cres itself (Walks 25 and 26), catching an early bus to Nerezine and returning from Osor. This would provide the additional benefit of staying at the same place for more than three nights, thus avoiding the standard 30 per cent supplement charged for stays of fewer than three nights. Although it is possible to stay in Martinšćica (and, at a pinch, Lubenice), this would necessitate lugging a full pack around, which seems rather unnecessary, and would again involve staying a single night at a number of different places, all with a 30 per cent supplement.

WALK 24
Osoršćica (Lošinj)

Time	4hrs 30mins
Distance	12km
Maximum altitude	589m
Rating	easy
Maps	None available – see sketch map.
Transport	Lošinj is connected to Zadar by ferry and to the island of Cres by road; Cres has catamaran services to Rijeka. Nerezine is easily reached by bus from either the town of Mali Lošinj, if you have arrived on the boat from further south, or the town of Cres, if you are approaching from the north.
Accommodation	For accommodation in Cres see www.tzg-cres.hr and www.cres-losinj.net.

A straightforward but attractive route over the ridge collectively known as Osoršćica, rising to 558m, and finishing in the small town of Osor, just over the bridge on the island of Cres.

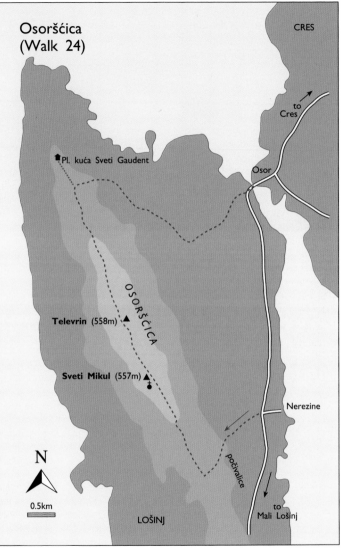

Osoršćica
(Walk 24)

CRES

to
Cres

Pl. kuća Sveti Gaudent

Osor

OSORŠĆICA

Televrin (558m) ▲

Sveti Mikul (557m) ▲

Nerezine

počivalice

N

0.5km

LOŠINJ

to
Mali Lošinj

235

The small church of Sveti Mikul on Osorščica

Starting from the small church on the bend in the main road at **Nerezine** (where there is a sign to Podgora), follow the trail markings inland up a small sealed road between the houses. Turn left at the end of the sealed road, after 5mins, onto an unsealed track; then go right and left onto a path. Follow this path, with views of the ridge above and ahead, and a view down over some stone ruins and the island of Cres beyond, which is soon spoilt by the appearance of a rubbish tip. A further 30mins brings you to a junction; ignore a path to the left to Čunski and continue straight ahead towards **Osorščica**, gaining the base of the main ridge. Here you come to a rest point, or **počivalice** (from *počivati*, 'to rest') before continuing up a rocky path through pines and over wild thyme, with the odd bit of scrambling along the spine of the ridge. The towns of Nerezine and Osor appear below on the right; the lovely looking island of Unije on the left; and there is a fantastic view back down the length of Lošinj behind you before the first summit (557m) is reached, an hour from the bottom of the ridge. There is a small church here (**sveti Mikul**), and an advertisement for the hut (Planinarska kuća sveti

Gaudent) at the far end of the ridge, which does its best to tempt you with the hypnotic words *hladno pivo* (cold beer).

Continue, following the path down behind the church (not straight ahead along the ridge, where there is no path). Ignore the turn-off to Nerezine on the right, continuing straight ahead towards Televrin and Osor, to reach a path to the cave (*jama* or *špilja*) on the right in 10mins. A further 20mins brings you, passing the radio antennae on the way, to the second peak, **Televrin** (558m). Although marginally higher than sveti Mikul, it is less attractive, and does not have the same view back along the length of the island.

Continue, following the path as it descends slightly on the left (west) side of the ridge before regaining its rocky spine, to reach a large cairn in 30mins. A further 15mins brings you, past more large cairns, to a junction, from where it is possible to continue straight ahead to Planinarska kuća sveti Gaudent (and its *hladno pivo*) in 20mins. There is little reason to sleep at the hut, unless for some reason you have been lugging a full pack across Osoršćica, and you are advised to continue to Osor as detailed below.

Turn right from this junction and descend towards Osor, with a view down over a small peninsula, which hangs like a teardrop from its narrow isthmus. Another 40mins brings you, past a small spring which is little more than a festering pool, to a junction where a path descends from the hut (Planinarska kuća sveti Gaudent) on the left. Turn right here, following a shady, walled track, to reach another junction in 15mins. The signs here are placed high in the trees and are easily missed; continue straight ahead, arriving on an unsealed road in 15mins. Turn right onto this, descending a further 15mins, past the large motor camp to the bridge, with the town of **Osor** on the other side, on the island of Cres.

Osor is a pleasant little town with a chequered history not atypical of the region. Once inhabited by the Liburni (the Illyrian tribe inhabiting the northern

The use of the fur of the *kuna* (pine marten) as a trading unit and method of payment (whence the modern unit of Croatian currency, the kuna) is first recorded in connection with Osor in a document from 1018.

Adriatic coast before the Roman conquest) and successively under Roman, Byzantine and Croatian rule, it was destroyed by the Genoese in 1377 and subsequently ruled by Venice, Napoleon, Austria and Italy, to become incorporated once more into Croatia in 1945. You will see a relief sculpture of the familiar Venetian lion (the lion of St Mark) as you enter the town, testimony to the long rule of Venice before the arrival of Napoleon. ◄

Catch the bus, hitch or walk back to **Nerezine**, a few kilometres along the main road, or return by bus to Cres if you are basing yourself there.

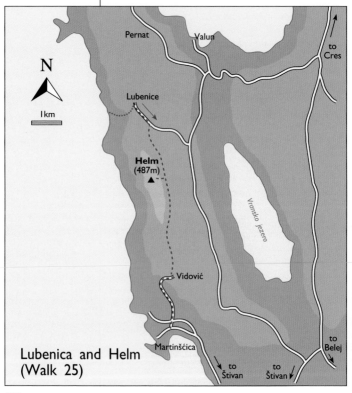

Lubenica and Helm
(Walk 25)

WALK 25
Lubenice and Helm (Cres)

Lubenice sits in a wonderful location, perched above the cliffs and looking down over the Adriatic. Originally a hilltop settlement of the Liburni, and now a tiny village scattered with churches, it remains a quiet and remarkably unspoilt spot, far from the madding crowds of Brač and Hvar. It is possible to stay here, rather unofficially, but people are unlikely to be interested in guests staying less than a week. Those interested should ask at one of the churches in order to be directed to prospective lodgings. The best position for taking photos is slightly down the hillside, to the left just as you reach the first small chapel (from where a path descends to the very alluring beach).

Time	2hrs 15mins
Distance	5km
Maximum altitude	487m
Rating	very easy
Maps	None available – see sketch map.
Transport	A catamaran service runs between Rijeka and Cres, which is more convenient than the ferry between Porozina and Brestova. Buses run from Cres to Lošinj, which is in turn connected to Zadar by ferry. Take a bus travelling south on the main road from Cres and get off at the turn-off to Valun. From here walk, or hitch, the 4.5km to the turn-off to Pernat and Lubenice. (Don't go all the way to Valun, or you will have to walk all the way back uphill again!) From the junction, it is a further 5km to Lubenice, passing the turn-off to Pernat on the way. Certainly in the summer months, hitching this section should be straightforward enough: leave Cres early to catch the morning traffic up to Lubenice.
Accommodation	For accommodation in Cres see www.tzg-cres.hr and www.cres-losinj.net. In Martinšćica – for those stranded! – there's the Hotel Zlatni Lav (www.hotel-zlatni-lav.com).

Cres harbour

An easy stroll on the island of Cres, from the cliff-top village of Lubenice (382m), over the wooded peak of Helm (487m) and down to the sea at the small town of Martinšćica.

Backtrack from **Lubenice**, walking 10mins on the main road to reach a small gravestone on a bend. Here a broad, rocky track on the right (marked 'Helm') leads off into the pines. This brings you to a gate in a few minutes, after which continue on a clear track through a rocky field, with the wooded peak of Helm ahead. Turn right through another gate and then continue straight ahead through yet another gate (marked 'Vid' for Vidović) and not right as implied by a sign reading 'He' for Helm. This leads to a forest road on the edge of the pines in 15mins, which you cross diagonally and continue on a path through the trees. A further 15mins brings you to a track on the right, marked by a large cairn and the word 'Helm' written in stones on the forest floor. Ascend this, following cairns and veering right to meet the forest road at the top of **Helm** (487m) in 10mins. ◄

The view is rather disappointing, being largely obstructed by trees, but Vransko jezero is clearly visible to the east, as is Osoršćica (on the island of Lošinj) to the southeast.

Return to the main trail and continue towards Vidović, veering left at a large cairn in 10mins before turning almost immediately to the right. The trail soon emerges from the trees, continuing over rock and scrub, and descending and veering right. Osoršćica is clearly visible ahead, as is the bay (but not the town itself) of Martinšćica and, closer at hand, the roofs of Vidović. You should arrive in the village of **Vidović** just under 1hr from the Helm turn-off. From here follow the main road a final 30mins (2km) down to **Martinšćica** on the coast.

There is a bus back to Cres around 3.30pm. Otherwise, you can try to hitch the 9km back to the main Osor–Cres road via Štivan.

WALK 26
Sveti Salvadur and Sveti Blaž (Cres)

Time	4hrs 45mins
Distance	8km
Maximum altitude	250m
Rating	very easy
Maps	None available – see sketch map.
Transport/	See Walk 25.
Accommodation	

A clearly marked and very easy walk from the town of Cres to the church of Sveti Salvadur and on to Sveti Blaž, following the slopes above the coast and returning along the waterfront from Sveti Salvadur.

Walk to the tower from the centre of **Cres** (along Put Fortice or Zagrebačka ulica, for example) and turn right to arrive at the main road. Cross over this and start up the broad, walled track, clearly signposted to sveti Salvadur and Sveti Blaž. This ascends gradually, sometimes winding but always clearly marked, heading roughly northwest and passing the occasional devotional shrine, to reach **Sveti Salvadur** in 40mins. The church, which dates from 1857, is set in a small garden surrounded by trees, with a view of the forested coastline and headlands further north, and Cres and its harbour back beyond the point.

Ignore the trail down to the left, by which you will descend later, and continue straight ahead. The path narrows considerably, descending and becoming rocky, with little in the way of views until it emerges onto open terraces with views back along the coast, including Sveti Salvadur, after 40mins. Continue across the terraces, re-entering forest cover as you round the headland, before beginning to zigzag down towards the sea at **Sveti Blaž**. Pass through some ruined houses to reach a grassy area above a rocky cove and pebble beach, 90mins from sveti

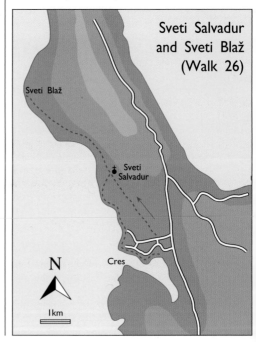

Sveti Salvadur and Sveti Blaž (Walk 26)

Sveti Blaž

Sveti Salvadur

N

Cres

1km

Salvadur. The grassy area is unfortunately littered, one assumes from the boat trips which come this way for a picnic, but it makes a nice spot for a swim.

Sveti Salvador

Retrace your steps back to Sveti Salvadur (90mins should be sufficient) and descend, following the path on the right, which leads down to the sea in 20mins, where you turn left towards Cres. From here there is a clear path around rocky bays (with plenty of opportunities for another dip), soon replaced by a concrete track. Continue past the large motor camp and frequent cafés before rounding the headland and striding back into Cres, a little over 1hr beyond Sveti Salvadur.

FURTHER POSSIBILITIES

Eco-Centre at Beli
There are a number of easy trails to and from the Eco-Centre at Beli (see page 41; maps at www.supovi.hr).

Boat moored at Račišće, on the island of Korčula

The routes in this book cover most, but not all of the mountain areas in Croatia, and have been selected as the most representative and impressive routes the country has to offer. However, a number of other areas may be of interest to those with enough time to see more of the country.

Dinara

As the highest mountain in Croatia, Dinara (1831m) may seem conspicuous by its absence from this guide. The main reason for its omission is the continued presence of landmines in the area; and although numerous Croatian hikers now head for the summit every year on marked trails which are perfectly safe, it cannot be commended with the same enthusiasm as Velebit or Gorski kotar. For those who do want to climb Dinara, it is important to stick to marked trails, and carry a decent map (SMAND Dinara 40). Start from Glavaš, near Kijevo SE of Knin, allowing at least 6hrs for the climb.

Omiš Dinara

Omiš Dinara (863m) is a peak above the town of Omiš, by the river Cetina gorge some 20km south of Split. The route heads up from the centre of town, first on a road then steps which eventually become a steepish path with occasional, very faint trail markings. It's a rather less pleasant walk than expected, with little shade and (at least on my last visit) large amounts of litter.

Vransko jezero

Vransko jezero nature park (www.vransko-jezero.hr), containing the largest natural lake in Croatia, is an important area for birdlife, and contains a number of the educational trails – although the latter are not particularly well marked. The park entrance is between Zadar and Šibenik.

Kamenjak, Rab

The island of Rab is clearly visible as you climb up the path to Zavižan in northern Velebit (Walk 11), and its highest point, Kamenjak (409m), makes a worthwhile excursion. The trail heads up from the town of Rab itself, through the villages of Barčići (on the road between Rab and Lopar) and Pahlinići, then across country. Good views of Goli Otok and northern Velebit beyond. This is one of the few islands for which SMAND publish a sheet, Otok Rab (20a).

Obzova, Krk

From Baška (famous for its Glagolitic tablet) on the island of Krk, it's possible to climb Obzova (568m) and

Hlam (461m). For Obzova head NW from Baška passing the village of Batomalj and the church of Sv Majka Bože; for Hlam head N from Baška.

Kornati Islands

The Kornati Islands National Park (www.kornati.hr) form one of the most heavily indented parts of the Mediterranean. Numbering around 140 (depending on who is counting them), including various islets and reefs, and scattered over an area of some 300km², they take their name from the largest island in the group, Kornat. After visiting the islands George Bernard Shaw wrote that, on the final day of Creation, God wished to crown his oeuvre, and from a mixture of tears, stars and wind created the Kornati Islands. A number of companies in Zadar offer boat tours of the Kornati islands; private accommodation can also be booked on some of the islands.

Brijuni Islands

The Brijuni Islands National Park (www.briuni.hr) were established as an Austro–Hungarian health resort at the close of 19th century, and later became the private residence of Tito, who introduced various exotic plants and animals to the islands. There are also Roman ruins here. The islands provide a pleasant enough day trip from the Istrian coast, with boat trips departing from Fažana near Pula.

APPENDIX B
Hut Details

PD = planinarski dom (mountain hut); Pl. kuća = planinarska kuća (mountain hut); sklonište = shelter; PDS = Planinarsko društvo sveučališta (hiking club); HPD = Hrvatsko planinarsko društvo (Croatian Mountaineering Committee); HPS = Hrvatski planinarski savez (Croatian Mountaineering Association); NP = national park

See the notes on Accommodation in the Introduction for an explanation of the difference between *dom*, *kuća* and *sklonište*. Some huts offer cooked meals, but this varies depending on time of week and season, and (particularly in more remote areas) **cannot** always be relied on.

Hut	Altitude	Capacity*	Season**	Contact details
MEDVEDNICA				
PD Grafičar	864m	sleeps 33	daily except Monday	HPD 'Grafičar' Zagreb Tel: +385 (0) 1 455 5844 mobile: +385 (0) 98 470 114
Tomislav dom (Hotel Tomislavov dom)	1000m	hotel with 42 rooms	open all year	www.hotel-tomislavovdom.com Tel: +385 (0) 1 456 0400
PD Glavica	420m	sleeps 8	weekends	PS 'Zagreba' Zagreb Tel: +385 (0) 1 481 8801
SAMOBORSKO GORJE				
PD Oštrc	691m	sleeps 32	weekends only	PD 'Željezničar' Zagreb Tel: +385 (0) 1 482 3044
PD Žitnica (Japetić)	815m	sleeps 38	closed in 2009	HPD 'Jastrebarsko' www.hpd.jastrebarsko.hr mobile: +385 (0) 98 905 3018
PAPUK				
PD Jankovac	475m	sleeps 66	by arrangement	Hrvatske šume d.o.o. UŠP Našice, tel: +385 (0) 33 618 050 mobile: +385 (0) 98 984 2375
UČKA				
Poklon dom	922m	sleeps 14	weekends only	PD 'Opatija' Opatija Tel: +385 (0) 51 712 785

* This remains an approximate figure in smaller huts and *sklonište*, which typically have mattresses in communal sleeping areas.

** Unless otherwise specified, *sklonište* are open all year.

Hut	Altitude	Capacity*	Season**	Contact details
GORSKI KOTAR				
PD Risnjak (Schlosserov dom)	1418m	sleeps 40+ (sklonište sleeps 6)	open 1 May – 1 Nov, every day except Monday	NP Risnjak, Crni Lug www.risnjak.hr Tel: +385 (0) 51 836 133
PD Snježnik	1490m	sleeps 14 (sklonište sleeps 3)	closed in 2009 (previously open weekends and public holidays)	HPD 'Platak' Rijeka Tel: +385 (0) 51 516 597
PD Platak	1111m	sleeps 90	open all year	Općina Čavle Tel: +385 (0) 51 230 908
PD Sušak (Platak)	1127m	sleeps 50	open all year	PD 'Stubičan' Donja Stubica Tel: +385 (0) 51 230 905
PD Hahlić	1097m	sleeps 20 (sklonište sleeps 4)	open weekends and holidays	HPD 'Obruč' Dražice www.pd-obruc.com Tel: +385 (0) 51 297 016 mobile: +385 (0) 91 726 1938 or +385 (0) 98 933 9612
PD Tuk (PD 'Bijele stijene' u Tuku)	875m	sleeps 54	open all year	HPS Zagreb www.plsavez.hr Contact Radojka Matijašić Tel: +385 (0) 51 833 589 mobile: +385 (0) 98 232 867
Pl. kuća Janjčarica	1236m	sleeps 17	by arrangement	HPD 'Bijele stijene' Mrkopalj Tel: +385 (0) 51 833 248 or +385 (0) 51 833 225
Pl. sklonište Jakob Mihelčić	1460m	sleeps 16	open all year	PD 'INA Bjelolasica' Zagreb Tel: +385 (0) 1 389 7384 mobile: +385 (0) 98 902 5745
Ratkovo sklonište	1185m	sleeps 10	open all year	PDS 'Velebit' Zagreb www.pdsvelebit.hr Tel: +385 (0) 1 485 1670 email: pdsvelebit@yahoogroups.com
Pl. kuća Bijele stijene (Pl. kuća na Bijelim stijenama)	1300m	sleeps 14	open weekends during summer (15 May – 15 Oct)	HPD 'Kapela' Zagreb www.hpd-kapela.hr Tel: +385 (0) 1 655 5440
Pl. sklonište Miroslav Hirtz	1280m	sleeps 20	open all year	HPD 'Kapela' Zagreb www.hpd-kapela.hr Tel: +385 (0) 1 655 5440
PD Klek	1000m	sleeps 38	open weekends during summer	PD 'Klek' Ogulin Tel: +385 (0) 47 521 206, mobile: +385 (0) 98 900 8670

Hut	Altitude	Capacity*	Season**	Contact details
Pl. sklonište Bitorajka (Bitoraj)	1303m	sleeps 20	open all year	HPD 'Bitoraj' Zagreb mobile +385 (0) 91 466 8141
VELEBIT				
PD Zavižan	1594m	sleeps 28	open all year	HPS Zagreb www.plsavez.hr Tel: +385 (0) 53 614 209 or +385 (0) 1 482 4142
Rossijevo sklonište	1580m	sleeps 8	open all year	PD 'Degenija' Zagreb www.degenija.hr Tel: +385 (0) 1 345 2023 email: info@degenija.hr
Pl. kuća Alan	1305m	sleeps 40 (sklonište sleeps 10)	open beginning June – end Sept, weekends only from October	Planinarsko orijentacijski klub Sljeme, Zagreb Tel: +385 (0) 1 467 4259, mobile: +385 (0) 98 921 8587 email: pavlic.irena@gmail.com
Pl. kuća Miroslav Hirtz (Zavratnica, Jablanac)	20m	25	open beginning May – end Sept	HPD 'MIV' Varaždin mobile: +385 (0) 98 174 3755
Pl. sklonište Radlovac	950m		closed (currently no plans to reopen)	
Pl. sklonište Ograđenica	1400m	sleeps 4	open all year	PD 'Đakovo' Đakovo www.planinari-djakovo.hr Tel: +385 (0) 31 814 119 mobile: +385 (0) 91 569 5677
Pl. kuća Kugina kuća	1180m	sleeps 24 (*sklonište* sleeps 8)	weekends beginning of June – end Sept or by arrangement	PDS 'Željezničar' Gospić Tel: +385 (0) 42 232 377 mobile: +385 (0) 98 961 0042
PD Ravni Dabar	723m	sleeps 50	weekends	Tel: +385 (0) 53 633 016 or +385 (0) 1 390 3226 mobile: +385 (0) 98 171 0933
Prpa	900m	alpine-style chalets	open all year	Vlado Prpić (HPD 'Prpa' Baške Oštarije) Tel: +385 (0) 53 674 012
Pl. kuća Vila Velebita (Baške Oštarije)	920m	sleeps 32	open beginning July – end Aug, and by arrangement Apr – June & Sept – Nov	PDS 'Željezničar' Gospić Tel: +385 (0) 53 574 065 mobile: +385 (0) 98 961 0042
Pl. sklonište Šugarska duliba	1212m	sleeps 10	open all year	PD 'Naftplin' Zagreb Tel: +385 (0) 1 630 1748

Hut	Altitude	Capacity*	Season**	Contact details
Pl. sklonište Tatekova koliba (Stap)	860m	sleeps 10	open all year	PD 'Paklenica' Zadar www.pdpaklenica.hr Tel: +385 (0) 23 397 582 or +385 (0) 23 301 636
Pl. sklonište Zavrata (Malo Rujno)	750m	sleeps 10	open all year	PD 'Paklenica' Zadar www.pdpaklenica.hr Tel: +385 (0) 23 301 636
Pl. sklonište Pećina (Bojinac)	c.1100m	sleeps 4	open all year	
Pl. sklonište Struge	1400m	sleeps 15	open all year	PD 'Paklenica' Zadar www.pdpaklenica.hr Tel: +385 (0) 23 301 636
Pl. sklonište Vlaški grad	1280m	sleeps 12	open all year	PD 'Paklenica' Zadar www.pdpaklenica.hr Tel: +385 (0) 23 301 636 mobile: +385 (0) 91 794 6578
Pl. sklonište Ivine vodice	1250m	sleeps 12	open all year	PD 'Paklenica' Zadar www.pdpaklenica.hr Tel: +385 (0) 23 301 636 mobile: +385 (0) 91 452 3340 or +385 (0) 91 112 2440
PD Paklenica	550m	sleeps 50	open June – September, and weekends otherwise	PD 'Paklenica' Zadar www.pdpaklenica.hr Tel: +385 (0) 23 301 636 or +385 (0) 23 213 792
MOSOR				
Pl. kuća Lugarnica	867m	sleeps 20	open weekends by arrangement	HPD 'Mosor' Split www.hpd-mosor.hr Tel: +385 (0) 21 394 365 Mobile: +385 (0) 91 250 2508 email: info@hpd-mosor.hr
PD Umberto Girometta	900m	sleeps 80	open weekends (call to check during winter)	HPD 'Mosor' Split www.hpd-mosor.hr Tel: +385 (0) 21 394 365 Mobile: +385 (0) 98 659 442 email: info@hpd-mosor.hr
Pl. sklonište Kontejner-Ljuto kame	1055m	sleeps 3–4	open all year	HPD 'Mosor' Split www.hpd-mosor.hr Tel: +385 (0) 21 394 365 email: info@hpd-mosor.hr

Hut	Altitude	Capacity*	Season**	Contact details
KOZJAK				
Pl. kuća Malačka	477m	sleeps 40	by arrangement	HPD 'Malačka' Kaštel Stari Tel: +385 (0) 21 231 240
PD pod Koludrom	325m	sleeps 10	open Sundays	HPD 'Ante Bedalov' Kaštel Kambelovac Tel: +385 (0) 21 221 402
Pl. sklonište Orlovo gnijezdo	598m	sleeps 5	open all year	Tel: +385 (0) 21 220 519 or +385 (0) 21 220 912
PD Putalj	460m	sleeps 72	open all year	PD 'Kozjak' Kaštel Sučurac Tel: +385 (0) 21 784 5399 mobile: +385 (0) 98 131 8481
BIOKOVO				
Pl. kuća Slobodan Ravlić (Lokva)	1467m	sleeps 20	by arrangement	HPD 'Biokovo' Makarska www.biokovo-hpd.hr Tel: +385 (0) 21 616 455 mobile: +385 (0) 98 165 8483 email: info@biokovo-hpd.hr
Pl. kuća pod Svetim Jurom	1594m	sleeps 18	by arrangement	HPD 'Biokovo' Makarska www.biokovo-hpd.hr Tel: +385 (0) 21 616 455 mobile: +385 (0) 98 165 8483 email: info@biokovo-hpd.hr
Pl. kuća pod Vošcem	1370m		closed	HPD 'Biokovo' Makarska www.biokovo-hpd.hr Tel: +385 (0) 21 616 455 email: info@biokovo-hpd.hr
PD Vošac	1425m	sleeps 14	by arrangement during summer	SAK Ekstrem, Makarska www.ekstrem.hr mobile: +385 (0) 98 968 7786
Pl. kuća Sveti Jure	1756m	sleeps 30	by arrangement	Biokovo Active Holidays www.biokovo.net Tel: +385 (0) 21 679 655 mobile: +385 (0) 98 225 852 email: biokovo@biokovo.net

The above list covers only those huts and shelters relevant to the routes in this guide. For a full list of mountain huts in Croatia see www.plsavez.hr.

APPENDIX C
Contacts and Useful Addresses

Transport
Croatia Airlines: www.croatiaairlines.hr
London Office:
2 The Lanchesters
162–164 Fulham Palace Rd London
Tel: 020 8563 0022
Zagreb Office:
Zrinjevac 17 10000, Zagreb
Tel: +385 (0) 1 481 9633

British Airways: www.ba.com
easyJet: www.easyjet.com
Ryanair: www.ryainair.com
Wizz: www.wizzair.com

Jadrolinija: www.jadrolinija.hr
Zagreb office:
Zrinski trg 20
10000 Zagreb
Tel: +385 (0) 1 487 3307
Split office:
Gat sv Duje bb.
Tel: +385 (0) 21 338 333

Zagreb bus station (with timetables):
www.akz.hr

Zagreb train station (with timetables):
www.hznet.hr

Train times in Croatia:
www.trazim.com/Putovanja.htm

Embassies and Cultural Centres in Croatia
British Embassy in Zagreb:
Ivana Lučića 4
PO Box 454
10000 Zagreb
Tel: +385 (0) 1 600 9100

British Consulate in Dubrovnik:
Vukovarska 22/1
Mercante centar
20000 Dubrovnik
Tel: +385 (0) 20 324 597

British Consulate in Split:
Obala Hrvatskog narodnog preporoda
10/III
21000 Split
Tel: +385 (0) 21 346 007

British Council in Zagreb:
Ilica 12
pp55
10001 Zagreb
Tel: +385 (0) 1 489 9500

French Embassy in Zagreb:
Schlosserove stube 5
10000 Zagreb
Tel: +385 (0) 1 4818 110

German Embassy in Zagreb:
Ulica grada Vukovara 64
10000 Zagreb
Tel: +385 (0) 1 6158 100

Croatian Diplomatic Missions Overseas
UK:
Embassy of the Republic of Croatia
21 Conway Street
London W1T 6BN
Tel: 020 7387 1144

Ireland:
Embassy of the Republic of Croatia
Adelaide Chambers, Peter Street, Dublin 8
Tel: +353 (0) 1 476 7181

USA:
Embassy of the Republic of Croatia
2343 Massachusetts Av NW
Washington DC 20008
Tel: +1 (0) 1 202 588 5899

Croatian National Tourist Board
UK:
Croatian National Tourist Board
The Lanchesters
162–164 Fulham Palace Road
London W6 9ER
Tel: 020 8563 7979

Croatia (Head Office)
Croatian National Tourist Board
Iblerov trg 10/IV
10000
Zagreb
Tel: +385 (0) 1 469 9333

Croatian Tour Operators in the UK
Balkan Holidays:
www.balkanholidays.co.uk
Tel: 0845 130 1114

Croatia for Travellers:
www.croatiafortravellers.co.uk
Tel: 020 7226 4460

Headwater Holidays:
www.headwater.com
Tel: 01606 720 033

Tourist Information Offices and Agencies in Croatia

Zagreb Tourist Information Office
Trg bana Jelačić 11
10000, Zagreb
Tel: +385 (0) 1 481 4051

Zagreb Tourist Board
www.zagreb-touristinfo.hr

Zagreb County Tourist Board
www.tzzz.hr

Rijeka Tourist Board
www.tz-rijeka.hr

Split Tourist Board
www.visitsplit.com

Makarska Tourist Board
www.makarska-info.hr

Dubrovnik Tourist Board
www.tzdubrovnik.hr

Accommodation in Zagreb

Hotel Ilica
Ilica 102
10000 Zagreb
Tel: +385 (0) 1 377 7522
www.hotel-ilica.hr

Hotel Jadran
Vlaška 50
10000 Zagreb
Tel: +385 (0) 1 455 3777
www.hup-zagreb.hr

Hotel–Pansion Jaegerhorn
Ilica 14
10000 Zagreb
Tel: +385 (0) 1 483 3877
www.hotel-pansion-jaegerhorn.hr

Hotel AS
Zelengaj 2
10000 Zagreb
Tel: +385 (0) 1 460 9111
www.hotel-as.hr

Hotel President
Pantovčak 52
10000 Zagreb
Tel: +385 (0) 1 488 1480
www.president-zagreb.com

Fulir Hostel
Radićeva 3a
10000 Zagreb
Tel: +385 (0) 1 483 0882
www.fulir-hostel.com

Buzz Backpackers
Babukićeva 1b
10000 Zagreb
Tel: +385 (0) 1 232 0267
www.buzzbackpackers.com

Foreign Language Bookshops in Zagreb

Algoritam
Gajeva 1
10000 Zagreb
Tel: +385 (0) 1 481 8672
www.algoritam.hr

Profil
Bogovićeva 7
10000 Zagreb
Tel: +385 (0) 1 487 7325
www.profil.hr

SMAND Map Outlets

UK
The Map Shop
www.themapshop.co.uk
Tel: 01684 593146

Croatia
SMAND d.o.o.
Varaždinska ulica 92
42205, Vidovec
Tel: +385 (0) 42 741 433

Mladost knjižara
Ilica 30, 10000 Zagreb

Mladost knjižara
Ilica 7, 10000 Zagreb

Walking and Mountaineering Clubs and Societies

PDS 'Velebit' (Zagreb)
Open Tuesdays, Wednesdays
and Thursdays, 19.30–21.00
Radićeva 23, 10000 Zagreb
Tel: +385 (0) 1 485 1670

HPS (Hrvatski planinarski savez, Zagreb)
Kozarčeva 22, 10000, Zagreb
Tel/fax: +385 (0) 1 482 4142
www.plsavez.hr

National Park/Nature Park Information

PP Medvednica www.pp-medvednica.hr
PP Žumberak–Samoborsko gorje
www.pp-zumberak-samoborsko-gorje.hr
PP Papuk www.pp-papuk.hr
PP Lonjsko polje www.pp-lonjsko-polje.hr
NP Kopački rit www.kopacki-rit.com
NP Risnjak www.risnjak.hr
NP Sjeverni Velebit
www.np-sjeverni-velebit.hr
Tel: +385 (0) 53 884 551
NP Paklenica www.paklenica.hr
Tel: +385 (0) 23 369 155
NP Plitvička jezera
www.np-plitvicka-jezera.hr
NP Krka www.npkrka.hr
PP Biokovo www.biokovo.com
NP Mljet www.np-mljet.hr
NP Kornati www.kornati.hr

Other Useful Information

Croatian Tourist Board www.htz.hr
Croatian Automobile Club www.hak.hr
Croatian Bureau of Statistics www.dzs.hr
Visit Croatia www.visit-croatia.co.uk
Cycling in Croatia
www.pedala.hr, www.bicikl.hr/bike-bed
Croatian Meteorological Service
www.meteo.hr

APPENDIX D
Croatian Language Notes and Glossary

A Note on Grammar

A full discussion of Croatian grammar is beyond the scope of this book; however, a few basic points should be mentioned. Nouns and adjectives are governed by seven cases: nominative (subject); accusative (direct object, and verbs of motion); dative (indirect object); locative or prepositional (used with positions); genitive (used with possession or amounts); instrumental (used with the word *s* or *sa*, meaning 'with'); and vocative (used in some forms of address). Thus the same noun (for example *kava*, a feminine noun meaning 'coffee') may take a number of forms, depending on its function within a sentence: *dobra je kava* ('it's good coffee' – nominative); *daj mi jednu kavu, molim* ('give me a coffee, please' – accusative); *u kavi* ('in the coffee' – locative); *s kavom* ('with coffee' – instrumental). Similarly, taking Zagreb as an example of a masculine noun: *Zagreb je lijep* ('Zagreb is pretty'); *idemo u Zagreb* ('we're going to Zagreb'); *ja sam u Zagrebu* ('I'm in Zagreb'); *on je iz Zagreba* ('he's from Zagreb').

Nouns may be masculine (usually ending with a consonant in the singular, and -i in the plural), feminine (usually ending with -a in the singular, -e in the plural) or neuter (-o or -e singular, -a plural). There are also a number of irregular exceptions to the above rule. Adjectives agree with nouns.

Pronunciation

Pronunciation is very important if you are to be understood clearly. As a number of Croatian letters are not found in the English alphabet, and some familiar letters are pronounced differently in Croatian (in particular j, which sounds like an English 'y'), a list of letters requiring particular attention is given below.

a   pronounced as the 'a' in father
c   pronounced as the 'ts' in cats
č   pronounced as the 'ch' in church
ć   very similar to č, but slightly softer, as the 'tj' sound in picture
đ   pronounced as the 'j' in jam
dž very similar to the above
e   pronounced as the 'e' in egg
g   pronounced hard, as the 'g' in give
i   pronounced as the 'i' in ill
j   pronounced as the 'y' in yes
lj pronounced as the 'lli' in million
nj pronounced as the 'ni' in onion
o   pronounced as the 'o' in hot
r   rolled slightly
š   pronounced as the 'sh' in shake
u   pronounced as the 'oo' in pool
ž   pronounced as the 's' in pleasure, or the French 'j' in janvier

Other letters are pronounced as they would be in English.

The complete Croatian alphabet is as follows: a, b, c, č, ć, d, đ, dž, e, f, g, h, i, j, k, l, lj, m, n, nj, o, p, r, s, š, t, u, v, z, ž. Note that there is no q, w, x or y.

Glossary

In the following list of vocabulary and basic phrases, 'Z' and 'D' have to indicate the Zagreb and Dalmatian dialects respectively. All other words and phrases are modern, standard Croatian. Alternative masculine/feminine/plural endings are given, where appropriate, as are some variations in meaning.

Greetings, Introductions and Basic Phrases

Hello/Good day	*Dobar dan**

* The old Serbo-Croatian greeting *Zdravo!* (literally meaning 'healthy'), although still included in a number of guidebooks, is not used, except occasionally for effect or in jest. Even in Belgrade, the preferred informal greeting is *Ćao*.

Hi/bye! (informal)	*Bog!* or *Bok!* (Z) (also used as a toast, from *zbogom*, 'go with God')
Good morning	*Dobro jutro*
Good evening	*Dobra večer*
Good night	*Laku noć*
Goodbye	*Do viđenja*
See you later!	*Vidimo se!*
Have a good trip!/ Safe journey!	*Sretan put!*
Yes	*Da*
No	*Ne*
Please	*Molim*
Thank you	*Hvala*
Thank you very much	*Puno hvala/hvala vam lijepo*
I beg your pardon?	*Molim?*
Sorry!	*Oprostite!/Pardon!*
Excuse me (when about to request something)	*Oprostite*
Excuse me (when trying to get past someone)	*Samo malo*
Just a minute!	*Samo malo!*

Greetings, Introductions and Basic Phrases

Here you are! (when offering something)	*Izvolite!*
Cheers! (as a toast)	*Živjeli!*
Do you speak English/ French?	*Govorite li engleski/francuski?*
I'm sorry, I don't speak Croatian	*Oprostite, ne znam hrvatski*
I only speak a little (Croatian)	*Samo malo govorim (hrvatski)*
I don't understand	*Ne razumijem*
I don't know	*Ne znam*
How are you? (formal)	*Kako ste?*
Fine, thank you	*Dobro, hvala*
Pleased to meet you!	*Drago mi je!*
Where are you from?	*Odakle ste?*
I'm English	*Ja sam Englez*
I'm from…	*Ja sam iz…*
I'm a… (teacher/ student/engineer…)	*Ja sam…(profesor/ student/inženjer…)*
Mr	*Gospodin*
Mrs	*Gospođa*
I like/I don't like…	*Sviđa mi se/ne sviđa mi se…*
Great!	*Odlično!*
Let's go! (plural)	*Idemo!*
Please could I have…	*Molim vas…*
I'd like…	*Ja bih…*
Do you have…?	*Imate li…?*
I/we need…	*Trebam/trebamo…*
How much does it cost?	*Koliko košta?*
I've already ordered, thank you	*Već sam naručio, hvala*
Can I order, please?	*Mogu li naručiti?*
Can I pay, please?	*Mogu li platiti?*
Can I have the bill, please?	*Molim vas račun?*

Greetings, Introductions and Basic Phrases	
This is for you	To je za vas
Can I help you?	Mogu li pomoći?
I'm just looking, thanks	Samo gledam, hvala
One ticket to…, please	Jednu kartu do…, molim
What time does the train to Delnice leave?	U koliko sati ide vlak za Delnice?
Which platform?	Koji peron?
Which number?	Koji broj?
There is/there are…/is there?/are there…?	Ima…/ima…?
There isn't/there aren't…	Nema…

Numerals	
0	nula
1	jedan
2	dva
3	tri
4	četiri
5	pet
6	šest
7	sedam
8	osam
9	devet
10	deset
11	jedanaest
12	dvanaest
13	trinaest
20	dvadeset
21	dvadeset jedan
22	dvadeset dva
30	trideset
40	četrdeset
50	pedeset

Numerals	
60	šezdeset
70	sedamdeset
80	osamdeset
90	devedeset
100	sto
125	sto dvadeset pet
200	dvijesto
300	tristo
1000	tisuća
first	prvi
second	drugi
third	treći

Time, Days of the Week and Months	
What time is it?	Koliko je sati?
09.25	devet i dvadeset pet sati
14.00	dva sata (or četrnaest sati)
minute	minuta
hour	sat
day	dan
week	tjedan
month	mjesec
year	godina
Sunday	nedjelja
Monday	ponedjeljak
Tuesday	utorak
Wednesday	srijeda
Thursday	četvrtak
Friday	petak
Saturday	subota
January	siječanj
February	veljača
March	ožujak
April	travanj

Time, Days of the Week and Months	
May	*svibanj*
June	*lipanj*
July	*srpanj*
August	*kolovoz*
September	*rujan*
October	*listopad*
November	*studeni*
December	*prosinac*
spring	*proljeće*
summer	*ljeto*
autumn	*jesen*
winter	*zima*
today	*danas*
tomorrow	*sutra*
yesterday	*jučer*
in the morning	*ujutro*
in the afternoon	*popodne, poslije podne*
in the evening	*navečer*

General Vocabulary	
after	*poslije*
and	*i*
beautiful	*krasan*
before	*prije*
big	*veliki*
black	*crni*
blue	*plavi*
closed	*zatvoreno*
cold	*hladno*
difficult/more difficult	*teško/teže*
easy/easier	*lako/lakše*
excellent	*odlično*
far	*daleko*

General Vocabulary	
fast	*brzo*
from	*iz*
from...to...	*od...do...*
green	*zeleni*
here	*ovdje/tu*
hot	*vruće*
how?	*kako?*
in	*u*
later	*kasnije*
much/many	*puno/mnogo*
near	*blizu*
now	*sada*
of	*od*
on	*na*
open	*otvoreno*
or	*ili*
red	*crveni*
slow	*polako*
small	*mali*
terrible	*strašan*
that	*ono/to*
there	*tamo*
this	*ovo*
to	*u* (sometimes *na* is used instead)
under	*ispod*
very	*jako/vrlo*
what?	*što? kaj?* (Z) *ča?* (D)
when?	*kad?*
where?	*gdje?*
white	*bijeli*
who?	*tko?*
with	*s/sa*
without	*bez*

General Vocabulary	
IN THE MOUNTAINS	
cascade, travertine fall	*buk*
cave	*špilja/pećina*
cliff	*stijena*
crag, bare limestone peak	*kuk*
dry stone wall	*suhozid*
field/cultivated area between limestone ridges	*polje*
forest	*šuma*
hill	*brdo*
lake	*jezero*
limestone depression	*vrtača, doline,* or (larger) *duliba, dabar*
limestone pit	*škrapa*
massif	*gora/gorje*
mountain	*planina*
mountain hut	*planinarski dom, planinarska kuća*
mountain range	*planinski lanac*
pass	*vrata* (lit. 'door'), *prijevoj, sedlo*
peak/summit	*vrh*
ridge	*greben, hrbat, kukovi*
river	*rijeka*
rock/rocky	*kamen/kamenit*
scree	*sipar*
shelter	*sklonište*
sinkhole	*jama*
small peak, hillock	*glava* (lit. 'head')
spring	*izvor*
steep	*strm*
valley	*dolina*
water	*voda*
waterfall	*vodopad, slap*

General Vocabulary	
ON THE COAST	
beach	*plaža*
cape/headland/point	*rt*
coast	*obala*
island	*otok*
peninsula	*poluotok*
sandy	*pješčan*
sea	*more*
stony	*šljunčan*
DIRECTIONS AND RIGHTS OF WAY	
Where are you going? (formal)	*Kamo idete?*
I'm/we're going to…	*Idem/idemo u…*
Excuse me, where's the path to…?	*Oprostite, gdje je put za…?*
How far is…?	*Koliko daleko je…?*
Is it marked?	*Je li markiran?*
I'm/we're lost!	*Izgubio sam se/ izgubili smo se!*
(on the) left	*(na) lijevo*
(on the) right	*(na) desno*
path	*staza*
road	*cesta*
way	*put*
WEATHER	
It's raining/snowing	*Pada kiša/snijeg*
It's getting dark	*Pada mrak*
It's windy	*Puše vjetar*
weather	*vrijeme*
cloud	*oblak*
fog	*magla*
frost	*mraz*
hail	*tuča*
ice	*led*

General Vocabulary	
lightning	*munja*
rain	*kiša*
snow	*snijeg*
storm	*oluja*
sun	*sunce*
thunder	*grom*

PLANTS AND ANIMALS

animal	*životinja*
bear	*medvjed*
beech	*bukva*
bird	*ptica*
buzzard	*škanjac*
cat	*mačka*
common viper	*šarka* or *šarulja*
cow	*krava*
cypress	*čempres*
deer	*jelen*
dog	*pas*
dormouse	*puh*
eagle	*orao*
flower	*cvijet* (not to be confused with *svijet*, 'world')
fox	*lisica*
goat	*jarac*
grass	*trava*
griffon vulture	*bjeloglavi sup*
horse	*konj*
juniper	*borovica* or *smrika*
leaf	*list*
lynx	*ris*
mountain pine	*klekovina, planinski bor* or *bor krivulj*
nose-horned viper	*poskok*

General Vocabulary	
oak	*hrast*
pine	*bor*
rabbit	*zec*
sheep	*ovca*
snake	*zmija*
tree	*drvo*
wild mountain sheep	*muflon*
wild pig	*divlja svinja*
wolf	*vuk*

TOWNS AND CITIES

apartment	*apartman*
ATM	*bankomat*
bank	*banka*
bed	*krevet*
bookshop	*knjižara*
bridge	*most*
castle	*dvorac*
chapel	*kapelica*
chemist	*apoteka* or *ljekarna*
church	*crkva*
citadel/old town	*stari grad*
city walls	*zidine*
door	*vrata*
exchange office	*mjenjačnica*
garden	*vrt*
graveyard	*groblje*
hotel	*hotel*
house	*kuća/dom*
monastery	*samostan*
post office	*pošta*
restaurant	*restoran/konoba/ gostionica*
room	*soba*
single room	*jednokrevetna soba*

General Vocabulary	
double room	*dvokrevetna soba*
shop	*dućan, trgovina*
square	*trg*
street	*ulica*
town/city	*grad*
village	*selo*
wall	*zid*
TRANSPORT	
aeroplane	*avion*
airport	*zračna luka/aerodrom*
arrivals/departures	*dolazak/odlazak*
bus	*bus*
bus station	*autobusni kolodvor*
bus stop	*stajalište*
by train	*vlakom*
car	*auto*
main (railway) station	*glavni (željeznički) kolodvor*
on foot	*pješice*
platform	*peron*
taxi	*taksi*
ticket	*karta*
single ticket	*u jednom smjeru*
return ticket	*povratna karta*
train	*vlak*
Equipment	
book	*knjiga*
boots	*čizme*
crampons	*dereze*
gloves	*rukavice*
guidebook	*turistički vodič*
hat	*kapa*
ice axe	*cepin*

General Vocabulary	
jacket	*jakna*
(mountain) map	*(planinarska) karta*
mountain guidebook	*planinarski vodič*
rucksack	*ruksak*
sleeping bag	*vreća za spavanje*
sleeping mat	*karimat*
socks	*čarape*
tent	*šator*
FOOD AND DRINK	
apple	*jabuka*
baked	*pečeno*
beef	*govedina*
beer	*pivo*
boiled	*kuhano*
bread	*kruh**

Of particular interest to the hiker will be *crni kruh* ('black bread'), *alpski kruh* ('alpine bread') and *raženi kruh* ('rye bread'), all of which keep much longer than the standard *bijeli kruh* ('white bread').

breakfast	*doručak*
cake	*kolač*
carp	*šaran*
cheese	*sir*
chicken	*piletina*
coffee with milk	*kava s mlijekom*
coffee	*kava*
cucumber	*krastavac*
dessert	*desert*
dinner	*večera*
dried meat	*suho meso*
eggs	*jaja*
fig	*smokva*
fish	*riba*

General Vocabulary	
food	*jelo*
fried/deep fried	*prženo/pohano*
fruit juice	*voćni sok*
grapes	*grožđe*
grilled	*na žaru*
ham	*šunka*
homemade	*domaće*
ice cream	*sladoled*
lamb	*janjetina*
lettuce, green salad	*zelena salata*
lunch	*ručak*
mackerel	*lokarda*
main course	*glavno jelo*
meat	*meso*
milk	*mlijeko*
mullet	*cipal*
mussels	*dagnje*
octopus	*hobotnica*
orange	*naranča*
pasta	*tjestenina*
pear	*kruška*
pepperoni-type sausages	*čajna*
plum	*šljiva*
potato	*krumpir*
red wine	*crno vino*
rice	*riža*
rock melon	*dinja*
salami	*salama*
salmon	*losos*
sauce	*umak/saft*
sausages	*kobasice*
soup	*juha*

General Vocabulary	
sour cherry	*višnja*
squid	*lignje*
strawberry	*jagoda*
strudel	*štrudla*
Swiss chard	*blitva*
tea with lemon	*čaj s limunom*
tea	*čaj*
tomato	*rajčica, paradajz* (Z)
trout	*pastrva*
tuna	*tuna*
Turkish coffee	*turska kava*
veal	*teletina*
vegetables	*povrće*
venison	*srnetina*
water melon	*lubenica*
white wine	*bijelo vino*

WARNINGS, DANGER AND EMERGENCIES	
Danger!	*Opasnost!*
Be careful!	*Pazi!*
Help!	*U pomoć!*
doctor	*doktor/liječnik*
ambulance	*hitna pomoć*
Please call a doctor!	*Molim vas pozovite doktora!*
I fell/he fell/she fell	*pao sam/pao je/ pala je*
sick/ill	*bolestan*
hospital	*bolnica*
snakebite	*zmijski ugriz*
blood	*krv*
broken	*slomljen*
landmines	*mine*
abandoned military installation	*napušteni vojni objekt*

APPENDIX E
Further Reading

Walking and Mountaineering Guidebooks

When this guide was first published in 2004, it was the only English-language walking/mountaineering guidebook for Croatia (apart from one translation mentioned below). Since that date, it has been joined by Sandra Bardwell's handy *Croatia. Car Tours and Walks* (Sunflower, 2006).

Within the country, there are a number of guides available in Croatian. The Croatian walker's Bible is *Hrvatske planine* by Dr Željko Poljak (Zagreb: Golden Marketing, 1996). First published in the 1970s and reprinted a number of times, this is an exhaustive guide to practically every walking and climbing area in Croatia – including a number now in neighbouring countries, but (at least before the war) easily accessible from the Croatian side of the border. Note that pre-1991–95 editions include a number of areas now unsafe to visit. The same author's *50 Najljepših planinarskih izleta u Hrvatskoj* (Zagreb: Školska knjiga, 2001) is a more compact selection from the above. (The latter publication has been expanded, with additional routes and information for foreign visitors, and published in English under the title *Mountains along the Croatian Coast*, Zagreb: Školska knjiga, 2002.) An excellent guide to the entire north–south route over Velebit is *Velebitski planinarski put* by Alan Čaplar, and the same author's *Dinarska Hrvatska* gives more extensive coverage of the Dinaric Alps. Also available is *Mrkopaljski planinarski put* (covering the MPP on Bijele stijene).

For those combining a visit to Croatia with Montenegro, there is Rudolf Abraham's *The Mountains of Montenegro* (Cicerone, 2007)

General Guidebooks

Numerous general guidebooks to Croatia have been published over the past few years, most of which have now run through several editions. Without any doubt the best is *Croatia. The Bradt Travel Guide* (4th ed; Bradt, 2010) by Piers Letcher, who has been visiting Croatia for 20 years (4th ed. updated by myself).

Others include *Lonely Planet Croatia* and *The Rough Guide to Croatia*. There are excellent little city guides to Zagreb and Dubrovnik, again from Bradt. For Dubrovnik there is also the *Visible City Guide* by Annabel Barber. French readers are well served by the excellent, colourful and informative *Croatie* from Guides Gallimard, which includes illustrated sections on wildlife, typical woodland trees and history; and are also referred to the *Guide Routard*.

A number of English-language guidebooks written while Croatia was part of Yugoslavia are available on the second-hand market, and several remain useful: Ante Pelivan, *Dalmatia: Natural and Cultural Sights* (Zagreb, 1985); Lazar Trifunović, *Yugoslavia: Monuments of Art* (Belgrade, 1988); and last but very much not least, J.A. Cuddon, *The Companion Guide to Jugoslavia* (London: Collins, 1968; 3rd revised edition 1986).

History

The Illyrians (Oxford: Blackwell, 1992) by John Wilkes is the most detailed account available of the Illyrian lands from prehistory through to the late Roman period. Dimitri Obolenski's *The Byzantine Commonwealth: Eastern Europe, 500–1453* (London: Weidenfeld and Nicholson, 1971) is a thorough account of the region during the medieval period, and also contains material on Croatia.

Two of the best accounts of the war in the former Yugoslavia are *The Death of Yugoslavia* (London: Penguin and BBC Books, 1995) by Laura Silber and Allan Little and *The Fall of Yugoslavia* (London: Penguin, 1992) by Misha Glenny. The latter author's *The Balkans, 1804–1999: Nationalism, War and the Great Powers* (London: Granta, 1999) is a detailed analysis of the formation of modern southeast Europe. Ivo Goldstein's *Croatia: A History* (London: C. Hurst & Co., 1999) is a good account of the country's history from antiquity to the present, although it concentrates primarily on the modern period. Fred Singleton, *A Short History of the Yugoslav Peoples* (Cambridge University Press, 1985; rep. 1989) is a balanced

account which finds equal favour among the present author's Croatian, Serbian and Montenegrin friends!

Language Courses, Phrasebooks and Dictionaries

The most comprehensive and easily obtainable Croatian language courses in the UK are *Colloquial Croatian: The Complete Course for Beginners* by Celia Hawkesworth with Ivana Jović (Routledge, 2005) and David Norris' *Teach Yourself Croatian* (Teach Yourself, 2003). In both cases material has been re-evaluated and updated from two earlier publications, *Colloquial Croatian and Serbian* and *Teach Yourself Serbo-Croat,* written by the same authors respectively. Also good is *Dobro Došli 1* by Jasna Barešić, although this is more easily obtainable in Zagreb.

Pocket-sized Croatian–English/English–Croatian dictionaries include the small, cheap and easily obtainable Langenscheidt Universal Croatian Dictionary. However, this fails to distinguish between the various possible meanings of a word, and these various meanings are not necessarily listed in the order you might expect – which can lead to considerable confusion! Somewhat better is the slightly larger pocket dictionary published by Školska knjiga (Zagreb, 2003). The most comprehensive Croatian–English dictionary is the weighty (and remarkably pricey) two- volume set by Željko Bujas, but this is obviously not something to pop in one's pack and carry up a mountain. Note that Lonely Planet's small *Eastern*

European Phrasebook, although published comparatively recently, contains inaccuracies in both modern Serbian and Croatian.

Natural History

The most detailed information on the flora of Croatia is to be found in Oleg Polunin's monumental work, *Flowers of Greece and the Balkans: A Field Guide* (Oxford: OUP, 1980; rep. in paperback Oxford: OUP, 1987). This includes detailed sections on the flora of Risnjak, Mljet, Plitvička jezera and Velebit/Paklenica, together with that of national parks in other Republics of the former Yugoslavia. More general and slightly smaller is the same author's *The Concise Flowers of Europe* (Oxford: Oxford University Press, 1972; reprint, based on Polunin's much larger *Flowers of Europe: A Field Guide*). Another more general field guide is Christopher Grey-Wilson & Marjorie Blamey, *The Alpine Flowers of Britain and Europe* (Harper Collins, 1979).

Birds of Europe, by Lars Svensson, Peter J. Grant, Killian Mullarney and Dan Zetterström (Princeton University Press, 1999), is an outstanding field guide. Collins' *Birds of Britain and Europe Field Guide* (HarperCollins, 2004) is also good.

An excellent field guide to reptiles and amphibians is E. Nicolas Arnold and Denys W. Ovenden, *Reptiles and Amphibians of Europe* (Princeton Field Guides, 2002). This was reprinted from the Second Edition of *Collins Field Guide to the Reptiles and Amphibians*

of Britain and Europe (HarperCollins, 2002), however the Princeton edition has the advantage of being in paperback.

Gerard Gorman, *Central and Eastern European Wildlife* (Bradt, 2008) is an excellent general guide with plenty of colour photos.

Travel Literature

Rebecca West's *Black Lamb and Grey Falcon: A Journey Through Yugoslavia* (London: Macmillan, 1942; reprinted Canongate Books, 1993) remains one of the finest accounts of the various republics of the former Yugoslavia, drawn from the author's travels through them on the eve of the Second World War. It's a vast tome, and should be more than enough to keep even the most voracious of readers busy for a whole trip. Fitzroy Maclean's *Eastern Approaches* (London: Jonathan Cape, 1949; numerous reprints) contains details of the author's exploits with the Partisans during the Second World War, sandwiched between material on the Western Desert and Soviet Central Asia. More recently, Dervla Murphy's *Through the Embers of Chaos: Balkan Journeys* (London: John Murray, 2002) recounts its intrepid author's travels through the region on a bicycle. Alberto Abbé Fortis's *Viaggio in Dalmazia*, originally published in 1774 and translated into English as *Travels into Dalmatia* (reprinted London: J. Robson, 1978; New York: Arno Press and New York Times, 1974), recounts the 18th-century Venetian traveller's experiences along the Croatian coast.

Accounts of travel in Dalmatia in the 19th century include Sir J. Gardiner Wilkinson, *Dalmatia and Montenegro* (London: John Murray, 1848; reprinted New York: Arno Press and New York Times, 1971, and Elibron Classics, 2001); F. Hamilton Jackson, *The Shores of the Adriatic – Austrian Side* (London: John Murray, 1908); and Robert Munro, *Rambles and Studies in Bosnia–Herzegovina and Dalmatia* (Edinburgh: W. Blackwood & Sons, 1894).

Croatian Literature

Croatia has an extensive literary tradition stretching back to the Renaissance. Of particular interest with reference to this guide is *Planine* ('The Mountains') written in 1569 by Petar Zoranić. The first secular prose work in Croatian, it sets out to imbue the mountains around its author's native Zadar with mythical history and legend, in the tradition of Ovid, or Sannazaro's *Arcadia*. Probably the most important Croatian writer of the 20th century was Miroslav Krleža. Works by Krleža available in English translation include *On The Edge of Reason* (New Directions Press, 1995), *The Banquet in Blitva* (Northwestern University Press, 2003) and *The Return of Philip Latinowicz* (Northwestern University Press, 1995). Other well-known modern Croatian writers include Ivan Aralica and Dubravka Ugrešić, a number of the latter's books also having been translated into English, including *The Culture of Lies* (London: Weidenfeld and Nicholson, 1998) and *In the Jaws of Life* (London: Virago, 1992). A good collection of short stories is S. Koljević (ed. and trans.), *Yugoslav Short Stories* (London, 1966).

Major poets include Antun Gustav Matoš and Tin Ujević. Although not about Croatia itself, *The Bridge over the River Drina* by Ivo Andrić remains one of the most highly regarded novels to emerge from the former Yugoslavia. Born in Bosnia, educated in Zagreb and finally settling in Belgrade, Andrić was awarded the Nobel Prize for Literature in 1961.

Sunset, Korčula

LISTING OF CICERONE GUIDES

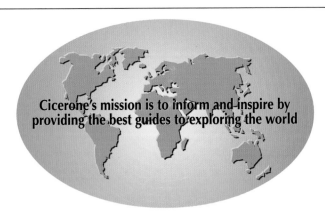

Cicerone's mission is to inform and inspire by providing the best guides to exploring the world

Since its foundation 40 years ago, Cicerone has specialised in publishing guidebooks and has built a reputation for quality and reliability. It now publishes nearly 300 guides to the major destinations for outdoor enthusiasts, including Europe, UK and the rest of the world.

Written by leading and committed specialists, Cicerone guides are recognised as the most authoritative. They are full of information, maps and illustrations so that the user can plan and complete a successful and safe trip or expedition – be it a long face climb, a walk over Lakeland fells, an alpine cycling tour, a Himalayan trek or a ramble in the countryside.

With a thorough introduction to assist planning, clear diagrams, maps and colour photographs to illustrate the terrain and route, and accurate and detailed text, Cicerone guides are designed for ease of use and access to the information.

If the facts on the ground change, or there is any aspect of a guide that you think we can improve, we are always delighted to hear from you.

Cicerone Press
2 Police Square Milnthorpe Cumbria LA7 7PY
Tel: 015395 62069 Fax: 015395 63417
info@cicerone.co.uk www.cicerone.co.uk

CICERONE